To Pap, With Love

As my father
would say "Take care
of yourself!"
Diane

To Pap, With Love

Diane M. McDonald

Writers Club Press
San Jose New York Lincoln Shanghai

To Pap, With Love

Writers Club Press
an imprint of iUniverse, Inc.

For information address:
iUniverse, Inc.
5220 S. 16th St., Suite 200
Lincoln, NE 68512
www.iuniverse.com

ISBN: 0-595-22749-X

Printed in the United States of America

For my family,
Without their help and support this story would never have
been written.

Not recognizing me.
Repeating herself.
cutting the food.

Contents

My Heartfelt Thanks

I had to look at my life in detail when I began writing our story. I am grateful to God, who allowed me to not only survive the fire, but provides constant help and direction. I'm thankful for my mother's selflessness in rescuing me, then returning for my brother. Even though I didn't live in a cottage with a white picket fence, I'm grateful for the sacrifices and support given by my father.

Needless to say, this story would not have been written without the help and support of my family: my husband, my children and their spouses, my grandchildren. Caring for a person with any illness is draining, Alzheimer's carries a stress all its own. Not only did my family live this story, they read and reread it many times as I committed it to paper. They even shared their computer skills when I floundered. I'm grateful to my daughter, Terri, for writing about some of her experiences.

I have tried to protect the privacy of the many people involved in our story. With their welfare in mind, I have not named our church, clinic, day care facility, hospital, or nursing home. Many people extended a helping hand or a needed smile during those years. Rather than naming them and inadvertently leaving someone out—I wish to acknowledge their helping hands—from the angel on the corner (our school crossing guard), our mailman, the doctors and nurses, social workers, staff at the Jewish Council for the Elderly, staff at the nursing home, to my friends and co-workers, to the clerks at the store and mechanics at the garage, to the people I met on the street. My heartfelt thanks. You know who you are.

My lamaze coach throughout the birth of this book, Catherine Scherer—words are not sufficient to express my feelings.

I also wish to thank Rika Keilson at iuniverse.com. We have never met but her clear answers to my e-mails helped me navigate through the submission maze.

Dream—When I began writing our story, I had a dream in which the name of this book appeared. As I left the church of the Angels, a bake sale was in progress outside. A woman, dressed in Scandinavian clothes sold cookies. They looked so good, I bought one. As I took the brown cookie from the woman's hand, I saw the words "To Pap, With Love" written on the cookie in red gel on top of the white icing.

Prologue

Dear Friend,

You won't believe what Pap did today!

There I go again, starting in the middle, and confusing you. I promise, this time I'll start at the beginning. But before I start, maybe I should tell you why I'm writing to you.

My youngest daughter, Sue, is the instigator. In the fall of 1993, she went away to college as a freshman. She was homesick, so to keep in touch, I tried to send two letters or cards a week. To make the letters interesting, I included stories about her grandfather's latest misadventures. After several months and many letters, Sue suggested that I write a book. I passed this idea off with a laugh. After all, I had a husband, a family, Pap (my father), and a full time job. Besides, I was taking two demanding courses at a community college. When I asked why I should write a book, Sue replied, "So others will know that they're not alone." I mentioned the idea to a few people, then forgot it.

In March of 1994, I opened a copy of *Guidepost* Magazine to an invitation—"*Would you like to tell a story?*" The magazine asked the writer to include a letter detailing his or her writing experience and plans for the future. I wrote my story, and while I was composing a letter listing my writing experience—or inexperience—to accompany it, I remembered Sue's suggestion.

I mentioned Sue's idea to a classmate. She asked what kind of book I was going to write. Self-Help? Biography? I spent quite a bit of time pondering that question. I have neither the credentials nor the knowledge to write a self-help book. My experience is limited to dealing with my father. What do I have to offer that other people would want to read?

Along with attending the same classes, my classmate and I shared the experience of living with an older parent who was dependant on our care. Many times she listened as I detailed the events of my day. One night, she was more frustrated than normal. As she told the story of her day, I understood and sympathized. Then I shared mine. She remarked that as bad as her day was, mine was always worse. She felt better after listening to my tale.

As I debated about writing our story, I remembered our Irish setter, Rusty. He was nine months old when he joined us and had already been in many homes and often returned to Anti-Cruelty because of his aggressive and destructive behavior. My husband, having heard me talk with fondness of an Irish we had when I was a child, brought Rusty home as a gift. We didn't know what we were getting into.

We raised our pets as we raised our children—with love, understanding, and a firm hand. This dog was full grown and no longer afraid of people bigger than himself. Rusty was not only stubborn but because of his many homes, he developed some undesirable habits. He picked up a sock or a plastic bag, decided it was his and dared anyone to take it away from him. He growled, barked and snapped until his treasured object was forcefully removed. He had learned how to be aggressive and get away with it. I was at my wit's end.

I went to the library looking for a book on training Irish Setters. I chanced upon a story by Gladys Taber—a funny tale about an Irish that an unsuspecting person was asked to board. The story didn't help with my problem, but I sympathized with the problems the dog-sitter experienced. It helped to lighten my load; I wasn't the only person having trouble raising an Irish. May this book help to lighten your load.

Rusty lived with us for many years, never giving up some of his bad habits. He never learned to "drop it." He kept his stubborn streak. I learned to be a lion tamer, using a chair to safely retrieve a treasured possession. I learned to adjust.

◆   ◆   ◆

I was raised in the Catholic faith. I attended Catholic school when Sister was the boss and we moved over on our seat to make room for our guardian angel. I have never been a "Sunday" Catholic. A long time ago I changed from formal prayer to informal conversations, mostly "Thank You" and "Help!"—whispered, spoken, or yelled as the circumstances dictated.

I am extremely grateful for the help I received from family, friends, and others. I depend on the constant help I receive from above. My shoulders are not broad enough to carry the full weight myself.

A person's ability to deal with his or her life is formed by all of the events that have transpired from birth up to that particular moment in time. With this in mind, I'll begin with my father's childhood. I would gladly leave out parts of my own childhood that still bring painful memories, but I'm including these experiences because they played an important part in our lives.

I read recently that the purpose of a memoir is to validate a life. That is one reason for writing our story. But other, bigger reasons exist than just to say that a very nice, gentle, kind, inquisitive man lived. He wasn't rich, didn't acquire fame while he was alive—no one would be interested in his life except for his family.

I believe three divine purposes were at work in his illness. The first was to teach me patience. IT DIDN'T WORK! The second was to leave slowly—if he died suddenly, it would have been much harder for me to handle. Besides sorrow in his passing, would I have felt guilty thinking that there was something I should have done? The third was to give us such a memorable experience that I would write about it and possibly write it well enough that it would be published—making many people aware of the help available from God, family and friends to get through an ordinary, rough day. Perhaps our story will help those who are currently living with someone undergoing the loss of their memory. Not that answers are provided in our story, but sometimes knowing that someone else has walked the same path is comforting.

I had to focus on the last four years of Pap's life in order to write in such a way that our story doesn't read like an instructional manual or a newspaper account. I had to remember some of the small things—how Pap always finished his coffee before leaving the house, even if we were already late; how he always had to say goodbye to the dogs. I had to go down into the mine of my memory again and again with my pick, looking for missed gems, gold, diamonds hiding under the dirt. It was very dark down there.

My father lived for almost 85 years, only four, possibly five years, were spent in a gradual drift. I will be happy to return to the light because Pap's last four years are overshadowing the other 80 years of his life. I want to remember the man—who always had time to listen to a problem or an idea; who guided me to develop my own answers rather than telling me what to do; who helped me to become my own person, even if that person is very stubborn. His guidance allowed me to stand on my own feet, listen to my own voice, feel good about myself when the world thought that I looked very different and didn't accept me. He lived with us for almost all of our married life. He had the good sense to allow my husband and I to make our own way, to stay out of family quarrels, to let us learn how to become parents by following our own path. That was no small feat. It is very hard to "Keep Thy Mouth Shut," to advise rather than to dictate, to let your family make their own mistakes.

In his late sixties, he had enough self-worth to look silly as he skipped with his grandson around and around the house. He had enough understanding to pretend that he needed the practice and was grateful for the opportunity. (He also needed to practice coloring and printing letters.) He did these things with a warm, loving, giving attitude. He seldom made you feel stupid, but when you screwed up, he helped you to see that you did. Then he helped you to pick yourself up, dust yourself off, and get going again.

His influence allowed me to develop my own child-rearing philosophies as we raised our four children. Since these values were so strong, I could rely on them when our roles reversed, when my father's memory declined and I became the parent instead of the daughter.

Pap had "good hands," which allowed him to improvise, to fix, to build many of the things that we are still using. Sometimes his methods were unorthodox; his habit of thinking about a problem, and then moving as if through molasses while he made the needed repairs could drive people to distraction. But if he was asked to fix something, he seldom forgot, and kept trying various ways until he got the problem licked. Whether it was a bike, a book bag, or the porch, it didn't matter. After fixing something, he didn't brag about his accomplishment or lord it over others, he thought of it simply as his contribution to the family.

He had an inventive, inquisitive mind. He was always open to new ideas; he didn't close his mind to the ideas of others so his thinking never became rigid. He was interested in self-improvement—how to write better, talk better, gain greater self-confidence. In his seventies, he was still trying to improve. He didn't sit in front of the television set and vegetate until his mind started to drift. The board games he invented didn't make any money, but in the grand scheme of things, they probably weren't meant to. But he kept trying, never gave up.

My father also had a stubborn streak, but that wasn't all bad. His stubbornness caused him to defy his mother's wishes (no small feat and not for the timid) to: A) become a Catholic, and B) marry my mother. It helped him to survive the tragedy of the fire that killed his wife and infant son, and then battle both families, his and my mother's, when he decided to raise me by himself.

I inherited my father's stubborn streak. Often I'm so involved with my own plans that I'm unaware of other possibilities. I frequently need help from other sources. Pap liked to help others—family, friends, neighbors. I know I received "help from above" while Pap was still alive and probably throughout my whole life. Many times I went to look for something for Pap, only to find something hazardous to his health or that warned me about a problem. Even though my father has passed over, I'm sure he still helps, we just don't see him.

So, gather your tea, coffee, or wine. Find your favorite place to sit for a spell. And let's talk. If you need to put this down for a while, I understand. I'll be here when you come back.

1

Childhood

William Everett Witting was the second son of eleven children, born on February 23, 1910, to Christian Swedish parents in Chicago, Illinois. His mother, Ellen, was born in Sweden and as a young girl immigrated to this country with her adopted parents. His father, Charles, was born in Evanston, returned with his family to Sweden as a child and came back to Chicago when he was a young man. Charles was born with a club foot which made walking difficult. Still, he walked over five miles each way, every day, to court Ellen. Stubbornness and determination have always been Witting trademarks. Ellen was short and very bossy; she wanted her own way and enjoyed arguing to get it. She was a stern disciplinarian but she had a sharp wit and loved to tease. She kept a straight face when she kidded, only the mischievous glint in her eyes gave her away. Charles was a printer by trade. The family made up for a lack of money with fun, high jinx, and imagination.

Ellen did not believe in nicknames or in shortening a Christian name. She always called my father William. He was Billy, Bill, Will or Wee Wee to his brothers, sisters and friends.

The family lived on the Northwest side of Chicago in a large six room rented house. They moved many times but stayed in the same neighborhood in order to be close to their relatives in Evanston.

Charles was born on October 31. Each year the family had a large Halloween party to celebrate. The children decorated the house from top to bottom, adding to the collection saved from the year before. Skeletons were constructed from mops and brooms. Bats, cats, and moons were made from cardboard, painted, attached to string and suspended from the ceiling. Spiders and their webs dangled from unlikely places. A few witches and ghosts were added for fun. Crepe paper was twisted into spirals and looped across the room. They carved a large pumpkin and placed it in the middle of the front room window to light after dark. When they finished, the house looked haunted. The children dressed in costumes and waited for the fun to begin. Friends and relatives crowded the house. The children bobbed for apples floating in the big wash tub. The party wasn't complete without homemade apple cider to drink, apple or pumpkin pie, donuts, and donut holes to eat.

In those days the children had many opportunities to be creative. Many of the streets and alleys were unpaved, so they were perfect for playing kick-the-can or marbles. In warm weather, whenever there was a breeze, the sky was littered with kites.

Billy was good with his hands. He spent his free time making kites, flying them, repairing them, or fixing their tails so that they would go higher. He built two different pushmobiles. One kind was constructed from a roller skate and some wood. A set of wheels was placed on the bottom at the front, the second set was attached to the plank at the rear. One foot would ride on the contraption, the other would push. The other pushmobile was made from a salvaged orange crate. Buggy or wagon wheels were fastened to the base and a rope or a board was attached to the front axle for steering. Each crate was customized using paint; Billy added a pillow for the seat, tin cans for headlights and a bicycle horn. One person rode while another pushed.

Billy had a mischievous side that often got him into trouble. He regularly climbed out of the bedroom window to continue playing when he was supposed to be in bed. Sometimes he was caught, but not often.

Alvin was Billy's older brother by almost three years. They were very close and did everything together. Saturday's they snuck into the neighborhood movie theater through the side door in the morning and stayed all day. One person paid a nickel for admission, then went to the bathroom, where he opened the side door for the rest of his friends. For spending money, they searched through the sweepings of the theater.

The brothers loved to play tricks on their father. They went down into the cellar and rang the doorbell by touching the wires together to get their father to answer the door. They could hear him get out of the rocking chair and walk to the door. They waited until they heard the creak, creak, creak of the chair before they rang the bell again. They kept this up until their father yelled, "Okay you kids in the basement, stop that."

During the First World War, Alvin and Billy dug a foxhole between the rows of corn in the garden to hide from the enemy. Their mother fell into the foxhole while harvesting the corn. Since it wasn't very deep, she didn't get hurt. They weren't punished but they had to explain where the enemy was.

Heating water for baths was a big project in those days, especially with so many children. They didn't have an automatic water heater, so water was heated in a big copper kettle on the stove. When the kettle was full of water, it was so heavy that it took two people to carry it. Since the park near their house had an indoor swimming pool, their mother sent her children there for a weekly swim, which was their bath. Swimming was not Billy's passion; when he could, he ditched the swim.

The family was resourceful and used ingenuity to stretch their income. The older children, Elsie, Alvin, and William, were sent with a wagon to the railroad tracks to search for coal for the furnace. They were warned not to return home until the wagon was filled to the top. Coal came in three kinds: hard, soft, and coke. As they picked, they sorted the coal into piles so that the proper kind could be used to control the fire.

Alvin delivered medicine for a drug store for three pennies a trip and Bill delivered groceries for a penny. Their bank was a mason jar buried in the basement. One day their mother stepped on the jar and broke it.

She was mad. The boys were punished for taking her mason jar, but not for hiding the money.

On Bill's twelfth birthday, Aunt Emma gave him a statue of a white goat with black spots that had its head down. A young boy was sitting on the ground, holding on to its long horns, either pulling or being pushed by the billy goat. (I always thought that the statue fit my father perfectly. I wonder if Aunt Emma thought the same?)

The family used an ice box to keep the food cold. It was William's responsibility to fetch the block of ice. He used a wheelbarrow to carry the ice since a block weighed 100 lbs. After one trip, while Bill opened the cellar door to put the wheelbarrow away, his sister Connie, who was his junior by nine years, decided to help him. The wheelbarrow got away from her and the axle gouged into her foot. Her foot was bleeding badly, and her mother, who was all dressed up and ready to go downtown, was not happy with the accident. Bill told his mother to go, he would take care of his sister. Taking his time, he cleaned and bandaged her wound. Connie still has a scar as a reminder of the day.

Bill was a runner in his youth, running four miles every day for practice. He participated in several races sponsored by one of the city's big newspapers. He stopped running after a couple of years when he didn't achieve the results that he wanted. (I was very surprised when I learned that my father ran in races. For as long as I can remember, the only exercise he did was to walk, and that was out of necessity not for recreation or exercise.)

Bill was a member of the debating team in high school. At the end of the year, the best members of the team competed against other schools in a contest. One year he took the pro side of the argument and won. The next year, the subject was the same. In order to make it more challenging, he took the opposite side and won that debate too.

Of the eleven children born, three boys and five girls survived childhood. They inherited their family's characteristics—short to medium height, slender build, fair skin, light hair and blue eyes. They inherited a love of God and of music. Bill loved to play the harmonica; he always had one in his pocket and played whenever the mood struck.

Bill and Edna were born with a lazy right eye. Bill's vision was worse than his sister's. Always resourceful, he memorized the eye chart so that he would pass the test for his driver's license. Because of his vision and family circumstances he wasn't drafted for World War II.

After graduating from Haugan High School in January of 1925, Bill went to work for the railroad repairing box cars. One day on the way to work, he stopped at Walgreen's to buy a package of cigarettes. They were giving away a car and gave him a chance with his purchase. He put the stub in his pocket. That Monday, his mother did the wash as usual. She picked up William's shirt to wash it, but it fell out of the basket. After the clothes were washed, she found the shirt laying on the floor and said it would just have to wait until the next washing day. Bill was very glad his shirt was still dirty; the winning ticket for the new car was in the pocket of that shirt.

After work one day, Bill went with his younger brother, Earl, to the woods. There they found a puppy with a noose around its neck, tied to a tree. They felt sorry for the dog and let it loose. After playing with it for a while they headed home and the dog followed. Connie said, "Mother was madder than a wet hen. She didn't want a dog." Tess, as they named the dog, initially lived in the yard; she gradually moved to the porch and was eventually invited to live inside.

Since the children were getting older, working and adding to the family income, the family bought a bungalow. One evening Bill and Edna took a load of boxes to the new house. Bill was very happy and after they locked up the house, he suggested to his sister that they sing. They stood outside on the porch singing some of the popular songs of the day with gusto. They lingered for hours, singing. Bill was in no hurry to leave.

Alvin and Bill were working for the railroad when the Depression hit and they both lost their jobs, drastically reducing the family income. Each Sunday, the family held a meeting and planned their meals for the week. The children voted on the menu and agreed to stick to it, including how many slices of bread each person would eat at each meal. Dinner was rhubarb sauce or applesauce on bread. The lost income also caused the loss of the bungalow. The family went back to renting.

Their mother belonged to a Swedish lodge. On the nights she attended meetings, the children used the time to do things that weren't allowed. One evening, Bill, who was learning to dance, closed the doors to the front room to keep the younger kids from watching, put music on the phonograph and was showing Edna the steps he had learned. Connie asked him when he was going to teach her to dance. Bill replied, "I will, I will."

That night his mother came home early. She was furious when she saw her son and daughter dancing. She spouted, "You're not making a dance hall out of my house. Dancing is only for worldly people, for people who don't have any thoughts in their head."

At the age of twenty-one, Bill wrote the following in his autograph book: "Roaming through this book brings back many memories, some happy, some a bit on the shady side, nevertheless I am glad it was as it was and if I had the power to change the past—relive the past—I would not ask to have it different than it was. My understanding of life has been made deeper because of those years. A laugh always follows a tear. To understand life we must live it, and sooner or later we will discover that no matter what the reverse, life is worth living and that happyness (sic) comes from simplicity. William E. Witting, Philosopher"

Bill wasn't practicing any religion when he met Marie, who was a Catholic, at a church dance. A short time later, Bill converted to the Catholic religion which didn't make his mother happy. She nagged him unmercifully. She stopped when Connie told her mother that it was better that Bill was a Catholic than no religion at all. Marie was so good and sweet that everyone loved her and she won over her mother-in-law.

Marie spent the week before my birth in bed in the hospital. She had lost her first child and the doctors didn't want to take a chance with me. I was born on October 4, the feast day of St. Francis of Assisi, patron saint of animals and the founder of the Franciscan order.

My mother was of Irish and German descent. Her father was a first generation Irish-American and her mother was a second generation German-American. Both nationalities are known for their stubbornness. Combined with the stubbornness I inherited from my father, I was a very determined child.

For the first four years, my life was normal. Before my first birthday we moved to the country, into a house built by my father. I became acquainted with chickens and rabbits and with other aspects of country life. I had my first dog, an Irish Setter named Rusty. I was already beginning to express my personality—inquisitive, determined. One morning I decided that wasps were not supposed to live in my tree and I knocked their nest down with a stick. My mother had to beat the wasps off of me with a broom. Sometime later, while my father changed a flat tire on a country road, I wandered into the pasture to "talk to the cows." That was the reason I gave my parents when they finally found me, a tiny girl surrounded and hidden by huge beasts.

After my third birthday, I received a brother for a playmate. A year and a half after his arrival, everything changed. My father was at work and my mother, brother, and I were taking a nap when our house caught fire. I woke to a smoke filled room and called my mother. She carried me outside, told me to roll in the snow, and returned for my brother. They never came out.

I had third degree burns over a large portion of my body. It required many months in a hospital in Chicago, but I survived due to the skill and dedication of my surgeon, Dr. Slaughter, and the rest of the medical team. They waited until I was stronger to tell me that my mother had died. Over the next two years, I had to return to the hospital a number of times for more surgery.

Our minds are selective. They hide many memories that give us pain. I don't remember anything from that time in the hospital except for these two things. The story of the death of my mother and brother in the fire and my survival appeared in the newspapers. Readers sent me many cards and presents. A person in Hawaii sent a brown musical bear, which I named Cinnamon Bear after the Christmas story. (I don't remember the cards or the presents but Cinnamon Bear, minus his music box, sits in a position of honor on top of the jewelry box on my dresser.)

I was still in the hospital in June. I wanted to buy a present for my Dad for Father's Day. I confided my wish to my favorite nurse who took me shopping. While we were out, my doctor stopped in. I missed his visit, but I got my father's present.

After I was released from the hospital, Dad and I moved to a neighboring town in the country. Their parish school didn't have a kindergarten so Dad talked to the Sisters and they agreed to keep me in the first grade for two years. During that time, we moved three times. Our first house was next to the school, then we moved to a house four blocks away.

From there we moved to an old chicken coop on the edge of town so Dad would have a place to work on his current game, Country Auction. He designed and printed a playing board complete with play money and activity cards. He made houses and wells to be auctioned off. His strong faith in God, his creative mind, and my presence helped him to survive the tragedy.

Soon after we moved to the edge of town, I lingered with friends after school and missed the school bus. I asked someone how to get home and was pointed in the right direction. I had a long walk—more than two miles, and I cried all the way. Dad met me when I was crossing the railroad tracks, almost home. I never missed the school bus again.

Whenever I got sick, I always ended up in double trouble. I had chicken pox with whooping cough, measles with the mumps. I don't know the reason—the double sickness, pressure from the authorities because of our living conditions, or if Dad just missed his family—but the summer before second grade, we moved back to Chicago. I went to live with Aunt Connie, her family, and Gramma Witting on the North side. My father rented a garage on the South side to use as living quarters as well as a workshop. It had a toilet and running water. Dad used shelves and equipment to divide it into living and working space.

I lived with my aunt's family for a year. Dad didn't have a car so on Saturday morning I caught the bus for the four mile trip to the South side to spend the weekend with my father. Sunday afternoon I took the bus back again.

Something happened during that year which made a lasting impression. Aunt Connie returned from shopping, bringing home clothes for her sons. I watched the handing out of the parcels with interest. My aunt said, "There's nothing here for you. You have your own father to buy things for you." Because of this experience, I have always made it a practice to include everyone who is at our house when I'm passing out things.

Before school began in the fall, I moved to the garage to live with Dad. My new neighborhood was a mix of cultures, nationalities, and religions. The Catholic church, St. Finbarr's, was the furthest away—across the street and around the corner. Behind us, on the other side of the alley, the members of a Jewish synagogue gathered for services on the Sabbath, High Holy Days and other occasions. In front of our garage, a store became a Gospel Church where the congregation met regularly for music, prayer, and fellowship. (I only lived with Dad part of the time but he lived in the garage for three more years.)

Aunt Elsie's husband didn't approve of how my father was raising me, neither did my maternal grandmother, Gramma M. They both tried to get custody and involved the courts and social workers in their quest.

In an effort to appease my relatives, Dad offered to paint the rooms of an elderly woman in exchange for my room and board. After the painting was finished, she told Dad that I was too much work for her, I couldn't live there anymore. Whenever I have tea with milk, I think of her. It was a grownup treat that I was allowed to have at her house.

I lived with an aunt's in-laws for a while; they lived in our neighborhood. I went to my father's place after school and returned to their house in time for supper and stayed the night. That arrangement was also short lived. They were childless at the time and she was very particular about her house and I sometimes wet the bed at night.

I spent a part of each summer vacation with Gramma M. in the country. She had a cinder block cottage on the swamp end of a lake in Wisconsin. The cottage lacked modern conveniences—it didn't have running water, electricity or a telephone. We had an ice box, an indoor chemical toilet, and a water pump connected to a well outside; we used kerosene lamps for light. There were no children nearby for me to play with. But the cottage was on the lake. I went down to the pier and looked for frogs and fish. I picked wild flowers by the armful. I helped Gramma plant and tend the garden. I learned about snakes and chiggers. We dug for worms in the compost heap to go fishing. We watched the stars at night.

Getting out to the main part of the lake in the row boat took a minimum of thirty minutes, if you didn't get lost. Since we were on the swamp end, we had to navigate through the islands of grasses and mud, zig-zagging our way until we got to deep water. We passed ducks, bird nests, baby ducklings, dragonflies, mosquitoes, swimming insects, bubbling mud, acres of water lilies, and island upon island of swamp grass. I never learned the way out to the main part of the lake, I was too busy looking at everything else. If the fish were biting, we caught a nice mess of crappie, lake trout, sunfish, or bullhead. I was allowed to help clean them for dinner.

Gramma M. was in her seventies. She was of medium height, with a stocky build and pure white hair. She was very independent and inquisitive and told everyone my "tragic" story. My grandmother didn't drive, she hitchhiked wherever she wanted to go. Many times we walked a couple of miles to the community hall before sunset, planning to get a ride home with a friend. If her friend wasn't there, she picked a likely candidate and begged a ride home, using me as the reason. She was well known in that part of the country so most of the time it was a neighbor who picked her up when she was hitchhiking on the highway to and from town, but sometimes it was a truck driver just passing through. Dad didn't like her method of transportation.

Although Gramma M. liked to tell my story to others, I tried to ignore my scars and do everything that the other kids did. I was a tomboy, always climbing fences and garage roofs. I skipped rope, played hop scotch and raced friends and buses. I was not handicapped by my scars, except that I needed to protect my back from the sun and I couldn't touch my toes. The fact that I was different from everyone else was very apparent—my scars were very visible. People, grownups especially, were always asking me questions…they weren't always kind.

One summer Dad had a surprise waiting for me when I returned from summer vacation in Wisconsin. In order to enter the garage, we had to pass through a small storage area. This time I had to detour around a huge doll house that completely covered a card table. Dad had built it out of wood while I was gone. It had a porch, doors that opened and closed, shutters on the windows, shingles on the roof and electricity. The only thing missing was furniture. Blocks of wood and my imagination took care of that.

The next summer a black and white Schwinn bicycle sat next to the doll house. Since Dad never had a bike as a child, he wanted me to have one. It wasn't new but I didn't care.

We always celebrated Christmas in the garage. Dad bought or was given a tree on Christmas Eve and we decorated it with paper ornaments, tinsel and a string of lights before going to Midnight Mass. Santa never stopped at the garage, but he always stopped at my Gramma M.'s apartment. In the wee hours of the morning one Christmas day, I thought I heard reindeer hooves on the roof. I was mistaken, Christmas morning the floor under the Christmas tree was as empty as the night before. That year Santa didn't stop at Gramma M.'s either. I was told I was too old for presents from Santa. (My relatives were mistaken, even though our children are now grown, Santa always stops at our house.)

Everything that we learn in school doesn't always come out of a book. In fourth grade I discovered that I have been blessed—or cursed—with a voice that carries well. Even when I try to talk softly, people hear me in another room. Our parish was small, the church was on the first floor with the classrooms located above. I was allowed to stay upstairs with a few other classmates to clean the room while my class attended Stations of the Cross in church. Everyone was talking, except for me. I told them that we would get in trouble if Sister heard us. I got in trouble, my voice was the only one that Sister heard. I had to come downstairs and join the rest of my classmates in church.

I had many adventures while we lived on the South side. An incident from the summer before fifth grade stands out in my memory: two friends and I went to Lincoln Park Zoo, which was two bus rides and ten miles away. We were to meet my father at a certain time, on a certain corner, for the ride home. Signals must have crossed that day because we never found my father. The garage didn't have a telephone so I couldn't call him. None of us had money for the bus ride and it was too far to walk. I was elected to tell our story to the bus driver. He must have taken pity on us because not only did he give us a free pass, but also transfers for the next bus.

I was lonely. A friend's dog had puppies and I asked if I could have one. Dad said yes. Queenie came to live with us, but she only stayed for a few weeks. I left her alone in the back yard while I went inside for my roller skates. When I came back, she was gone. I called and called, looked and looked but didn't find her. Someone must have cut through our back yard and picked up the puppy on the way. She couldn't have gotten out by herself.

My uncle felt sorry for me and adopted a mixed collie from a shelter. We only had her for a short time when Tippie caught distemper. It didn't matter what remedy Dad tried, she kept getting worse. One day when I came home from school, she was gone.

I still wanted a dog. A friend told me about Penny, a wire haired terrier mix that her cousin had. They were moving and couldn't keep the dog. I asked my father. He said no because he was afraid Penny would catch distemper from our garage. I didn't give up, I pestered and pestered. Dad finally gave in. Penny wasn't a pretty dog but she had character. She was black and white with a white mane on top of her head, white eyebrows and a white goatee. She was very talented. She caught mice and brought them to me for a present. (Three must have been Penny's lucky number, she lived with us for sixteen years.)

When I was in fifth grade, Dad got a night job at a bowling alley setting pins, leaving me home alone with Penny. He always cautioned me to lock the door, to be very quiet, and not to let anyone know that I was there. As the weeks and months passed, my relations became very upset that I was alone every night. My father's younger sister, Ruth, came to the rescue and stayed with me until Dad came home from work.

The summer before I started sixth grade, Connie convinced her brother, Bill, that it was his turn to live with his mother in her North side apartment. We moved again and I returned to the same school where I had spent second grade. They had two rooms for each grade, even and odd. In second grade I was on the even side and when I returned, I was placed on the odd side. Unlike today's students, who switch classes and know everyone in the same grade, we stayed in the same room for the entire day. We didn't talk to the students on the other side nor did we change sides for the next school year. We remained on our side until we changed schools or graduated. I had a difficult time making friends, most of my classmates had been together since first grade.

After we moved in with my grandmother, Dad got a regular daytime job with a tool company and we lived in an apartment like other families. We even had our first television set. Until that time, I watched only an occasional program at a friend's house. Instead, I read books or listened to the radio. I begged to be allowed to stay up to listen to a favorite program, only to be told that I could listen, if I got ready for bed and laid down. Of course, I often fell asleep before the program ended.

My grandmother's apartment was on the third floor. Dad rented our landlady's garage for a workshop. As grandma got older, she found climbing the stairs exhausting. This gave Dad some privacy; he spent evenings and weekends in the garage, working on his games and other inventions.

Since I was getting older, my relatives became more concerned about my spiritual welfare. My father's family were Christians; some were Methodist and the rest belonged to a Bible church. They didn't understand how I could be "saved" since I was a Catholic. The differences in our respective religions caused many disagreements. Vatican II, when some of the rules of the Catholic church were changed, was still in the future. We didn't eat meat on Fridays or on the eve of certain Holy Days. We fasted from Midnight, no food or drink, except water, before receiving communion. Often Dad and I ate tuna fish casserole while the rest of the family had Swedish meatballs or a roast. When we lived with Gramma Witting, my aunts and uncles gathered on Christmas Eve to celebrate and exchange presents. The family gatherings often lasted past midnight and we had to pass up cake, cookies and pudding if we were attending Mass in the morning.

In eighth grade, I had to choose my high school. I picked Alvernia, an all-girl Catholic school. I looked forward to high school. I thought that since everyone was going to a new school, it would be easier to make friends. I didn't know that many of my new classmates went to the same high school that their friends did. Once again I would have a hard time making friends.

Several of my grammar school classmates attended Alvernia, meeting at the corner store in the morning. I wasn't invited, but I arrived early so that I could go to school with them, and met them after school for the bus ride home. This lasted for about a month until one morning they met extra early so that they could go to school without me. I was told, "You weren't invited to come with us, you were only tagging along." I was very shy during those days and after this episode, I stayed more to myself.

Dad had two romantic involvements while I was in school. The first was with a woman who worked in the cloakroom at the bowling alley. I don't know if they ever went out on a date but Dad really liked her. He explained that he did not want me to have a stepmother so he wasn't going to ask her to marry him. The second woman conned my father but he was not aware of it. He signed up for ballroom dance lessons and developed a crush on his teacher. She pretended to be interested in him…then she informed him that she could be fired if she saw him outside of class. It was a ploy to convince Dad to sign up for extra lessons. It worked. When he finally realized her true motive, he quit and hired a lawyer to break his contract.

We lived with my grandmother for four years. Dad got tired of her nightly comment, "Oh, it's you," and decided that we should move. He told me that it was for my well being since she and I fought like two cats. Dad didn't know that Gramma prevented me from entering the apartment when she wasn't home by putting a chair against the back door. She said I didn't need a key to the front door. Gramma was in her eighties and listened to religious music on the radio. She was having a hard time adjusting to a teenager who enjoyed dancing and listened to Rock-N-Roll music. I think Dad was also tired of his job because he soon quit. I told him "no garages".

I was a sophomore in high school when we found an apartment with a store in front that Dad converted into a printing shop. I inherited the duties of cook, dishwasher, housekeeper, laundress, and shopper while I continued to go to school. Money was tight, so I got a part time job as a waitress at a dimestore to earn spending money.

Penny liked the new apartment but she missed my grandmother. When we lived in the garage, we gave her rye bread which she often hid to eat later when she was hungry. We heard the crunching late at night. Gramma put butter on the rye bread before giving it to Penny. Penny didn't want to go back to eating dry rye, she wanted butter or gravy on her bread.

During high school I became aware of one of Dad's habits. Although he was always on time for Sunday Mass, he had a tendency to be late for everything else. Ready to leave, I listened to the clock tick as I waited for him, realizing we would be late again.

Dad gave me two very good pieces of advice. One I listened to and the other I ignored. The first was, "You don't eat garbage, why speak it?" I have been careful to use clean language since that time, except when I'm angry my words tend to become more colorful. The other piece of wisdom concerned smoking. My father smoked three packages of cigarettes a day. He said, "You're foolish if you smoke." I was foolish, I smoked.

I was still very self-conscious about my scars, especially after a boy I cared for broke up with me to date a beauty queen. I visited the doctor who performed the operations when I was a child to investigate plastic surgery. The doctor and his staff were amazed with what I had accomplished. They didn't think that I would ever have the flexibility to raise my hands over my head. I hadn't known that I wasn't supposed to be able to do it. I abandoned the idea of surgery and decided then and there that a few scars were nothing to be ashamed of. If people did not like me as I was, then it was their loss, not mine.

I didn't expect a graduation present from my father, I knew we didn't have any money. His printing business was struggling. Once again Dad surprised me. Before we left for graduation, he gave me a tiny diamond pendant.

After graduation from high school, my scars caused another problem when I applied for a job at Blue Cross. Even though I had been in perfect health since the accident except for childhood diseases, they declined to hire me. They didn't give a reason, but I think they were afraid I wanted plastic surgery.

It is ironic how the same circumstances affect people differently. Dad was affected negatively by many of the setbacks that we faced and continued to dwell upon past disappointments instead of putting them aside. I, on the other hand, have usually been able to maintain a positive outlook on life. I have a cheerful, sunny disposition unless I am worried about some molehill that I have allowed to reach mountainous proportions. I am more apt to count my blessings than my disappointments.

2

Pap

My husband and I were meant for each other. That explains why a boy from the mountains of Maryland fell in love with a girl from the big city of Chicago while in California. My girlfriend and I planned to go to Hawaii until we phoned a travel agent and learned the cost of the trip was more than we could afford. We were looking for someplace to go when a co-worker mentioned she wanted to visit her fiance, who was in the army, stationed in California. She didn't want to go alone. We joined forces for a trip that changed my life.

It had been a long plane ride from Chicago to California. All I wanted was to take off my heels and get into comfortable clothes. Instead, I was sitting in the back seat of a dark blue Cadillac waiting for our friend's fiancee to come out of a house. He was only stopping for a minute. He would be right back, he told us. That was a half hour ago.

Instead, a tall, skinny young man emerged. He wore green army fatigues tailored to fit his body, the pants tucked into black combat boots. His ash blonde hair was cut military fashion, a little long on top and very short on the sides. His face and hands were tanned from the sun.

As we watched, he closed the front door, walked down the steps and turned the corner headed for the back of the house where he picked up a garden hose. Turning on the water, he proceeded to squirt the occupants of the house through the open screened window.

This was my first look at the man who was to become my husband.

Tom and my father hit it off right from the start. This was very fortunate since, except for the early years of our marriage, my father lived with us until the month before his death. During our first year of marriage, Tom and I lived in California where our oldest daughter, Kathy, was born.

All new parents receive their education from their offspring; we were no different. I had a copy of Dr. Spock's book to which I referred in times of doubt. Kathy broke all the rules. According to Dr. Spock, newborns sleep most of the time; they only wake long enough to eat. Kathy didn't know she was supposed to sleep most of the time. She thought she should be awake when her parents were awake, otherwise she might miss something. Girls are dainty and quiet, not our daughter. She was very curious and climbed like a cat to investigate anything that sparked her interest. She broke us in well—I put Dr. Spock away.

Soon after Kathy's birth, Tom was transferred overseas and our daughter and I followed. We were in Germany for a year, during that time my husband decided not to reenlist. While I could still travel, I returned to my father's apartment in Chicago to await the birth of our second child. Dad was living in an apartment in a row house and had a separate location for his printing shop. Tom planned to join us in two months, after he received his discharge.

Before we left for Germany, we sold our car to Dad for a dollar. Shortly before Kathy and I flew home, Dad had problems with the car. The brakes went out. He was able to safely drive to a garage but they weren't able to work on it right away. Not wanting to drive the car without brakes, he left it overnight. In the morning, the mechanic didn't know the brakes were gone and smashed the car into a telephone pole. The garage should have been responsible for replacing the car but they were Dad's friends and he didn't want to pursue it. Dad didn't want to tell us about the car in a letter, preferring to tell us himself. Since Dad didn't have a car, he asked Aunt Ruth to go with him to pick us up at the airport.

While we waited for our baggage, Aunt Ruth confided she was glad I was home because Dad was getting into trouble without me. I never inquired as to what kind of trouble, but she hinted—a woman.

I made a novena to St. Joseph when I was dating Tom and promised that our first son would be named after him. Our son, William Joseph, was born in March. I liked how the name Billy Joe fit together. (If I had known the trouble I was causing using William for his first name, he would have been called Joe Billy.)

We lived in Dad's apartment for six months before we searched for a house to buy. We were cramped in the 4-room apartment with three adults, two children and two dogs. We hunted throughout the suburbs for a house but we couldn't find anything we liked and could afford. We finally found a nine-room house on the North side of Chicago. On our first visit we knew the house was for us.

The door from the foyer opened on a beautiful open wooden staircase which led to the second floor bathroom and bedrooms. Turning to our right, we walked into a double parlor where wooden pillars supported the archway separating the rooms. The only drawback was a tiny kitchen, just big enough for the stove and sink with a cabinet for dishes—the refrigerator was in the pantry. We couldn't eat in the kitchen but our family and guests would fit comfortably around the table in the adjoining dining room.

The house belonged to a retired couple who were moving to a small cottage on a lake and didn't need all of their belongings. We offered to buy their house and their excess furniture. Along with many beautiful paintings, beds, dressers, a couch and chairs, we acquired an old refrigerator in the basement. We decided to keep it and use it for storing milk and pop. My husband invited my father to live with us.

Besides his own house, Tom wanted a garage in which to work on his car. He had his garage for two years, then my father was forced to give up his printing shop because they were tearing the building down. Tom told Dad to move his equipment into our garage until he found another place.

A year later, my father's stuff was still in the garage. He announced (didn't ask) that he had bought a new printing press. I thought he had picked up a small press, the size of a card table. Wrong! When it was delivered, we discovered he purchased a huge, German press. It took up most of the garage and towered over me. It was wired for the current in Germany and needed a converter to run on our electric.

Dad figured out how to rewire the press so it would work. He insulated the garage, planning to run a printing business from home. No sooner was the insulation up when a couch in the alley caught fire and spread to our garage. Although the press wasn't damaged, all of the insulation was burned and the garage doors needed to be replaced. My father had to start all over again. Soon after, new technology in the form of photocopying revolutionized the printing industry, making his plans for a printing shop impractical. Dad got a job working the second shift at a company that printed envelopes.

The year Dad turned 57, he was involved in a car accident that was serious enough to require a visit to a doctor. The only injury he sustained was a whiplash to his neck but during the examination, the doctor discovered my father had developed Emphysema from years of heavy smoking. When Dad celebrated his next birthday, he decided he had smoked long enough; with the help of a no-smoking aid, he quit.

Although I had tried various ways to earn money working at home, I didn't earn enough money to make a difference. It didn't matter how I stretched Tom's paycheck, I always ran out of money. A neighbor told me about her evening part time job and suggested I work there. Tom and I discussed the problems that would arise if I worked away from home. Our main concern was the care of our children. Working nights would allow me to be home with the kids during the day and Tom would be home with the kids at night. I could make supper before I left. We could use the extra money. We decided I should try it.

The company had an opening, I applied and was hired. My first night at work, I was invited by the girl who was training me to join her group for break. The next day she didn't say anything, so I stayed by myself, I thought they didn't like me. Luckily, after break she asked me why I hadn't joined them. I made up some excuse, and told her I would join them the next day. I was still a loner, shy and slow to make friends.

Soon after I began working, I became pregnant again. Our daughter Terrina was born in the fall. After her birth, Tom and I discussed our options, we decided I should return to work. The extra money helped.

Dad retired at 62. Now he had time to develop his inventions, putter around the house, and spend time with his three grandchildren.

My father had a special relationship with his grandchildren. They looked up to him not only as a grandfather but as a friend. He didn't do traditional grandfather things—tell stories or take them special places. He was always there to listen to a problem or an idea, fix a book-bag or toy, or tie a shoe. The kids called him Pap.

Our son was very shy when he was young and didn't like to try anything new in front of strangers. Pap practiced skipping with Billy so he would be comfortable skipping with his class in kindergarten. Pap also needed practice in other things: printing letters and numbers, singing songs, and coloring.

The year Dad retired, my husband and I made one of the best investments of our lives. A new camping resort located 100 miles from the city invited us to tour their facilities. When we arrived, we could see that the campground was still being developed, most of the roads were dirt. The salesmen used jeeps to take their guests on tours, traveling through the hills and mud. But we were impressed with what we saw. It had a huge lake and another was under construction. As we sat on the dam between the two lakes, the salesman asked if we could picture ourselves fishing on the lake. We could. A swimming pool and a playground were already built. The resort was located on wooded, rolling hills. The camp sites were spacious, we didn't feel as if we were on top of our neighbor. Even though we had never gone camping or owned any camping equipment, we bought property. We purchased a canvas pop-up trailer from a friend and started a weekend retreat that was to become our second home. My father didn't like the country so he stayed home with the pets while every other weekend in the summer our family went camping.

My husband came from a large family of thirteen children; I was raised as an only child. Strangely we didn't have too many differences of opinion about child raising. We both loved children but did not want brats. My husband's family believed in the strap or the stick; my father seldom hit me. Tom was afraid he would hurt our kids if he hit them so he left the job of disciplinarian to me. I used a combination of spanking and chair sitting when they were young and grounding as they grew older. We decided to send them through the Catholic school system and told them a good education was their inheritance. This combination must have worked. Our son feels they won't need a psychiatrist because they have good feelings about their own self-worth. We enjoy the individuals they have become.

My father never interfered in our decisions concerning our children, nor did he get involved or take sides in our arguments. He always left it to us to work it out. If we were involved in a heated discussion, he vanished. Tom and my dad only had three arguments in the thirty years he lived with us. All three concerned the printing press and the garage.

My husband and I saw the play *A Fiddler On The Roof*. I was impressed with the way the father, Tevye, talked to God as a friend. I thought if he could do it, so could I, and I traded formal prayer for informal conversations. They usually began, "Please help me…" or "Thank You for…"

When we bought our house, we thought it was huge, but now it wasn't big enough, and our three children were growing. We had a large unfinished attic that was tall enough for an adult to stand in. Pap decided to finish it. He insulated the walls and ceiling, widened the staircase, and laid a floor. When it was finished, he moved into the back to use as a combination bedroom/workshop and gave us the front. Tom used the space for a den before we gave it to Billy for a bedroom.

We needed more living space in the country too. We had two double beds in our pop-up but the children were getting too tall to sleep three to a bed. We never returned the pop-up to its compact traveling size and replaced it with a sixteen foot travel trailer. Our new country home had a furnace, a four burner stove and an ice box—everything but a bathroom. We bought a porta-pottie for emergencies. Now that we had a furnace, we were able to run away to the country earlier in the spring and camp later in the fall.

◆   ◆   ◆

At the age of four, Terri came home from playing to ask her father if a friend could plant a garden in our back yard. Tom gave his permission and Terri brought "Muscles" home. His real name was Earl Wallace but he got his nickname from his physique. He was a very dark, tall, muscular, older black man. My father didn't raise me to be prejudiced but my husband was from the South, with very biased parents. The years he spent in the service had exposed him to people of many races and softened his views. Even so, Tom was very surprised when he saw our daughter's friend. We didn't know it but our family was soon to be adopted by this gentle man. He became part of our lives until his death fifteen years later.

Muscles loved to see things grow. He needed acres to plant—the first summer, our postage stamp garden contained more than 48 tomato plants. Often, our tomato plants were taller than the garage. Muscles took care of the garden and Pap took care of the lawn. They shared the back porch, kids, and pets. Muscles and Pap drank many cups of coffee together on the back porch while they watched the garden grow. They both liked to comb the alley for good stuff they brought home because they knew we needed it. They always had a very good reason why their latest treasure should not be returned to the trash. We never knew where Muscles lived, but he appeared at our house regularly.

When Pap was 64, too young for Medicare, he developed a bad cold. We were very concerned since he appeared to have trouble breathing. It didn't matter how much I pestered, he refused to go to the doctor. One night he couldn't breathe when he went to bed and finally agreed to go to the hospital. The doctor diagnosed a severe case of pneumonia. It was three weeks before he was well enough to be released from the hospital. He told me not to worry, he had insurance. I searched through his papers and found two insurance policies that paid twenty-dollars-a-day if he was hospitalized. The hospital social worker applied for financial assistance through welfare for him. Pap was so sick we thought we were going to lose him. X-rays showed a large dark spot on one of his lungs, but his weakened condition made surgery impossible. After he was released from the hospital, Pap made it a practice to walk up and down three flights of stairs many times a day. This exercise helped because when he returned for x-rays the spot was gone.

Pap was always interested in self-improvement; he bought books and tapes on many different subjects. He read books on preventive medicine and took an assortment of vitamins. He tried different ways to clear his lungs, from eating more of one food group to limiting his intake of another. He thought I should take vitamins and quit smoking.

Although I inherited many traits from my father, the ability to play a musical instrument wasn't one of them. In order to satisfy my love for music I collected record albums. On any given day, the sounds coming from the phonograph might be jazz, folk music, dixieland, classical, the Boston Pops, Elvis, show tunes, Dean Martin, country, Harry Belafonte, or gospel music. I varied the music to suit my mood. If I was happy, the music would be light; if I was troubled, I stacked the phonograph with religious music.

One of the traits I inherited from my father's family was a love of cooking. I collected cookbooks like I collected records. The subjects were just as varied. Except Tom was a particular eater, a regular meat and potatoes man. His favorite breakfast was pancakes, which we had every Sunday and holiday. I could add apples or blueberries to mine, just as long as I didn't fool around with his. Although Tom grew up on a farm, he didn't like many vegetables. I read cookbooks like I read mysteries, always searching for new recipes that my family would eat.

When we married, Tom and I talked about children. We agreed four was a good number. Time passed—we had three children interspersed with a couple of miscarriages. I said we would continue to try for children until the last one was in school, then that was it. Terri started kindergarten. I felt we should be happy with three healthy children and stop trying for any more. Wrong! Our fourth child, Susan, soon joined our family.

Our sixteen foot trailer in the country was not big enough to accommodate four growing children. Tom said we could keep it but if it rained, we were going home. Or we could get something larger. I had quit my job to stay home with Susie so money was tight. We went shopping and found a 35' burnt out unit. The fire was confined to the back bedroom, the rest of the trailer was smoke damaged. We planned to convert the bedroom to a bunkroom for the kids. Tom and I would sleep on a couch in the front room. It had a refrigerator with a freezer—we could have ice cubes and ice cream. It had a stove with an oven. The kids said, "Good, no more Hamburger Helper." The water heater had rusted out because the trailer wasn't winterized after the fire, we had a bathroom but couldn't use the fixtures, so we used our portapottie for emergencies. (The comfort station was right down the street complete with toilets and showers.) The furnace was damaged by the fire, so we bought a space heater. Our new country home even had air conditioning. We named it "The White Elephant." Our trailer came with extra guests—wasps. We called an exterminator. Now we had more room—we could take the dogs, the kids could bring a friend, we were able to take Muscles.

Our family continued to escape to the country at every opportunity. Sometimes we took the dogs, often we left them home with Pap. He still didn't like the country; he said he had too much to do in the city. He only went to the country with us if we needed his help. Muscles loved to go; he liked to fish, pick berries, plant flowers, and rake leaves. He wanted to plant a garden, but Tom wouldn't let him.

Now that Pap had free time, he purchased a red, three speed bicycle, to ride for exercise. He only had it for a short time when Billy asked his friend to go riding. Billy's friend didn't have a bike so Pap let him use his. After riding for a while, the boys stopped in a store for pop, leaving the bikes outside. While they were inside, someone stole Pap's bike. The parents of Billy's friend didn't have the money to replace it, so he was without a bike again.

When Susie was in first grade, a friend offered me a part time job. Tom and I talked it over and we decided it was a good opportunity to earn some extra money. Since it was only twenty hours per week and close to home, I had nothing to lose. We had a family conference and asked everyone to help with the housework.

Our neighborhood was fortunate to have a crossing guard, Angel, who was very friendly and enjoyed people. She knew the families that crossed her corner going to either the Catholic or the public schools, as well as the people who regularly went to church or waited for a bus. Through our kids, she met Pap. We lived six blocks from their school. If it was raining, snowing, or very cold, they were very long blocks. When I was working, Pap took pity on the kids and drove them to school or picked them up afterwards.

Our second daughter, Terri, was a happy child; she was always whistling. Whether it was the competition in school or being displaced as the youngest of the family, she started to dwell on the negative things that happened to her. I didn't want her to develop the habit of negative thinking. When she returned from a Girl Scout or school outing, she told me about the trip, emphasizing all the bad things. I was sad, she didn't have fun. Then I asked her to name one good thing for every bad one. I wouldn't feel so sad and neither would she because it sounded like she really had a good time. Terri told me she still thinks of one good thing for each bad one when things start to pile up.

Tom liked animals as much as I did so we always had more than one dog. When we lost one, another always appeared, needing a home. We noticed Tammy, our Belgian Shepherd, was having trouble laying down, getting back up. The vet said it was arthritis. Rather than allow her to suffer, we had her put to sleep. Tom knew I had an Irish Setter as a child and remembered the dog with fondness. A friend of Tom's had an Irish that was too much for them to handle. Tom asked if I wanted him. I said yes. Little did I know the adventure we were getting into. We named him Rusty. He was housebroken but that was the extent of his training. He was full grown—stubborn, aggressive, impossible. He was not afraid of anyone. He took possession of something and dared you to take it. I felt sorry for the dog since he had spent so much time alone; I didn't want to send him back to Anti-Cruelty, but I wasn't sure we could live with him either. Soon after he came to live with us, Rusty got into a fight with one of our other dogs. When Tom tried to break them up, Rusty bit him and Tom knocked him out. He developed a respect for Tom.

Rusty loved Muscles, he carried on like a young pup whenever he was at our house so Rusty listened to him too. Rusty liked me—I did the cooking, I was his person—but he didn't listen to me. He always questioned my authority. He stole a shoe, a piece of food, or some other treasure and growled, snapped, and barked—daring anyone to take the article away from him. If either Tom or Muscles was home, I got Rusty to behave by asking them to call the dog. If neither were home, I had to use devious means to retrieve his treasured possession.

If someone opened the door, Rusty was gone like the wind. He ran up and down the streets, around blocks, daring anyone to catch him. He never got tired—he liked the game of catch-me-if-you-can. He turned on a dime. When we were able to catch up with him, if we had the van, he got in without any coaching to go for a ride. He liked car rides.

One day he escaped into the van as we were getting ready to go to the country and wouldn't get out. Neither Tom nor Muscles could get him to move. From his first trip, he loved the country and we had a hard time leaving him home after that. He always sensed when we were going to the camper, and invited or not, managed to claim his space in the van.

Pap was very busy mopping up water when I came home from work one evening. I asked what had caused the flood. I learned Rusty had jumped into the tub in the second floor bathroom, and turned on the water to get a drink. Of course, he didn't turn the water off when he was finished. A washcloth stopped up the drain so the water over-flowed, through the bathroom floor into the pantry below and also out the bathroom door, through the hallway and down the stairs. Water was everywhere. We thought it was an accident that wouldn't happen again. We were wrong. Rusty remembered how to get a drink and turned the water on again with the same results. This time Pap installed a shut off valve by the tub so we could turn the water off. We cautioned the kids to turn the valve off after they were finished taking a bath. Rusty was just too smart. (Rusty lived with us until arthritis made him yelp in pain. Once again we took a dog to the vet for the last time.)

During the summer, our campground held a "Let's Paint" craft session using the techniques of Bill Alexander and "his mighty brush." (He demonstrated his method on television using big brushes to paint an oil landscape in a half hour.) I admired the ability to draw and paint, but I couldn't draw, so I assumed I wouldn't be able to paint. Here was an opportunity to test my theory. More than twenty people gathered that morning. We brought our bodies and everything else was provided: canvas, paint, brushes…along with instruction by a very talented and patient woman. Each person finished a painting of the Indiana sand dunes complete with a sailboat and clouds in a little over two hours and each painting was very different. To my amazement, my painting looked very good. I discovered a hidden talent and realized you don't have to draw in order to paint. I bought painting supplies and "How to Paint" books, and spent hours exploring the world of landscape and seascape in oil on canvas.

Pap loved to read and investigated various ways to earn money. He tried a mail order business without much success. He ordered quantities of various items to be ready for the orders as they poured in. They never did. In order to get rid of this merchandise, he rented a space at an indoor flea market and spent his weekends selling stuff. Then he needed more things to sell, so he frequented an auction and came home with boxes of lamps and broken appliances to fix and sell.

Pap had an old van which he used to haul his merchandise to the flea market. When the flea market closed. Pap didn't look for another one. He kept the van to pick up the kids from school. One day, he hit a car as he was leaving school. No one was hurt, the car only had minor damage, but he brought the van home and didn't drive it again. Then his driver's license expired and twice something happened to make Pap postpone his trip to renew his license. My father decided it was a sign to stop driving. He didn't want to get rid of his van and thought our kids might want it. He continued to buy license plates, until a few years later, the city towed it away.

Pap got into the habit of meeting his friends from the flea market for a couple of beers once or twice a week. One night they stopped at a tavern run by a widow. Her place was a few miles from our house, but it could be reached by taking one bus. My father struck up a friendship with the owner that lasted for a long time. He seriously considered asking her to marry him. He always enjoyed helping people and went to the tavern early to help and stayed late. As he made friends with more of the customers, his drinking escalated. Often, he fell asleep on the bus, missing his stop. Most of the time, he came home after the family was in bed. We found the strangest concoctions of food on the table or in the microwave. It was as if he had taken a little bit of everything in the refrigerator and piled it onto a plate. When we tried to talk to him about his drinking and the various things he did, he never remembered them. He didn't think he was drinking too much. After many years, the tavern was sold and Pap quit drinking.

Pap was not a person to see a doctor, he was seldom sick. Since his hospital confinement with pneumonia, he was more concerned with medical insurance. He investigated various options and decided to switch to Share, which was an HMO, (Health Maintenance Organization). Share covered all of the costs of his examinations, tests and hospital stays as long as it was authorized by his primary physician. He had to switch doctors but he thought the benefits were worth it.

Pap didn't stop with just changing his medical insurance. Stories appeared in the newspaper reporting problems with the mail, alerting senior citizens to watch for their checks. Thieves were stealing Social Security and pension checks from the mailboxes. Social Security announced a program to stop the theft—the monthly check would be directly deposited into the recipient's bank account. My father took advantage of their offer and no longer worried about his check being stolen. He also opened a joint checking account and a savings account in both of our names.

Pap continued to explore various ways to make money. He invented two or three different games. He tried selling various instruction manuals through the mail including a booklet on the steps to copyright an invention. His last project was a system to find the highest scoring words, arranged alphabetically, for the six-letter mystery word game puzzles. He spent hours in the attic working on his list. His system was compiled on a typewriter, Pap didn't know how to use a computer.

◆   ◆   ◆

At the camper, my husband and I were extremely tired of sleeping on a couch that made into a bed. The crossbar hurt our back when we were sleeping. We tried padding the bar and laying in a different direction, but nothing worked. I went looking for a new bed. Tom was at the lake fishing when I told him I finally found it. "Go buy it," he told me. "I want you to see it first," I replied. He was surprised when he saw the bed, it was surrounded by a bigger trailer. Our old trailer's furnace didn't work, so we only went camping from spring until fall. Our new trailer had a working furnace and air conditioning, now we could camp year round. We had a separate bedroom and a separate bunkroom, early risers had a place to go unless someone was sleeping on the couch. We could sleep eight people, not counting the floor space.

When things are running smoothly, something usually happens to change it. The number of hours I was working increased, although I was still working part time. Our household had barely adjusted to my new schedule when Kathy, our oldest daughter, decided to get married. I knew I would miss her help around the house. Like me, she loved to cook, and often made dinner on the days I worked.

Then the company I worked for moved to the suburbs and invited me to go with them. It meant working full time. We talked about our options. The country was in a recession and jobs were hard to get. Our budget had adjusted to the money I earned. We decided I should try it. Instead of working 10 minutes from home, my commute changed to twenty miles one way—an hour to get to work in the morning and from one to three hours to return home at night. I looked for alternative routes so I wouldn't have to spend my life in the car. I found different streets to take when the radio announcer gave travel times of over an hour on the expressway. The longer I worked in the suburbs, the more comfortable I became with my alternate routes. One morning, traffic was really backed up, we stopped and waited more than we moved. I became impatient and looked for a faster way to get to work. I was very surprised when I realized I could go North on a street I always drove South on coming home. I had never thought of it. It wasn't a one-way street but I had become rigid in my thinking, always doing things the same way. I vowed to take steps to become more flexible.

Our household was soon reduced by another person—Terri decided to get married. I lost my right hand, twice. Tom was working long hours, Bill was attending college and working part time, Sue was very busy in school—they didn't have time to help. Pap felt sorry for me and did more to help. He considered it his responsibility to keep our house supplied with milk. A large grocery store was near our house but the store Pap preferred, because it had better prices, was almost a mile from home. He found an old, broken shopping cart and rigged it to bring back the groceries. He took out the garbage and washed the towels. When no one came home early, he cooked supper and then did the dishes.

There weren't enough hours in the day to do everything that needed to be done. We fell into a pattern that included where we stored the various pieces of mail, books and magazines we wanted to look at but didn't have time to put away. Bill had the top of the china cabinet; Pap had one side of the buffet and I had the other. Sue had a shelf on the shadow box. Since I loved books and magazines, my pile had a habit of growing. Pap found a small three drawer chest which he put in the smaller room of our double parlor to keep tools and other things he used regularly.

Because of Pap's help and my family's support, I was able to start a new project. Soon after our marriage, my husband began a campaign to convince me to go to college. I always had reasons why it was impossible—the kids, my job, no time. I had earned several promotions at work and realized if I ever wanted to switch companies and get a comparable job, I needed more education. I enrolled at a community college.

I didn't know which Associates Degree to focus on: Accounting, Marketing or Management—all three fit my job description. I didn't know where to start, which course to take. Kathy and Bill had taken Economics in college, and it was required for all three of the degrees that interested me, so I registered for Macro Economics. The first night, our teacher asked everyone to introduce themselves, tell where they were from and their major. I started writing down the countries my classmates came from; but quickly gave up. Out of thirty-three students, only three were from the United States.

I didn't have a hard time learning when I was in high school but time changes many things. I spent seven hours reading a chapter of the economics text and still didn't remember what was in it. For a test I had to reread the whole chapter all over again. I was fortunate, our teacher was very good, and I enjoyed the class—both the subject matter and my fellow classmates. I received an A and I was hooked.

I often took my books and ran away to the camper for the weekend. It was quiet and peaceful, no telephones, no distractions; I did homework and studied for tests.

I liked our larger trailer in the country. I liked our separate bedroom with the door that could be closed when someone wanted to sleep late. I had the side of the bed next to the wall and didn't like climbing over Tom to get in or out. My knee was already starting to stiffen; I worried as I got older I would have more trouble getting out of bed. I wanted to be able to get out easier. In order to do that, we would either have to move our bed into the middle of the room or get bunk beds. We didn't have room to move our bed and I didn't want bunk beds.

Since our trailer was the maximum size allowed in the park, the only solution was to build a room addition, adding a bigger bedroom and a large family room. We listed the advantages. We would have room for our children and their spouses and it would be paid for before we retired. We found a contractor and visited the bank. After the room addition was built, we were able to move our bed into the middle of the new bedroom. Because of college and work, Bill seldom had the time to go to the camper. We gave Sue our old bedroom.

One of the advantages of working, other than earning money, is talking to other people. Since many hours are spent at work, co-workers become as close as family. Conversations cover a wide variety of topics—work, family, food, television programs. One day we began talking about religion. The person I was talking with shared my feelings; we were of different religions but she too often had informal conversations with God, talking to Him as a friend or her big brother, sharing her problems, asking Him for help. She said when they met, He would know her voice, they would not be strangers. I laughed because I knew He would recognize my voice too.

The drive to work in the morning wasn't getting any easier. My husband liked to tease that he could get to work in five minutes. I didn't want to think of how long it was going to take me. I began to reward myself for the long drive by stopping at McDonald's for a sausage biscuit. It was a small reward but the biscuit called my name as soon as I got in the car every morning. I waited until I got off the expressway in the suburbs before I detoured to McDonald's.

For Lent, I decided instead of giving up candy or chocolate, I would give up my morning sausage biscuit stop. To play fair, I wouldn't have a sausage biscuit on Sunday's either, I would wait until Lent was over. I didn't realize what I was giving up. Every morning for forty days, when I got in my car, I smelled the hot, fresh biscuit; I smelled the spicy sausage. I had to remind myself daily that I had given up sausage biscuits for Lent. I thought, after a while, the smell would disappear—it did, on Easter Monday, the day after Lent ended.

Throughout my childhood and the early years of my marriage, my father seldom missed Mass on Sundays or Holy days. But after he started drinking, he quit going to church. Then as his drinking escalated, he returned to Mass on Sundays. It wasn't long before he was going to Mass every morning. Soon after the tavern closed and he quit drinking, he struck up a friendship with a married woman he met at morning Mass.

On a Saturday morning the summer after Pap turned eighty, he returned from church to tell me he was going to the hospital. He had experienced chest pains during his morning walk and decided to have it checked out. I offered to drive him to the hospital and wait with him while he was examined. He accepted the ride but didn't want me to wait. He said I had enough to do without waiting for him, he would get home by himself. Later that afternoon, he called to tell us the doctors had transferred him to another hospital for tests. He stayed in the hospital for two weeks while they tried to clear the spot they found on his lungs.

While Pap was hospitalized, he phoned with a strange request. His friend from church was stopping by to pick up a copy of his game Country Auction. Would I please give it to her. By way of explanation he said she was very interested when he explained his game. He thought she was a newspaper reporter who was going to write a story about it.

That same year, Muscles spent the night at our house, fell onto the floor the following morning and couldn't get up. We called an ambulance and the paramedics took him to the hospital. The doctors said he had a stroke and his right side was paralyzed. He was transferred to a Veterans hospital and after some time, he was moved to a nursing home. My whole family visited Muscles when we had time but my father went to visit him regularly. He took care of his affairs until he passed away in May, at planting time.

My father and I divided up the tasks in the garden. We thought of Muscles as we planned the garden and planted the tomatoes. Pap pounded in posts for the pole beans and tied on the string, I planted the beans. I planted and weeded, he watered, we both picked the produce.

The printing press lived on and on in our garage. Whenever we talked about getting rid of it, my father would tell us about the plans he had to develop and sell his game or his newest invention, which always involved using the press. He threatened to move if we got rid of it. He always blamed the garage fire for his lack of success. Finally we wore him down. He said Tom could do anything he wanted with the press. We advertised in the paper; we tried to donate it to a school; we couldn't give it away—no one wanted it. We finally disposed of it through a salvage company. My father was very upset, but we did the best we could. After twenty years my husband finally got his garage back.

Pap had many opportunities to brush up on his cooking skills since he was cooking almost every night. Sue often asked Pap to do her a flavor. The favor was always to make a grilled cheese sandwich for her. And he always did. He even taught her to make the sandwich herself. I tried to make it easy for him. I bought frozen entrees and fish sticks. We ate a lot of Polish sausage and hot dogs. Thursday became hot dog day. Anything that would be easy to make, that my family would eat, I bought. Many times I made a stew or roast he could heat up. His suppers gave us the first clue something was wrong, but we just thought he was getting older.

3

Early

I was very tired of the long drive to work and the longer drive home. Rumors were flying that our company was going to close and I was trying to stay until the end. I thought regular exercise would be the best way to get rid of the stress from the daily drive and the tension at work. I decided to give myself a birthday present—a membership in a health club.

One evening Pap gave me some literature on an exercise bike. "What do you think?" he asked. Since it was the same bike I used at the health club I offered my opinion. It was an expensive bike. I didn't think I would use it but it would allow him to exercise at home. "It looks like a good deal," I told him. I was very surprised when he gave me the bike for my birthday. Now I could also exercise at home.

Every day at work, the discussion at lunchtime was always the same—the closing—and I was tired of talking about it. So I brought up a new subject…miracles. I had read an article in which the author wrote many miracles occur daily that go unnoticed. You don't think of it as a miracle when you miss hitting a car that you didn't see while driving—you swerved but you don't know why. Maybe you were delayed and just missed having an accident. Perhaps you find something important after searching for days without any results, or someone stops to help when you have car trouble. The list goes on and on. When we think of miracles, we think of the big ones, someone regaining their sight or recovering from an illness. The rest is just luck or coincidence or fate. Or is it?

On a beautiful Indian summer weekend in October, Sue and I went to the campground for Fall Festival. I lost my watch and couldn't wander freely if I wanted to be on time for some of the scheduled activities. Saturday was a warm sunny day. I didn't want to stay inside while I waited for the next event. I put a tape on our tape recorder and studied outside at the picnic table. A friend stopped to talk as I was preparing to leave. While I listened to his problems, I decided to skip the magician show. After he left, I continued to study until the end of a tape alerted me to the time. If I wanted to go to the flower arranging class, I needed to leave.

I was still at our camper when our neighbor came by looking for help; her sister had collapsed—they thought it was her heart. I used our CB radio to report the accident and request medical assistance. Hurrying to the scene of the accident, I stood talking to a friend when the buzzing of a yellow jacket caught my attention. After I cautioned her to be careful, the friend mentioned my neighbor had been stung that day. I told her to tell the paramedics, it might be important. After my neighbor left in the ambulance for the hospital, I proceeded to the flower arranging class. The person in charge told me I was too late, all the supplies had been given out…I should have come earlier. "That's all right," I replied, "I wasn't meant to do this today."

On my ride back to our camper, I reflected on everything that had happened during the day and realized how true my statement was. I had been delayed by unseen hands, directed to be where I needed to be, when I needed to be, to be of assistance to my neighbor. Goosebumps covered my arms as the full impact hit me. I felt very privileged to have taken part in the day's events. I have always believed in God, talked to Him often, and tried to live a Christian life. I have not always gone to church. I decided to try to attend Mass weekly to say thank you.

My neighbor fully recovered. At the hospital, the doctors discovered she had been stung five times that day, her blood sugar count was very high. It wasn't her heart after all.

Every morning, Pap walked to two different churches. His lady friend attended Mass at our church or at a neighboring parish depending on her schedule. Pap attended both Masses, hoping to see her. He told Angel, our crossing guard, that he was going to marry her but they were going to wait until her children graduated from school. The fact she had a husband didn't seem to make a difference. If for some reason Pap wasn't going to Mass at our church, he always stopped to tell Angel so she wouldn't worry. Over the years they had become good friends.

Pap liked to work outside. In the spring he raked, weeded and planted new grass. When the weather warmed up, he added watering and weeding the garden to his activities. Our yard was very small—it didn't require much work. Since he liked to help people, Pap mowed and raked our neighbor's front lawn too. He battled dandelions, our's as well as our neighbor's, from spring through the fall, digging out the young plants as soon as they sprouted. In the fall he traded his digger for a rake. The leaves on the ground became his personal responsibility. When winter brought snow, Pap found a discarded snow plow on wheels and used it to shovel the snow off the sidewalk for half of our block. If anyone needed help painting or repairing something, he was always available.

I was making progress in school, but I still had a few more courses to take before I received my Associates Degree. Sue attended high school and was extremely busy, active in sports and school activities. Bill's schedule was full, Tom's job had become more demanding. Life was normal, but we were starting to notice little things going wrong.

One afternoon, Sue called me at work with an unique problem. Pap was locked in the bathroom and couldn't get out. He had accidently turned off the lights when he got out of the shower. The downstairs bathroom didn't have a window and he was in total darkness. She had heard his call for help. What should she do? I told her to call her father, since he only worked a mile from home, or to try using a credit card to unlock the door. She called her father. By the time Tom got home, Pap had figured out how to turn the lights on and unlocked the door.

My father was always very modest. The only time we saw him in his underwear was when, in the middle of the night, he went to the bathroom. He never wore pajamas and always got fully dressed before coming downstairs. He didn't wear summer shorts and only exposed his bare chest when the temperature rose above ninety.

One afternoon, Tom was the first one home. He walked into the front room just in time to catch a glimpse of Pap's bare butt disappearing around the corner into the kitchen. Tom didn't believe what he had seen and followed him. He wasn't seeing things—Pap didn't have a stitch of clothes on. When Tom asked him why he wasn't wearing any clothes, Pap replied, "I've lost them."

Tom helped Pap search for his clothes. He found them in the downstairs bathroom, where Pap had taken them off to take a shower.

Pap became more imaginative in his cooking; he added homemade soup to his repertory. My family was very particular in what they ate, but Pap was not particular in what he added. Sometimes the soup was very good with barley, carrots, onions, peas; at other times it was an adventure. You never knew what you were going to find. I described one of Pap's soups to the girls at work as a pot of warm water. A new saying crept into my vocabulary, "For the life of me I don't know what he put in it."

Pap's cooking was never gourmet but it was edible. He had various dishes he made regularly. Most were easy recipes that contained only a few ingredients such as tuna fish casserole. I thought it was fool proof and always kept the ingredients on hand: elbow macaroni, peas, tuna fish, mushroom soup.

Pap made the dish successfully many times; in fact, it was a family favorite. One night, Pap altered the recipe. I don't know what he did but it was very soupy and didn't have much flavor. I cooked it in the microwave to reduce the liquid but it didn't help. Later, Pap confided he forgot to drain the water after he cooked the macaroni. He made the recipe many times after that. Sometimes he got creative on purpose, sometimes it was an accident. He used different ingredients: spaghetti…corn…Sometimes it was successful, many times it was not. Sometimes I could salvage it, many times I cooked something else. I got in the habit of tasting the dish before I announced supper was ready.

Another easy recipe my father made was hamburger beans; it contained hamburger, tomato sauce, beans, and mustard. No matter how late we returned from work or school, it didn't dry out. He changed that one too. Maybe he added hot sauce, maybe pepper, maybe both. He adjusted the recipe often; once it was loaded with oregano. The last time he made it, whatever he added, no one, not even the dogs, would eat it.

Many nights when I came home from work, dinner was cold. I thought I was late and dinner had cooled off. Even when I arrived home on schedule, the food was cold. I found out later Pap was making dinner at 2:00 in the afternoon, so it was ready to eat and he wouldn't forget.

Or nothing had been made for dinner. I tried to keep staples in the house for meals that could be made quickly. As I drove home in the evening, I planned what I would fix, just in case.

We started to find things, especially food, in places where it didn't belong. I bought two packages of hot dogs and put them away in the upstairs refrigerator. One evening I wanted to make them for supper and searched the shelves and bins of the refrigerator—no hot dogs. I thought my memory was playing tricks on me…maybe I forgot to buy them…or someone ate them. A couple of days later, I was looking for something in the basement and found the packages of hot dogs sitting on a shelf.

We never knew what we would find in the basement. When I went to wash clothes, two gallons of milk were sitting on the washing machine. Pap went to the store, bought milk, put them on the washing machine to close the basement door and forgot them. I opened the basement refrigerator to get a gallon of milk and saw a package of fish sticks on the shelf—they should have been in the freezer. Next to the fish sticks were two cans of pork & beans. Pap and I had a talk about the importance of putting things in their proper places, especially refrigerated or frozen food.

Strange things were also appearing in the microwave and oven. I found Pap's socks in the microwave—he was drying them. In the oven, I found a sponge; later, I found a bowl of a charred, solid substance that had lost all trace of its identity. I asked my family to look in the oven before they turned it on.

Pap washed his own clothes. He also washed the towels, which in our household were washed many times a week. Strange things started happening to the drier in the basement. Often after work, when I went to the basement to fetch something, I noticed the drier was running. A few hours later, the drier hadn't turned off. Investigating, I always found the wrong button had been pushed, air instead of heat, or the tumbler was turned off. Maybe the control was set for a sensor stop but the companion button was not pushed, so the drier ran on and on. Weeks passed and the drier behaved, then it ran on and on again. I looked for a solution to our problem, it was hard on the drier and a waste of energy. I used brown tape and taped the air only and tumble control buttons so they couldn't be pushed easily, with a big NO written on the tape. This action eliminated two problems, but left the rest. I got in the habit of opening the basement door when I arrived home to listen for the drier, and if it was running, I investigated.

◆   ◆   ◆

I have always loved Christmas and decorating our house. When we first moved to our home, we bought an artificial tree that I filled with ornaments. Each year the tree's appearance became more lifelike as the branches bent from the assortment. I added strings of popcorn and cranberries for harmony, and ropes of beads to catch and reflect the

light. My family teased me. "Where are you going to put another orna-
ment? There's no more room." It was a question asked every year as I
added to my collection on the tree. We always put the tree up a couple
of weeks before Christmas and left it up until after January 6.

Over the years, our Christmas decorations spread throughout the
house. Garlands of holly woven with lights spiraled up the stairway to
light the hallway. Garlands of evergreens laced with lights looped
across the archway. The stable, complete with pine trees, shepherds
and sheep, graced a spot in the dining room. A wreath decorated the
back door and an angel surrounded by lights hung on the front door.

Our family traditionally opens the gifts on Christmas Eve and Santa
comes on Christmas Day. Aunt Ruth and her husband joined us every
Christmas Eve since we bought the house. Our married children and
their loved ones returned for the evening. The Christmas of 1990,
Uncle Alvin journeyed from Wisconsin to surprise us and Aunt Edna
drove in from out of town to complete the group.

To start the new year off right, the announcement was made at
work that our company would close in four months. I didn't want to
lose my job but I was glad my long commute was ending. I didn't want
to work that far from home again. Sue and I planned to spend the
summer in the country and I would get a job in the fall. I didn't take
into account the economy was in a recession and many companies were
downsizing. It would be over a year before I returned to work.

◆   ◆   ◆

My father lived in Chicago most of his life. For years he took public
transportation and was very comfortable traveling around the city on
the bus. When other people needed help getting from here to there, he
was able to give them directions. He knew which bus to take and when
it would be better to take a train. He knew the location of all the main
streets on the North side of Chicago, both north-south and east-west
streets.

Pap became concerned about his loss of hearing and decided to get a hearing aid. He saw an advertisement for Miracle Ear on television and made an appointment to have his hearing checked. Their office wasn't in our neighborhood, Pap had to take two buses to get there. Their examination revealed he needed hearing aids for both of his ears. He ordered them and made an appointment to return for an adjustment when they were ready. The day he went to pick up his hearing aids he returned home very upset—he couldn't find their office. He said he walked up and down the block, must have passed it a number of times, but never found it. I offered to drive him but he turned down my offer; he was determined to go on the bus. He phoned their office, made a new appointment, got instructions, and made the trip successfully. He was very happy with his new hearing aids. When they were not in his ear, they emitted a very high pitched squeal that was very irritating, especially at night. We were constantly telling him to fix his aids or put them back in.

I noticed Pap was having trouble using the telephone. At first I thought he had trouble hearing. But then he couldn't reach the Miracle Ear office by phone. He was upset, he knew he was dialing the right number but he kept getting a recording. I offered to help and looked at the paper. The number Pap was dialing was an 800 number. Maybe Pap wasn't dialing "1" first. I explained how to dial long distance and dialed the number for him.

Over the next year, Pap's aids played a recurring part in our lives. Pap lost one of his aids—he said it fell out of his ear. Then I almost stepped on the other, while it was laying on the floor. Since Pap and Bill shared the attic, Bill was continually telling Pap to put his aid away because he played with it throughout the night, waking Bill up. Pap couldn't hear out of his remaining aid. He successfully made the trip to the doctor's office where they showed him how to clean it to remove the ear wax. Then he lost it and visited the office to have his aid replaced, using his hearing aid insurance to pay for it. Pap's aid continued to show up in unlikely places—on the coffee table in the front room, on a couch cushion, on his plate in the dining room, on the floor. He didn't know how his aid got there, he said he always put it away where it belonged. Then he needed new batteries and got lost on his way to get them. I told Pap we would drive him whenever he needed to go to the Miracle Ear office. Then he lost his aid again. When he called the office to report the loss, he was told he had used up his insurance and he would have to pay to have the aid replaced. He decided not to.

After searching for many months, Terri and her husband, Bob, finally found a house in the suburbs they liked and that fit their needs. Their new house was twenty-five miles from ours. It would take longer to get there—we wouldn't be able to just stop by for a minute.

Terri and Bob took advantage of the warmer weather and invited everyone to a barbecue in their yard to celebrate their new house. Storms were forecast for Saturday. In the morning, the sky was grey, dark clouds arrived but sped by on a brisk wind, and white clouds followed, along with a blue sky. By early afternoon, it was a beautiful day.

Long tables were set up in the back yard. As family and friends gathered, chicken and hot dogs were roasting on an enormous grill, pop and beer were cooling in washtubs filled with ice, and a huge coffee pot had just finished perking. Chips, pickles, and salads were ready to be set out. Aunt Ruth drove, bringing Aunt Connie and Aunt Edna with her. Most of Pap's family was there—except Elsie, who was in a nursing home, and Shirley, who lived in California. Alvin, who lived in Wisconsin, sent his regrets.

I invited Pap to sit down at the table with his family and made him a plate of food. Pap enjoyed visiting with his sisters. Wherever they went, he followed. When they decided to go home, he followed…he was ready…they were leaving…he was going too. I caught up to him as he was following them out the door and explained he was going home with us. "Thank you for telling me," he said.

Sue and I spent the summer in the country as planned. (Our room addition was well used.) We bought a bird feeder, placed it outside, where we could see it while sitting on the couch in the family room, and became acquainted with our feathered and furry neighbors. Sue and her friends watched scary movies on television—I closed the door and listened to music and read in the trailer. I had time to paint...an activity school and working far from home had curtailed. We returned to the city for what I laughingly referred to as my weekend: Monday and Tuesday. Grocery shopping, household tasks, sending out resumes and job interviews were scheduled for the time I was in the city.

In the twenty years we camped in the area, we never explored the whole region. Most of the time we remained at the campground or drove south to Starved Rock State Park. Now that we had more time in the country, we explored. I was pleasantly surprised by the beautiful state parks and river areas that surrounded us.

The Nature Club at our campground received a flyer advertising the second annual "Autumn on The Prairie" to be held at Nachusa, a six hundred-acre preserve purchased by the Nature Conservancy that was being restored as a prairie. I was intrigued by their description of the area and wandered there to investigate. Arrows on paper plates attached to sticks pointed the way. The surface of the road turned to gravel, then became steeper as I drove up and down the hills. The prairie was located well off the main road, hidden among the hills. Tents were set up on a hill, marking the location. Hundreds of people gathered to explore the prairie. Guided tours were conducted by knowledgeable people through the tall grasses and onto the sandstone knolls. Standing on top of a knob, you could see for miles without a house or a barn in view. I had a marvelous time and vowed to mark the date for the third "Autumn On the Prairie" on my calendar. I just hoped I would be able to find it again.

During the summer, the events taking place at Queen Of Heaven cemetery, in Hillside, made the news. Many unusual photos were taken of the crucifix near the war memorial. These photos revealed images that could not be seen by the naked eye. It was reported that rosaries were turning to gold. Hundreds of people were gathering daily to experience these unexplained events and pray the rosary.

A former co-worker and I drove to the cemetery to investigate. Groups of people were saying the rosary. It was very peaceful. We talked to people, listened to stories and looked at photographs. On some of the photo's the figure of Christ on the cross was bleeding, or the figure or the cross appeared gold. On others, the Virgin Mary mingled with people standing near the cross. The doorway to heaven in the sky emerged on other photos—empty or filled with images of people or a golden chalice or a red bleeding heart surrounded by green thorns.

My friend and I set a date to revisit the cemetery, then meet another co-worker for lunch. My friend had to cancel because of a death in her family. I decided to go to the cemetery by myself and then keep our lunch date. Before leaving my house, I searched for an old rosary I knew was around…somewhere. I had the rosary for years but couldn't remember where I had gotten it. I finally found it buried in an old jewelry box on a shelf at the back of my closet. I barely remembered the rosary which had a silver figure mounted on a mother of pearl cross, a silver chain divided the mother of pearl beads.

I visited the cemetery and stayed to say the rosary for my friend. I was surprised I had forgotten some of the words to the prayers. I had become so comfortable talking to God informally, I seldom said formal prayers. I lingered to talk to people and to look at pictures. Everyone had his or her own story to tell.

Later, when I talked to my friend, I shared my day—the stories I heard and the pictures I'd seen. She suggested we set a new date to visit the cemetery.

Our next visit was on a beautiful, warm October day. We were discussing our experiences at the site with three women when we smelled a strong fragrance of roses—suddenly we were in a rose garden. We sniffed the air and each other, looking for the source of the scent. Someone had brought a bunch of roses and placed them at the foot of the cross, but the aroma did not come from there. No one was wearing rose perfume, but we all experienced the strong fragrance. We found out later that the Virgin Mary's flower is the rose and the scent of roses signals Her presence.

A group started the rosary and we decided to join them before leaving. I stood next to my friend...sometimes I could hear her voice... sometimes I couldn't. When I couldn't, I glanced at her. She was gazing at her beads with a puzzled expression. After we finished the rosary, I asked her if anything was wrong. She showed me the clear crystal beads on her rosary—three had turned amber. I looked at my own rosary and was astonished to see that the silver figure on the cross was now gold and so was the chain. I decided to say the rosary every day for a month to say thank you.

Halloween hadn't arrived, but Christmas decorations were already appearing in the stores. The gentle reminder had begun: Christmas is coming—time to shop. I wanted to give my children something for Christmas, but since I still didn't have a job, I couldn't plan on having extra money to spend. I knew from past experience that if I was going to make something I had to start soon. I decided to gather all of my family's favorite recipes and compile my own cookbook. I could type them on Bill's computer and print them on his printer. All I needed was time, which I had plenty of, a disk, paper, and a ribbon. I would receive an added benefit from the project. My typing had never been good, I would get some needed practice.

My whole family loved chocolate—candy, ice cream, milk. They preferred their candy cold and kept bars in the refrigerator or freezer. Pap loved chocolate and Snicker bars. Any chocolate in the house was fair game. Pap bought Snicker snack size by the bag and hid them in the basement, on a shelf. He often disappeared into the basement for a snack.

Since I wasn't working, I became aware of how much Pap was eating. Leftovers didn't remain in the refrigerator. He went through boxes of cereal every week. I watched the advertisements for cereal on sale. It was not unusual to buy three or four family size boxes of different cereal at the store and run out before the end of the week. When the checker commented that I must have a large family, I replied, "No, I have Pap."

Then our can opener died. We had an old electric can opener that was mounted on the wall in the kitchen. It was easy to use but after years of service it stopped working. I searched the city looking for a can opener similar to our old one but wasn't successful. I finally bought one that sat on the kitchen counter. The only trouble was that my father didn't know how to work it. We showed him again and again but he didn't remember. I finally bought a manual can opener and left it on the counter for Pap.

My father was a true Swede, he loved his coffee. He always made a pot in the morning so I could have a fresh cup when I woke up. The coffee pot stayed on at our house all day.

Then Pap started having trouble making coffee. Sometimes he forgot to put in the coffee grounds and made hot water. Sometimes he used double the amount of grounds and made very strong coffee. Maybe he forgot to put the pot back on the unit and we had coffee all over everywhere. Sometimes he forgot he had added water and added some more, then we had water everywhere. After cleaning up the mess for the umpteenth time, we decided to make coffee before he did. I made a pot at night before going to bed so he wouldn't have to make coffee in the morning.

Pap noticed that he was having trouble with his vision. He went to visit his primary physician at the Clinic and was referred to an ophthalmologist. Although Pap didn't have trouble visiting the Clinic, the eye doctor's office was located in a big medical building in a different place. Since my father was experienced in traveling around the city, he wasn't worried. I offered to drive him for his appointment but he insisted he was capable of getting there by himself.

Except he got lost. He was very upset and the story he told didn't make sense. He said he knew where he was going, he knew the city, he didn't know what happened. He called the doctor's office and made a new appointment. I explained that I didn't have anything special to do the day of his appointment and I would drive him—he could come home by himself. After much discussion, Pap finally agreed.

The doctor's office wasn't difficult to reach, but the bus stop was a little tricky. The bus turned and went through a park at the place where my father had to get off. Once he saw the bus route, I didn't think he would have any more problems.

When Pap arrived back home, he was content. He had made another appointment a couple of weeks away and he knew he could get there unaided.

The day of his next appointment came. I offered to drive him and was turned down. He insisted he was perfectly capable of getting there by himself. We discussed what bus he was going to take and where he was going to get off. He set off and was gone for a long time. I had to go out and when I returned, I found a message from Pap on our answering machine that didn't make sense. It sounded like he thought he was talking to me, not a machine, and I began to worry.

When Pap came home, he was very upset. He got turned around again, he didn't know what happened. From his story, it sounded like he had taken the train downtown, but that wasn't where the doctor's office was. I gave Pap a choice, I would call the doctor's office and explain…or…I could drive him to the doctor's office and he could talk to them in person. He wanted to go for a drive.

While we were driving, I told my father I would park the car and meet him in the doctor's office. If the doctor didn't have time to see him, I would drive him home. He argued with me. He insisted he could get home by himself and I agreed. "But," I replied, "I'm already here and it is silly for you to wait for a bus when I can drive you." He finally agreed he would wait for me. Even if the doctor didn't have time to see him, he wouldn't leave without me.

I dropped Pap off at the corner and drove down the street, looking for a place to park. I was lucky, before 5 minutes passed, I found an empty space. I walked back to the medical building and went to meet my father. Pap told me the office was on the first floor. I didn't know the doctor's name but I didn't think I would have trouble finding him.

Entering the building, I walked down the ramp, past the information desk and took the elevator to the first floor, where my father said the doctor's office was. The door was locked, it was dark inside—no one was there. I thought I made a mistake and went back downstairs. I stopped at the information desk and asked for the room numbers of all the eye doctors with offices in the building. I visited the offices of the other doctors, their waiting rooms were full of people but Pap wasn't one of them. I asked the people in the waiting rooms if they had seen my father. No one had. I went back to the information desk to ask if they saw someone of my father's description. They hadn't. Then I called our house, but no one was home?—I left a message on the answering machine. I continued to search the building. I didn't know what to do, my father had said he wouldn't leave without me, I didn't want to leave without him. I spent more than two hours—calling the house, first getting the answering machine, then talking to my son, walking up and down the ramp, going outside to smoke a cigarette, searching the building, checking with the information desk, going up and down in the elevator, and repeating everything I had done one more time. There were four floors in the building with many offices, I thought Pap must be waiting for me, somewhere. There were two hospitals within walking distance of the medical center. I visited each one, but I couldn't find my father. "Where did he go?" I asked myself…over and over. I finally decided to go home.

When I arrived home, my family said Pap had just walked through the door. We surmised that he was so upset with himself when he saw the dark doctor's office he forgot to wait for me. He took the elevator down and went outside and boarded a bus. (One of the few times a bus is there when you want one.)

I decided I had had enough fun. I would get involved with the eye doctor whether Pap wanted me to or not. I didn't want to interfere with his independence but I didn't want to play that game again.

In order to become involved with the eye doctor, I had to find out who he was. I called the Clinic and received the needed information. Then I called the ophthalmologist and discovered my father had gotten completely mixed up. The doctor related the story. Pap came to see him about his loss of vision in his right eye and admitted he had a lazy right eye and never was able to see out of it. After the examination, the doctor discovered a cataract on Pap's right eye, but that wouldn't cause a complete loss of vision. He ordered an ultrasound to rule out the possibility that a tumor or a detached retina had caused Pap's loss of sight. Pap had to visit his primary physician and get the necessary approval for the test—he went to the wrong doctor's office.

I drove Pap to visit the Clinic. I met his primary care physician and a nurse took the preliminary blood tests. The nurse said they would get approval for the ultrasound and make the appointment with the hospital. They would call our house when everything was set.

◆   ◆   ◆

Ready or not, Christmas was coming. I hadn't realized the project I was undertaking when I began to put together my cookbook. I collected recipes throughout my life—from every place where we lived, every job I worked at, many of the parties and school functions I attended. I decided to include them also. I couldn't believe the stack that piled up as I pulled scraps of paper from here and there. I had more than 100 typed pages when I finished—a sizeable book.

I bought binders, dividers and plastic covers for the pages. I planned for extras so I could share with my aunts and close friends. Pap offered to help me as I assembled the books on the dining room table. I explained what I was doing a couple of times, but I always lost him somewhere. He didn't understand and shook his head in amazement as he watched me put the books together. I was surprised at his confusion. The project was easy, he had done similar things in the past. But Christmas was coming—I had to study for finals at school, and there were the cookbooks to finish, the house to decorate, and cookies to bake. I had so many things to do that I didn't question his inability to grasp what I was doing. I just thought he was getting older.

Christmas arrived on schedule. Our family gathered at our house for dinner on Christmas Eve. My children enjoyed their cookbook and the comments I added to some of the recipes. They liked the boxes of home-made cookies that they could take home. We enjoyed watching our first grandchild, Brittany, open her presents. We ate cookies and fudge, and sang carols.

◆　　◆　　◆

Pap still considered it his responsibility to buy the milk for the week. When the weather started to get cold, I offered to drive him to the store. A few times we had a lengthy discussion about the snowy, icy sidewalks before he agreed. After that he often asked for a ride or hinted we were low on milk hoping I would offer to drive him. He preferred to ride rather than walk.

Pap received the phone call from the Clinic scheduling his ultrasound and didn't tell anyone. He probably thought he would go by himself and didn't need to bother us. Except he forgot the appointment, a couple of times. I wasn't aware of the missed dates until I answered the phone one day and talked to the representative at the hospital. I scheduled an appointment for the following month, February, marked my calendar, and informed Pap of his new time.

I had to cancel February's ultrasound appointment. Tom and I had to go out of town because of a death in the family, and I didn't want Pap to go by himself. I rescheduled the appointment for March.

I decided to give myself another birthday present—better health. I was going to quit smoking. Of course, I made the decision after finishing a cigarette and it took five months before I attempted to quit. When Lent started, I decided I would give up cigarettes. On Ash Wednesday I stopped smoking, on Thursday I had a couple of cigarettes. On Friday, I didn't smoke as many, but I smoked more than zero. I decided I wasn't going in the right direction. Saturday I went to the camper by myself. The temperature was in the single digits and snow covered the ground. I left my cigarettes in the car. After the camper warmed up, I took off my boots and socks and put on slippers. Whenever I wanted a cigarette, I told myself I had survived without them so far, but I could have one after an hour passed if I really wanted one. After the hour passed, I told myself that I was still alive but I could have a cigarette after an hour passed if I still wanted one. Then I repeated the whole process again and again. When I returned to the city on Sunday, I hadn't smoked a cigarette since Friday night. I had watched a program on television where a doctor had said one cigarette was to an ex-smoker what a drink was to an alcoholic. I wanted to be an ex-smoker. I talked to my Friend. I told Him that I was not going to be able to quit smoking without His help. I also told Him that daily temptations like the sausage biscuits were not fair.

The morning of the ultrasound appointment, the city was hit by an unexpected snow fall. More than 6 inches of snow fell, covering the city and snarling traffic. The snow was falling so fast, the plows weren't able to keep up with it. My husband suggested I cancel my father's appointment. After all the trouble we had with his appointment, rescheduling was the last thing I wanted to do. I told my husband I was sure we would be able to get to the hospital safely. We would leave before most of the rush hour traffic was on the streets. With any luck we would be at the hospital before the traffic got too bad.

We arrived at the hospital at 7:30 A.M., in plenty of time for my father's appointment, except the doctor was delayed by the snow. Due to the specialized nature of my father's test, this doctor was the only one who could do it. At 9:00 A.M. we were still waiting. Finally word came that the doctor had arrived and we continued to wait. The nurse, who had kept us informed on the lack of progress, stopped by to tell us there was a problem, the hospital didn't do an ultrasound on the eye. They didn't know who had scheduled the test or why no one had noticed the error. The doctor apologized for inconveniencing us. I spoke to the hospital spokesperson to try to figure out what had happened. When she called the ophthalmologist's office, she was informed the ultrasound was always performed in the same building as their office. The nurse at the ophthalmologist's office didn't tell anyone the location of the test because she assumed they knew. Murphy's Law: "If anything can go wrong, it will."

A new appointment was made for my father's test. Before the appointment, I found a card at home that showed Pap's membership in Share and placed it in my wallet. Then, I drove him for the test—I didn't want to take a chance he would get lost again. The receptionist in the specialist's office asked many questions that I couldn't answer, but I had Pap's insurance card and knew his Social Security number. Pap's Social Security card had disappeared from his wallet, along with his insurance card. (While I was helping him search, I found a filled out Emergency Card. That made me feel better.)? The receptionist asked if my father had Medicare. I didn't know and he didn't understand the question. After she made a phone call, she told me my father only had Share, but they covered everything.

I went with Pap into the examining room. The doctor invited me to stay and explained everything he did. He had the results of the tests in less than an hour. My father didn't have a tumor or a detached retina, the lazy eye coupled with the cataract was causing his loss of vision.

During Pap's next appointment, the ophthalmologist made the decision to wait before operating on his right eye. His vision in his left eye was good and not much would be gained by removing the cataract if he had never had good vision in his right eye. We made an appointment to return in three months.

Several months later, I answered the phone to receive a message confirming an appointment for my father at a different eye doctor's office. When I asked Pap about it, he explained that his friend said he should have his eye operated on; the doctor would be able to restore his vision so it would be as good as new. He made an appointment to see the doctor. I got excited, remembering all of the fun we just had. Trying to stay calm, I reminded him of the various tests he had just completed and the results the doctor had discussed with us. He replied that he hadn't understood, but now he did. He would cancel his new appointment. Good!

I had been out of work for over a year when an opportunity to work part time presented itself. My old boss had purchased a company and needing help, he thought of me. After a few months, he offered me a full time job as office manager. My husband said, "I won't tell you to take the job—our bills will." My life became hectic again. At least this time I was working in the city, closer to home.

Before I started working full time, I painted one more picture. My son had hinted that he would like a painting of the Flying Dutchman but I wasn't talented enough to paint the mythical ship. I found a picture of an old sailing ship coming out of the fog that I thought I could do. As I worked on the painting, it became mine—I felt like I was that ship, coming out of the storm into calmer waters, a new job. Little did I know I was in the eye of a hurricane—rougher waters were ahead.

4

Middle

Working full time presented problems at home. While I was without a job, I resumed the task of cooking our evening meal, except on Thursday, which remained Pap's night to make hot dogs. I really didn't want Pap to cook every night and neither did my family.

Pap still wanted to help. One night Bill walked into the kitchen just as Pap was starting supper. He had taken a package of On Cor Salisbury Steaks-In-Gravy out of the box, out of the cooking dish and placed the frozen block on a cookie sheet in the oven. Another night, Bill found a package of frozen breaded fish sticks defrosting in the dish drainer.

Pap and I got into the habit of discussing each morning what we would have for dinner that night. I always had something planned so I could tell him not to worry about supper—I would cook. Many evenings I cooked a pot of chili, or soup, or stew for the next night.

Pap's lunch was a problem. Bill had seen Pap eating a frozen fish stick fresh from the freezer. Fishsicles? Pap knew how to work the microwave but not the can opener, not even the manual one, so I planned leftovers Pap could eat for lunch. I made big pots of hearty soup and stored them in the basement refrigerator. Before leaving for work in the morning, I dished out a bowl and left it for Pap to find in the kitchen refrigerator. If I was out of homemade soup or leftovers, I opened a can of soup, placed it in a bowl and left that in the refrigerator. I was careful to use only microwave safe containers to store the food. We kept a bowl full of fruit on the dining room table.

A new expression crept into my vocabulary: "Guess what Pap did today?" The answer could be anything. On separate occasions, I found socks, the kitchen sponge and a handkerchief in the microwave. Did he think it was the dryer? I found a bunch of bananas in the microwave. Was he cooking them? Trying to ripen them? I found a bowl of dry cat food on the dining room table. Was he going to eat it? I found a box of frozen, breaded chicken in the oven and the oven was on. Was he inventing a new way to cook?

Pap continued to buy our milk but he didn't go to the store by himself. One of the last times that I drove him to the store, he took me on a tour and pointed out everything that he bought. I was surprised when he opened the door to the refrigerator case, stepped over the sill, and standing inside the case on a steel crate, he chose each gallon of milk and handed it to me.

The grocery store Pap preferred was very busy on weekends so I asked Bill to drive Pap during the week. Most of the time the visit was uneventful, but once, Bill told me Pap got in line as soon as he entered the store without picking up anything. Bill reminded Pap that you have to get what you want to buy before you pay for it. He left Pap standing in line and fetched the milk so Pap could pay for it. After Bill's experience, we took over the job of keeping the family supplied with milk.

Bill liked his room in the attic because he was away from the hustle and bustle downstairs. Bill didn't like some of the noises that were invading his domain—he was a light sleeper. First it was Pap's hearing aids, now it was his alarm clock. Pap's alarm was ringing in the middle of the night, waking Bill and sometimes waking me. When Bill woke up, he told Pap to shut off his alarm or got up and shut it off himself. This occurred a couple of times a week. I finally asked Pap, "Why are you setting your alarm clock for 4:00 A.M.? Why do you have to get up so early? You are retired." He said he could think better when he got up early.

One evening I noticed Pap was rubbing his bare feet as he sat at the dining room table. When I asked him if something was wrong, he said his feet hurt. "Let me take a look," I offered as I sat down on the floor. I wasn't surprised his feet hurt, his toenails had grown so long they curled under his toes, and a few were ingrown. "When was the last time you cut your nails?" I asked before I got the clippers. I cut his nails the best I could, then made an appointment with his primary physician, Dr. D., at the Clinic for his ingrown toenails.

When we arrived for the appointment, Dr. D. said they didn't take care of feet at the Clinic. We had to visit a podiatrist to have the ingrown toenails removed. Dr. D. authorized the visit and the nurse forwarded the request to the main office for approval and the request was denied. When the nurse informed me of the decision I became angry, "Who was going to take care of Pap's feet? It hurt him to walk." I asked the nurse for the name and phone number of the podiatrist. I called and made an appointment for Pap with the nurse, stressing that Pap's insurance didn't approve the visit, but we would pay for it.

I took time off from work the day of Pap's appointment. After I filled out the necessary paperwork at the doctor's office, including the insurance information, I informed the nurse that we were going to pay for the visit ourselves since Pap's insurance denied it.

When Pap's turn came, I accompanied him into the examining room, where I told the doctor the story that brought us to his office, mentioning we would pay for the visit. He said we couldn't pay for the visit, he was an HMO doctor and wasn't allowed to privately bill his patients. I started to get angry. How was Pap going to get his ingrown toenails removed? The primary physician wouldn't cut them, Pap's insurance wouldn't approve a specialist and the podiatrist wouldn't let us pay. I quickly calmed down when the doctor asked my father's age and said that he would submit the bill for payment. At my father's age, with his circulatory problems, Pap's insurance would pay. He removed Pap's ingrown toenails and advised me not to cut his nails again because I could cause an infection. I should make an appointment with his nurse whenever his nails needed cutting.

I had planned to drive Pap home when we were finished and return to work, but as we left the doctor's office, I realized that driving Pap home would take too much time. We were half-way between work and home, so I took Pap to work with me. I gave him a cup of coffee and some cookies and he sat in a chair in my office while I finished my work. Then I took him for a tour of the facilities and introduced him to everyone. They were surprised at my father's trim figure. From my stories of his eating, they expected a much larger man.

My schedule was very full with home, work and school. I didn't have time to go to the health club but I wanted to continue to exercise. I only used the machines at the health club because I didn't have enough stamina to make it through an aerobic class. I decided to buy a 30 minute low impact aerobic tape to play on our video recorder and exercise at home. The first time I put the tape on, I made it through the whole session. I was happy with my progress and exercised every morning before going to work, buying more aerobic tapes for variety. But after a couple of months, my heavy schedule wore me out and I gave up exercising for an extra half hour of sleep.

◆   ◆   ◆

Tom and I visited an older couple we had known for many years. Both Tom and her husband liked to tease and shared a love for mischief. When we went to a restaurant, his wife and I often felt sorry for our waitress when our men joined forces. Now he was past ninety and his health had deteriorated. His wife warned us that her husband might not recognize us and that his conversations didn't make sense. She shared some of the problems that they were experiencing due to her husband's loss of memory. He took their money and hid it, turned up the thermostat on the furnace to eighty or ninety, and was very fussy with food. They had trouble getting him to eat. He got up in the middle of the night, wandered around or reorganized his clothing. They were having a rough time.

When we told her about my father's activities, she cautioned us to watch him. I wasn't concerned about Pap's money, it was his, we didn't use it. But changing the temperature on the thermostat, wandering, and getting into trouble during the night—that concerned me. I knew we wouldn't have trouble with Pap's eating habits, he was eating everything in the house.

The *Wall Street Journal* published a five part series "*Mapping The Mind.*" The third part reported the results of an operation where part of a person's brain was removed for medical reasons. This individual has been the subject of many studies. One of the things they discovered was that he "lacks the ability to record 'internal states', such as a feeling of hunger…They quietly placed a tray of food in front of him a minute after he had eaten his usual dinner. He methodically ate the second dinner, soon forgetting which meal he was on, as well as what and when he had eaten—then 20 minutes later said he felt somewhat hungry." The person didn't know he had eaten or that he was full. When I read the article, I thought they were talking about my father.

Tom worked for the same company for twenty-five years, earning six weeks vacation. Since I just started another job, I wasn't eligible for a vacation. Tom took advantage of his time off and went to the camper to fish. Whenever Tom was gone, my father was more difficult and more things seemed to go wrong. This time was no exception. Pap didn't have anyone to watch television with, so he tried to be more helpful.

This year as in other years, Pap and I planned and worked on the garden together. Except Pap added another activity to his list…weeding. He weeded everything. The things he pulled out weren't always weeds: squash, Swiss chard, marigolds—all gone. The tomatoes, green peppers, and green beans were safe, he let them grow.

Naming my son after my father was proving to be a bad idea. Everything was fine when Bill was Billy but now he was getting mail under his formal name—William. Pap didn't always look at the full name. He saw the first name on an envelope, and decided the mail was his. If Pap didn't want it, he tore it up and threw it in the garbage. We explained to Pap that he had to look at the complete name on the letter before discarding it. We asked him not to tear up the mail. We always got the same response: "I didn't do it, I NEVER touch anything that isn't mine. I don't know who did."

I developed new habits: taking out the garbage each morning, checking the garbage for mail each evening. I asked Pap not to tear up the mail until we had a chance to look at it. I placed a basket on the dining room table and stapled a sign to the handle: "MAIL". I asked Pap to put ALL of the mail in the basket. Sometimes he was very good and my son got his letters. Then there was the rest of the time when Pap only took "his" mail.

Time was going by very quickly. Summer had flown by, "Autumn on the Prairie" at Nachusa had come and gone, Thanksgiving came before we were ready, and all of a sudden it was Christmas.

The previous year, I didn't have money to buy presents for Christmas. This year, I had more money but no time. I rushed between work, school, and home. In all of the activity, we still managed to get the house decorated and the shopping done. Our family gathered for dinner on Christmas Eve. We enjoyed the camaraderie, and the food, and the store bought cookies.

Pap received but didn't give presents to anyone. He felt bad, he didn't know what happened, he forgot. We told him not to worry about it…it wasn't important. But he remembered to buy a box of candy for his lady friend. He took it with him each morning when he went to church and returned with it when he didn't meet her.

Problems with the mail continued but we were more vigilant so Bill got his mail more often. Pap became more inquisitive. Often, he searched through piles of paper that didn't belong to him. When I caught him, I told him the stuff belonged to me or Bill or Sue—there was nothing of his in there.

Because Bill had grown taller than his father, he was able to keep his mail and books on the top of the china cabinet. Pap, however, became very interested in the place where Bill kept his stack. Often I found Pap rummaging through Bill's pile. I reminded him time after time that the stack was not his, the stuff belonged to Bill. He left it alone, only to go through it again…later. When I asked him what he was doing. He answered, "I'm looking for something…I'm just checking to see if anything is mine." He was drawn to it like a magnet.

When I came home from work, I noticed the china cabinet top was clear, Bill's stack was gone. I looked in the garbage and found all of Bill's mail—in pieces. Bill was very upset, many important papers were torn in two. I tried to find the matching pieces and taped them back together. I talked to Pap about the mess and of course he didn't do it, he didn't know who did.

Enough was enough!

Talking to Pap wasn't doing any good. We bought another mail box, one that had a key. Bill hung the new box next to our old one. I watched for our mailman and explained why we had another box and why it was so important to keep our mail separate from my father's.

If Pap noticed the new mailbox, he didn't mention it and Bill got his mail. Problem solved.

The time came for Tom's winter vacation at the camper. He traditionally took a week's vacation by himself during February; he enjoyed the solitude, the peace and quiet of the country. I knew he deserved it but I wasn't looking forward to his absence. I knew my father would get into more mischief without Tom's presence.

When I came home from work on the second day of Tom's vacation, Pap was searching through the end-table drawers in the front room. After I told him his stuff wasn't in there, he declared, "The tables are mine…they contain my papers, I always keep my things in them…I don't have any drawers in the attic to keep my papers." No matter what I said, I couldn't convince him that they weren't his. Just a few days before he had taken possession of my son's stack, ripped his papers, and tossed his stuff in the garbage. I was afraid of what he would do to my papers. I didn't want him to keep the impression that his stuff was all through the house, that he could do anything with it. It would be impossible to Pap-proof our whole house.

I lost my temper. I don't yell very often. I usually let off steam slowly, perking like an old-fashioned coffee pot, but I was yelling then. I wanted to hit him. After I got very angry, my father decided I was right—the stuff wasn't his.

I wasn't surprised that I got angry but I was surprised at the force of my anger. Now I understood why older parents were abused.

Neither Bill nor Sue were home, I didn't want to be home either. I wanted to go out but I was afraid to leave Pap roaming through the house by himself. I called friends just to talk and no one was home. I had to calm down by myself. After Pap had supper and watched a few television shows, he finally went to bed.

The rest of the week that Tom was on vacation was uneventful. My explosion did some good—Pap stayed out of our stuff. This made me very happy. I wasn't sure how I would have handled many more stressful evenings. Luckily Tom was only gone for a week and returned home in time for Pap's birthday.

◆   ◆   ◆

Vatican II brought many changes to the liturgy of the Catholic church. Members of the congregation took a more active part in the Mass, including bringing up the gifts of bread and wine. My father and I participated in this activity a few times and considered it an honor. The woman in charge of recruiting volunteers phoned, inviting us to bring up the gifts on Sunday. I thanked her for the invitation, mentioning that Sunday was my father's eighty-third birthday.

When the time came to bring up the gifts at Sunday's Mass, I gave my father the bowl containing the bread to bring up to the altar. He thanked me and as I watched, he reached in, took a piece out and was about to eat it. "Don't eat that!" I commanded. I couldn't believe what I had just witnessed. Why was he going to eat a piece? Did he forget where we were, what we were doing?

Pap followed me to the altar but when the priest reached for the bowl containing the bread, Pap drew it back. The priest pulled and once again, Pap pulled back. I couldn't believe what I was witnessing—a tug of war over the bowl of bread. "Give it to him," I whispered to Pap. Thankfully Pap released his grip, then followed me back to our pew.

In the afternoon we had a family party to celebrate Pap's birthday. Our married children and their spouses came to our house along with our grandchild. The party proceeded normally until Terri and Bob left with our granddaughter. After they left, Pap told me, "I'm ready anytime you are."

"Ready for what?" I asked.

"Ready to go home," he answered.

"You live here, this is your home," I replied. The morning's events coupled with this statement really upset me. It seemed that even though I was looking at my father, he was gone.

I decided to have Pap examined by Dr. D. at the Clinic. Something must have happened to cause his confusion. I was concerned that he might have had a slight stroke.

Dr. D. said Pap's blood pressure, pulse, and weight were normal—he didn't see signs of a stroke. He had hardening of the arteries, arteriosclerosis, which was normal for a man his age, emphysema, and sclerosis, a slight curvature to his back. The doctor assured me that considering his age, Pap was in fine health and I shouldn't worry.

But I was worried. Dr. D. hadn't explained what caused Pap's actions on his birthday. I didn't know what the problem was, but it seemed something was definitely wrong.

The company I worked for moved into a bigger subbasement. It was a small company and my boss turned the thermostat down every night to save money. Due to the dampness and coolness of the space, I had a constant sore throat. I finally got tired of not feeling well and went to see our family doctor. Dr. T. had delivered three of my four children and knew our family well. Pap had been his patient before he switched to the HMO.

While I was there, I discussed my father's memory lapses and mentioned our recent visit to his physician. Dr. T. said from what I told him, it sounded like Pap had the beginning of a form of mental dementia and the disease was progressive. He reminded me that today was as good as it gets and that tomorrow would not be as good. He suggested I plan for the future—investigate day care, look at nursing homes, and find a support group.

I was taking a Psychology class in school. Our professor stressed the need for a person to take care of himself, not to sacrifice his own health in caring for someone who was dependent, physically or emotionally, on his care. We discussed, in detail, unhealthy emotional dependency. Our discussions became heated as I debated the subject with him. He was thinking about physically or emotionally abusive people—alcoholics, drug users, or a domineering parent or partner. I was thinking of my father. He handed out several self-help lists that he had adapted for class: *How To Know If You Are Emotionally Dependant, Guidelines For Dealing With Angry Feelings,* and *Empowerment Means.*

We wrote a class paper about a personal problem that we were trying to solve. The following is an excerpt from my paper:

> My father is suffering from cerebral arteriosclerosis (a chronic brain disorder). He is spending a large portion of his time taking care of his primary drives: eating, sleeping, and watching television. His favorite occupation is eating, followed by sleeping. He forgets that he has eaten, therefore, he must be hungry so he eats again. He is regressing to the point where many things are his, whether they are or not.
>
> The problem is that my father lives in our house, and we are trying to allow him to continue to have independence without hurting himself, getting lost, or damaging our property. He is very

frustrated with his inability to remember things. We are trying to help direct his life without interfering: arranging to drive him to doctors' appointments and the store, leaving food that he likes to eat within sight, finding things that he has lost.

It is difficult for those of us who live with him to deal with his condition. There is a great deal of sadness when we think of the man who used to be. At times we still see a glimmer of that person. The only thing that we can expect is that his condition will continue to deteriorate.

It is hard to come up with a permanent solution for my problem. I have a support network with my husband and children.... We are trying to maintain a sense of humor and are investigating day care possibilities for the time when it will not be safe for him to stay at home by himself.

I wrote we were investigating day care but the reality was that it was a thought in my head that I hadn't acted on. I knew what should be done but I wasn't frustrated or angry enough to do it. I didn't want to interfere in Pap's life. I wanted him to have freedom to do the things he liked for as long as he could.

Winter finally ended and spring arrived. Day after day the skies opened to water the grass and the flowers and the trees and the roofs. Water spilled down from our roof in buckets. It overflowed from the gutters, drenching anyone going up or down the stairs. We thought that our gutter might be clogged with leaves and branches from the tree but we needed a dry day to check out the roof.

When we bought our house, we discovered that the apartment building next door was built on our property line, our roof butted against the side of their building. To reach our roof, we used their stairs. After a few years, to make access easier, my father built a trap door into our roof in his part of the attic.

On a clear Saturday afternoon, Tom decided to clean out the gutters, climbed the stairs to the attic and went out on the roof. He enlisted Sue to help. She came downstairs and announced, "Mom, Pap has a lot of money upstairs. You'd better come up and look."

I climbed the stairs to the attic, went back to my father's workshop and saw stacks of money all over the place. I started counting a stack—over two hundred dollars in fives, tens and twenties. Other stacks were scattered around the room—two or three on his desk, another one or two on a cabinet, a few more on a shelf. My father never had any money to speak of. Where did it come from? I went downstairs to get my father.

When he came upstairs, I asked him where the money came from. "I printed it," he replied. "It's mine."

"No, you didn't. This is real money." Years ago he had printed play money for his game, Country Auction, but these were American greenbacks. I sat down and started sorting it into stacks of fives, tens, and twenties.

"I always keep money around for my business," Pap insisted. "I never told you because there wasn't a need for you to know. You don't know everything I do."

I counted two thousand dollars in small bills. I knew Pap never received that much money from his mail order business. I was very uncomfortable with all that cash in the house—it made a very large pile. After putting a rubber band around it, Pap and I went for a walk to the bank. The main bank was already closed but the drive through was open.

Pap always waited until he saw his statement from the bank before withdrawing money for the month. I tried to convince him that his money was available on the first of the month but he felt more comfortable when he saw the amount in his account. I remembered seeing Pap's bank statement in the morning mail and looked at his balance before we walked to the bank. When I asked the teller to run a check on his balance, two thousand dollars were missing. Now I knew where the money came from. Pap always withdrew two hundred dollars each month in small bills. He just added another zero when he made out his check and no one questioned it. I kept two hundred dollars for Pap and deposited the rest of the money. On the walk back to the house, Pap and I talked about the dangers of walking around with a large sum of money in his pockets. He said he hadn't withdrawn the money, he didn't know how it got into the house.

The image of this little, old man walking down the street with two thousand dollars in small bills sticking out of his pocket gave me a sinking feeling. I said thank you to my Friend for keeping my father safe. I could just picture Pap playing with the money in his workshop. Making stacks…counting it…rearranging the stacks…to count it all over again. I don't think he ever had that much cash in his life.

I reasoned Pap's money would be safer if we moved it from his checking account to his savings account, except his bank book was missing. Tom thought that I should move the money to an account in my name but I didn't want to do that. I didn't want to interfere with my father's independence; I just wanted to prevent his accidental withdrawal of large sums of money. We had to wait until the main bank was open to get another savings book before I could transfer the money.

I took time off from work and went to the bank with Pap. After I explained our problem to a personal banker, we received a new bank book. I was surprised to discover that most of Pap's money was in his checking account. I left a few hundred dollars in his checking account and transferred the rest to savings. Since I kept the new passbook, I thought the money would be safe.

Pap thought he had eight thousand dollars in the bank, not five and kept asking what happened to three thousand dollars. He wanted to know who took his money. In desperation, I told him he spent it on his hearing aids. (Later I found out that was exactly what he did.) A few minutes later we had the same conversation all over again. He was convinced that he had eight thousand dollars in the bank.

I became concerned about my father's bills. Did he have any? Was he remembering to pay them? When we moved into our house, we left the gas and electric bills in my father's name to save the deposit money. When the bills arrived each month, he gave them to us to pay. It was no longer safe to leave the utility bills in Pap's name—he was tearing them up or forgetting to give them to us. I called the companies and transferred billing to our name. But what about his health insurance? I didn't think he had life insurance.

I looked at my father's bank statement and noticed his health insurance was paid automatically. That was a weight off of my mind. I asked my son to look through Pap's papers and see if he could find a will, an insurance policy, or the deed for the cemetery lot. Bill found Pap's will—everything was left to me, a deceased uncle was my designated guardian. Bill also found the papers for the cemetery. I put both of those in a safer place. Bill didn't find any life insurance policies.

A couple of weeks later, an envelope fell onto the floor from my father's stack. When I picked it up, I noticed it was a letter from Colonial Life Insurance stating that his premium was past due. I was very surprised my father had life insurance. I made a phone call and although they would not tell me how large a policy my father had, they said he'd had it for more than ten years. When I remembered his twenty-dollar-a-day hospital insurance, I didn't think his policy was worth very much. But some money is better than none. I wrote out a check and mailed it that day. Then I marked my calendar to watch for the bill the next time the premium was due.

Sometimes when we arrived home from work or school, we received a surprise. They weren't always pleasant, and they were occurring more often—especially when Pap was home alone.

When Bill came home from school, he was greeted by waves of water flowing down the stairs from the second floor. Rushing upstairs, he saw the plug in the bathtub drain. Water gushed from the faucet, into the full tub, and overflowed onto the floor. The water leaked into the pantry below and from there to the basement where it soaked all of my Christmas decorations along with some clothes that had been hung to dry. Pap had decided to take a bath, started running the water, went downstairs to watch television and fell asleep. He forgot all about his bath. By the time I got home, Bill had cleaned up the water on the stairs, in the bathroom, and in the pantry below. He left the items on the pantry shelves and the soaked stuff in the basement for me.

I tossed out boxes of food, dried off the cans and washed the shelves in the pantry. I rewashed the clothes in the basement. I completely unpacked my boxes of Christmas decorations—lights, garlands, two big boxes of assorted ornaments, Nativity set, candles, wreaths. I dried and rewrapped all the ornaments. They still felt damp so I left Christmas in its new boxes upstairs to dry completely. I didn't want to take a chance that the humidity in the basement would cause mildew.

Most weekends when the weather was nice, Tom and I went to the country. This weekend we stayed home at Sue's request. She asked if a group of friends could spend the weekend at the camper to celebrate their graduation from high school. We liked Sue's friends and reasoned that soon she would be going away to college. We gave our permission after setting some guidelines.

Our phone rang before eight o'clock on Sunday morning. Answering the phone, I barely recognized my uncle's voice—he was very upset. Aunt Ruth was sick and she wouldn't let him call the doctor. Would I come?

When I arrived at their house, I realized that my aunt was more than sick, she needed to go to the hospital. She was laying in bed and had a hard time moving. She could talk but her words were slurred. My uncle explained that she fell Saturday night when she went to answer the phone. Somehow she got to bed by herself—she didn't want his help. She became angry whenever he picked up the phone to call someone. So as not to upset her further, he didn't call anyone until morning when he called me. Then he confided that they didn't have insurance. I thought she had had a stroke and informed both of them that she needed more help than I could provide. I was calling an ambulance.

The diagnosis at the hospital was a stroke caused by very high blood pressure. We were told that the first six hours after a stroke are critical and too much time had passed before she had received treatment. Before the doctors were finally able to get her blood pressure under control, her brain had been severely damaged. She wouldn't recover enough to be able to return home and my uncle didn't have the necessary skills to take care of her. She would have to be transferred to a nursing home when she was released from the hospital.

I urged my uncle to stop feeling guilty about not calling the ambulance right away. He did the best that he could. Right or wrong, he followed my aunt's wishes. When he talked about the papers that he needed to sign, I advised against life support.

The social worker at the hospital walked my uncle through the steps of making decisions for my aunt. He had to decide about life support, choose a nursing home, and file for financial aid. He had to make a list of all their assets, find their insurance policies and bank accounts, arrange for the nursing home deposit. My aunt always made their decisions, he didn't know what to do. He needed help but I could only give him advice and moral support. My hands were already full.

Only three weeks had gone by since we found the money in the attic when Bill saw Pap with more money. I looked in the top drawer of his cabinet in the little room of the double parlor and found two hundred dollars. How did he get the money? Did he cash a check? I had his passbook but I had left a small amount of money in his checking account.

We decided to let him keep the money, but I asked Bill to keep his eyes open. The next day, Bill told me that Pap went to the bank again—he withdrew another two hundred dollars. How? There wasn't that much money in his checking account. He was going to the bank every day.

Sure enough, four hundred dollars was now sitting in the top drawer. I took two hundred dollars and visited the bank. "How did my father withdraw money from his account without his passbook?" I asked the teller. She explained that as a service to seniors, the bank allowed them to withdraw one hundred dollars at a time without their passbook. That explained how he was getting money, but he had more than one hundred dollars. How was he getting $200—each day?

When I told Tom what happened, he said, "now maybe you'll do what I asked you to do. Put Pap's money in your name."

I decided to listen to Tom and moved Pap's money. We didn't want his money, but we didn't have the money to pay his bills or the deposit for a nursing home if it became necessary. I didn't want him to throw away the little bit of money he had. I left $500 in his savings account.

◆   ◆   ◆

One of the advantages of owning a home is having a yard. Yards are useful for many things: gardening, sunbathing, visiting, hanging out clothes, a place for children to play, and a place for dogs to exercise. Our dogs enjoyed our yard. Two gates kept them inside. If one of the gates was left open, the dogs took advantage of the opportunity to explore our neighborhood. They didn't like to come home by themselves, someone always had to find them.

Pap forgot to close the gate. The gates were left open more often and the dogs were wandering regularly and looking for them was becoming a habit. We were afraid for their safety, they didn't look for cars before crossing the street or alley. We reminded ourselves, and each other, to make sure the gates were closed before letting the dogs out.

◆   ◆   ◆

We continued to visit Pap's ophthalmologist regularly. Whenever Pap knew we were going to the eye doctor, he became worried. He told both me and the doctor that his right eye was getting better. He could almost see as well out of it as he could his left eye. I was concerned by

Pap's statement. During the next visit, I asked the doctor why Pap thought his vision was getting better. He didn't have a cataract on his good eye. The doctor replied, "He is getting a cataract on his left eye but it is still too early to remove it. He can see well enough for his needs. I will keep an eye on it." Before leaving his office, we made an appointment for the fall.

Our church had joined the Market Day program, a program designed to provide good food at reasonable prices while providing a non-profit group a way of earning extra money. Orders for fish, meat, poultry, breakfast items, pizza and other assorted foods were placed at the church and picked up once a month on a designated day. My family was partial to their pizza, hamburgers and pancakes. Before Sue became so busy at school, I gave the order to her to drop off. When Sue didn't have time, I gave the order to Pap to drop off at church. One month I went to pick up our order and it wasn't there, they hadn't received it. Pap forgot? I didn't want to take a chance of missing our order again, so I started taking it to church with me on Sunday.

Our oldest daughter, Kathy, often placed a Market Day order at our church for some of the things they liked. I picked her order up with mine if I was in the city; otherwise, she picked up our orders.

Friday morning, I realized I had forgotten to take our Market Day orders to church on Sunday. After work, we were going to the camper for the weekend. If we didn't want to miss out on our monthly orders, I had to get them to church. I decided to drop them off on the way to work.

Leaving church, I saw Angel, our crossing guard standing at her corner. I hadn't seen her in a year. After we talked about my children, we talked about my father. Angel said, "Pap is one of my guardian angels. He always has something good to say, something to cheer me up."

When I told her about some of the things that were happening at home, Angel confided, "I've noticed that Pap seems to be confused at times. He only goes to his girlfriend's house in the mornings. Last week, I saw Pap walking toward her house in the afternoon. When I asked him where he was going, he said that he was going to work at his girlfriend's house. So I told him that it was afternoon, it was too late. You're right, he said, I guess I messed up. Then he turned around and headed home."

Before I left, I asked Angel to keep an eye on my father. She said she would ask some of the people in the neighborhood to keep an eye out for him too—he would have a few human guardian angels.

Kathy and her husband, Mike, went out of town for the weekend so I picked Kathy's Market Day order up with mine. She ordered chocolate chip granola bars along with a few other things. I told her I would keep her order at our house until they returned. I didn't think Pap would bother her granola bars but, just to be safe, I put them in the hall closet. When Kathy came to pick up her granola bars, all that was left was an empty box. Pap found them and taste-tested.

The day finally came, our youngest child was graduating from high school. After years of parent/teacher conferences, mother/daughter dinners, bake sales, permission slips, registration forms, cheerleading, basketball and volleyball games, we were done.

The number of tickets for the ceremony at night was limited and I knew from experience that the church would be crowded. I debated with myself about taking Pap to graduation. I didn't know if Pap would remember that Sue had graduated. Pap's memory was always worse at night when he was tired. He was going to bed early, before 8:00 P.M. We held a family conference and decided to take him to the graduation Mass in the morning rather than the ceremony at night.

As Pap left for church the morning of Sue's graduation, I reminded him to come straight home, Sue was graduating and we were going to her Mass. (Ever since my graduation from high school, the graduation Mass always meant more to me than the regular ceremony at night.)

I waited for my father as long as I dared, then I assumed that he decided to stay at church. While driving, I kept my eyes open. I looked for my father walking down the street, but I didn't see him. Before entering church, I stopped to ask Angel if she had seen Pap. She said he was just there and she had reminded him about the graduation. "You're right," Pap told her, "Di told me this morning but I forgot." He turned around and headed for home. I drove back home, looking for Pap on the way. When I got home, Bill said Pap had been there and just left for church. Missed him again. Once again, I drove back to church, still looking for Pap. As I parked my car, Pap walked up to the corner. I hadn't seen him walking down the street.

We were on time for the entrance of the graduates. As usual, I thoroughly enjoyed the special liturgy and songs for the Mass, but I didn't think Pap knew Sue was graduating. I was proud of my daughter but sad as well. My youngest was growing up and my father was losing his memory. I knew that, if he could remember, Pap would be proud of his youngest granddaughter. She had excelled in school and received many awards for her achievements.

I was becoming more concerned that my father would get lost. When I asked him our address and phone number, he remembered both which made me feel better. But when I asked to see his wallet, I discovered that the emergency card I had put in it was gone, and so were his credit cards and the rest of his papers. He was carrying around an empty wallet.

I wanted to get an identification bracelet for Pap. I looked in the phone book and came across a listing for the Department of Aging. When I called the number, the person answering the phone was very helpful. She informed me that the police had an ID bracelet program and gave me the phone number to call. She offered to send me some other information along with a listing on senior day care centers.

When I phoned the police station, I was told that I could get an ID bracelet for my father for a nominal sum. The bracelet would have an identification number and the police phone number. The policeman added that the seniors liked the bracelet, so they wore it. I asked him to please send me the form. I decided that I would order two, in case one got lost.

I noticed Pap occasionally searched the house looking for something. He inspected his stack in the dining room, investigated his drawers in the little room, then went upstairs to continue his search. It was evident that he was looking for something. It was also obvious that he wasn't finding it because he became more agitated. When I asked what he was looking for, he said his check was missing. I reminded him that it was directly deposited into the bank, it wasn't lost. Then he relaxed—until the next time.

Pap stopped writing out checks; he withdrew his money from his savings account instead. At the beginning of the month, I tried to add money to my father's savings account and discovered he had closed it. He transferred his remaining money into an account in his name only. I could put money in for him, but I couldn't withdraw any. I made it a practice to put two hundred dollars into his account each month.

Sue opened a savings account at the bank where her brother worked. She gave him her passbook and asked him to withdraw some money. When he returned with the money, she absent mindedly left her passbook on the dining room table with the money inside and it disappeared. We looked all over the house without any success. We asked Pap if he had seen it. We got his standard answer, "I don't take anything that doesn't belong to me. I haven't seen it."

Right!

On a hunch, Bill checked upstairs in Pap's workshop. He found Sue's passbook with the money still in it. When Bill gave it back to Sue, Pap confided, "I was keeping it safe. I was afraid that it would be stolen laying on the table, so I put it up."

One evening I received a phone call telling me Aunt Elsie had passed away. She had suffered a paralyzing stroke a few years before and was confined to a nursing home. Stroke followed stroke as her health continued to deteriorate. Her mind wasn't affected, it was still very sharp and she kept her sense of humor. The lights in her blue eyes were always dancing.

I told Pap his oldest sister had died but I wasn't sure he understood. I wasn't sure he recognized her at the wake. He talked to his brother, sisters, nieces and nephews but I didn't know if he knew them. Pap always enjoyed talking to people. While I talked to our relatives, I kept an eye on Pap. I didn't want him wandering away. After the services and the ride to the cemetery the next day, we stopped with the family for lunch at a Bohemian restaurant. Pap needed more help. The meal was family style—Pap needed help serving himself, cutting his meat. Once again, I kept an eye on Pap as I circulated among cousins I hadn't seen in a long time. Pap thought that I had left. He got up from the table and was leaving himself but I "headed him off at the pass."

That year, as in other years, I planted green pepper and tomato plants. I planted marigolds and impatiens. I bought carrot, green bean, squash and Swiss chard seeds to plant after the ground warmed up. I put the seed packets on a shelf in the house to plant later. They disappeared. I never found them. I figured they must have disappeared for a reason and didn't replace them.

5

Lost

I always registered during the spring for my fall classes, committed myself to return to school after the summer. But this term was different. Because of a restricted budget my school reduced the number of courses available. Then, because of the public's uproar, they restored some of them. Their juggling of classes made Spring registration impossible—no schedules were ready. Finally, I received the notice I was waiting for—early registration for the Fall term would be held the last week of June, the same week as our vacation.

I didn't have a choice. I had to give up part of my vacation to return to the city to register. I only needed three more courses, Introduction To Finance was one of them. It was required for my degree and only offered in the fall term on Saturday at noon. For the past few years, I had been watching the schedule of evening classes for the course but it was never offered. I didn't want to go to school on Saturday, especially for a three-hour class starting at noon. It would screw up my whole day! I wouldn't be able to go to the camper, I would have to give up "Autumn on the Prairie."

I needed Finance if I wanted to get my degree the following spring. I also needed Biology, which was a four-hour class including the lab. My fellow classmates warned me that Biology required a lot of work, they advised me to take it by itself. I planned to take it in January.

Taking Finance along with another class would mean that I would be at school two nights a week plus Saturdays, or all day Saturday. I didn't want to be at school all day Saturday. Since my choice of courses was restricted, I knew I had to be at school for early registration. I couldn't take a chance that the Finance class would be filled.

We had a new issue to consider when we planned our summer vacation—Pap. Should we take him with us to the country or leave him home? When we asked Bill what he thought, he said, "Pap doesn't get into trouble during the day and I'll be home at night when he is tired. He can stay home."

Tom, Sue, and I left for the camper on Saturday morning. Pap stayed home with Bill. Sunday morning, our niece and her husband arrived from Maryland to join us for the week. Sunday night, I drove back into the city, checked on Pap, registered for my classes on Monday morning and drove back to the camper Monday afternoon.

We don't have a telephone at our camper. Phone calls are received at the front gate and messages are delivered by security to the various lots. Monday night we received a message to call home. I had an uneasy feeling when I saw the guard, we didn't get messages from home unless there was a problem.

Tom knew something was wrong as soon as Bill answered the phone. "I'm glad you called...Pap has disappeared...I went upstairs after supper and when I came back downstairs around seven, Pap was gone. He must have gone for a walk. It's after ten and Pap still isn't home. I'm getting worried. What should I do?"

We told Bill to call the police and keep us informed. He said he would ask Kathy and Mike to help him look for Pap. When he tried to call, their phone was busy so he drove to their house. Kathy was already asleep. The boys let her sleep and they each took a car to search for Pap. They kept stopping at our house to see if Pap had returned, leaving notes for each other about where they had been and where they were going. Bill checked the neighboring hospitals to see if someone of Pap's description had been admitted. When we called home at midnight, Pap still wasn't home.

Tom thought one of us should drive home; I thought we should wait until morning. It was one of the worst nights I have ever had. I spent most of the night storming the gates of Heaven verbally. I wrapped my father up in beautiful paper and tied him with a bow, then I gave him to God. Other times I just dropped him off like a sack of laundry with a plea to please watch out for him, to keep him safe. I knew God was the only one who could help my father and get him safely home. We were helpless…we didn't know where he was and we were a hundred miles away. Whenever I woke up, I said another prayer and eventually drifted back to sleep. I really wanted a cigarette.

When we called home early the next morning, Bill had good news—the police had brought Pap home at five o'clock. They found him sitting under a viaduct at the lake front, a few miles from home. He was complaining that his head hurt and he was limping, but otherwise he was unharmed.

As Pap walked up the front stairs with the policeman, Bill asked, "Where were you?"

"I spent the night upstairs in my room," Pap answered.

Bill was relieved when he heard that I was driving home to get Pap. He said he would stay up until I arrived, then he was going to bed. He and Mike had spent most of the night looking for Pap without success. They had searched all the streets and alleys in our neighborhood and the surrounding area. I wasn't surprised that they hadn't found Pap. I remembered looking for him on the day of Sue's graduation, on the street that I knew he had taken—without success.

Since my visit to Queen Of Heaven cemetery, I kept my rosary in my purse. While driving home, I said a rosary in thanksgiving for my father's safe return. I was glad our camper was so close to the city. It seemed that I was spending my whole vacation in my car—driving back and forth.

Before I drove Pap out to the camper, I called his primary doctor to schedule a check up. After I relayed what we knew of Pap's adventure, I mentioned that Pap seemed to be listing to the left. Dr. D. examined Pap's back and his legs looking for bumps and bruises. After the examination, Dr. D. said Pap was fine, just a little sore.

For the rest of the week, Pap asked every day to go home. He was worried about the dogs...who was taking care of them? He was concerned about his girlfriend...she didn't know where he was.

Each day, we told him he was on vacation with us—he would go home when we did. Bill was home, taking care of the dogs. We had phoned his girlfriend, she knew he was with us. We reminded him that he had gone for a walk and got lost. He said he didn't know what happened but he wouldn't do that anymore.

We gave Pap one of the beds in the bunkroom. He never remembered where his bed was, we had to direct him each night. Often he wandered back and forth between the trailer and the family room looking for something. When we asked what he was looking for, Pap replied, "The stairs. I want to go upstairs to go to bed." We explained he was at the camper, there was no upstairs. We left a night light on in the bathroom so he would be able to find his way. I left a bowl of fruit on the table along with boxes of cereal and a bowl.

Tom and our nephew took Pap fishing—he sat in a chair at the lake and watched. Pap confided to Tom that he was never a fisherman, his brother Alvin caught all the fish.

After our relatives departed, I looked for my glasses. They weren't on the table where I left them. I searched everywhere...without any luck. Where did they go? Did our niece accidently pack them with their stuff? Then I happened to notice that Pap's shirt pocket was bulging. I looked in his pocket and what did I find? My glasses. He found them on the table, thought they were his and took possession.

I was finally notified that Pap's ID bracelets were ready. I had ordered a small size for my father, but the bracelets were very small, too tight for him to wear comfortably. When I called the police station to ask for advice, a policeman recommended a jewelry store near our house that made adjustments. After a couple of links were added, I gave Pap one to wear. He had stopped wearing his watch and the bracelet took its place. I impressed on him the importance of wearing the bracelet at all times. He said he would, and I checked daily to make sure.

I was concerned about leaving Pap home alone and phoned the Department of Aging again. After I told my story, I was informed that my father's case would be referred to Catholic Charities. I wrote down the phone number of Catholic Charities Northwest Case Management so I could contact them. I was worried that the case worker would reach Pap and he wouldn't tell us. When I called Northwest Case Management, I spoke to the supervisor and learned that the person who would be handling my father's case was on vacation. I decided to write a letter to the case worker, telling her about my father's problem and my desire to get him into a day care facility and stressing the need for my involvement in his case. I relayed my fear that she would phone when I wasn't home, my father would forget she called and we would never know.

The case worker reached me at work and thanked me for sending the letter describing our situation, saying that it was helpful to have some background on a new case. We scheduled an appointment for her visit. I said I would stay home to make sure that she would be able to interview my father.

Pap wasn't allowed to stay home on weekends anymore if both Tom and I were going to the country. He always protested—he had too much to do in the city. I told him that what he had to do could wait; I reminded him that he got lost and couldn't stay home. Then he said he was worried about the dogs and his girlfriend. I replied that Bill and Sue would watch the dogs. I would call his girlfriend. Once, I actually called her and received the impression that my father's leaving didn't matter. After that, I just told Pap that I called. I didn't want his feelings to be hurt.

"I'm working on my memory, it's getting better," Pap said. It didn't do any good to remind him of all the things that were going wrong, so we agreed with him. I didn't tell him in advance that we were going to the camper, but about an hour before we were to leave I asked when he would be ready. I always insisted that he was coming with us. Luckily, after some verbal fencing, he usually came willingly.

On one of our trips to the camper, Pap took a bottle of yellow pills out of his pocket. I asked if I could see them. They were over-the-counter sleeping pills. I took possession.

Many activities were scheduled at our campground during the summer. Line dance instruction was held on Saturday mornings, various live bands played on Saturday nights. I took Pap with me to both. He enjoyed watching the line dancing and often tried a few steps on the side. He commented that it was good exercise but hard work. Sometimes at night Pap and I danced to a slow song.

In the camper, Pap sat on the couch and watched the birds and squirrels outside at the bird feeder. The squirrels always provided entertainment. We put movies on the VCR for him to watch while we went swimming or for a walk. He always worried about the dogs and asked when we were going home or he said he was going home. I always told him when we were going home and that he was going home with us.

Apparently our camping trips made an impression on Pap. One day when I came home from work, Pap said, "I think you should know that I'm not going to be home for a few days." His comment surprised me so I asked where he was going. He answered he was going camping. So I asked who he was going with. He replied, Diane. "I'm Diane," I told him. Then he said that he was going with Bob and Dick, they came by the house and invited him to go with them. (Bob and Dick were my mother's brothers. One had passed away, the other lived in California. My father hadn't seen them in years.)

Pap and I discussed his trip. It was decided that he was going to tell them that he couldn't go. Instead he was going to go camping with me on the weekend.

It was hard to have Pap with us all of the time. Terri offered to take Pap for the weekend to give us a break. We took advantage of her offer and escaped to the country. We visited some of the natural wild places where we couldn't take Pap.

After I started writing down our adventures, I asked Terri to write down her feelings about that weekend. Here in her own words is the tale:

The First Weekend

Pap came to stay with us for the weekend. Brittany wanted to take him to see a little park we called the elephant park. It got the name because there was a little slide that was made to look like an elephant.

Off we went. On the way to the park, Pap told Brittany how to take weeds out of the grass. At times he would stop at someone's lawn (whether they were out or not), get down on his knees and start pulling out the weeds, explaining to Brittany and myself everything that he was doing. It was hard to remember that he suffered from any kind of mind affecting disease.

When we got to the park, Pap had a good time with his great-granddaughter. He went on the swings with her, he climbed up the slide and went down, he was just having fun. He was reliving his childhood with Brittany and it was fun to watch. We all laughed and giggled at how silly he was acting but he said, "What's more fun than kids? More kids." Well he was being more kids.

After a while we started back home and we were back to our lessons in lawn care. When to remove weeds, how to remove weeds, what they look like and when to take them out.

The day was lovely. The only time Pap seemed to show any signs of being sick was when he was standing in the kitchen and couldn't find the kitchen. Other than that he did really well.

On Sunday, my mother and father were going to pick him up. However, he had other ideas. He was adamant that he was going to take the bus. This was not a good day. He kept forgetting my mother and father were coming to pick him up and every few minutes he just got ready to go and asked where he was supposed to catch the bus to go home. He had things to do, people to see. He thought his friends would start to worry if he wasn't there for church. I guess he had forgotten that he went to church that morning with my daughter and me.

Well, Mom and Dad eventually got there and took him home. It seemed like a very long day.

Both Pap and Terri were very happy to see us when we arrived at her house. Pap wanted to go home; Terri wanted to relax. She confided that Pap wanted to take the bus home—all day. We didn't stay to visit, we took Pap home.

I wanted the house to be presentable when the case worker came to interview Pap. The Christmas boxes were still upstairs from the flood. I knew I couldn't do anything with the stacks of books, magazines, and other stuff, but I could move the boxes. I did, back to the basement where I put them back on the big, empty table where I stored them.

When I came home from work, I received an unpleasant surprise, we had flood #2. Pap had once again turned on the water for a bath, sat down on the couch and gone to sleep. Water…water…water…everywhere! The boxes I had just put back in the basement where soaked again. Back to square one. This time we turned off the main water supply to the tub. I made a big sign, "NO," and hung it from the faucet. Enough Fun!!

The case worker arrived for the interview. She talked to my father and asked him some questions. I listened, but kept my mouth shut. Without his knowledge she gave him the Mini Mental test. He knew his name and birth date, but not his age. He knew it was summer but didn't know the month, day or year. He knew his address and phone number. He had no idea who was the president of the United States; it wasn't important to him. He qualified for three days at day care and his income was low enough that Catholic Charities would pick up part of the cost. His doctor had to sign a form stating that he was physically able to attend before we could proceed. I was very happy with this news. Our bills required me to work and I knew that Pap's days of staying home safely by himself were numbered.

Pap wore his ID bracelet—I checked daily to be sure. After the doctor signed Pap's medical form, he would go to Adult Day Care. But what were we going to do in the meantime? What would happen if Pap got lost and someone tried to call our house and no one was home? We decided to remedy this situation. Sue added a postscript to the message on our answering machine: "If you find a cute little old man wandering around, you can reach his daughter, Diane, at _____ (my work number)."

One day I noticed that Pap's ID bracelet wasn't on his wrist. I began to search. I looked on the dining room table, on his stack on the buffet, in his three drawer chest in the little room—without success. I climbed the stairs to the attic and found not only his bracelet next to his bed but also his house key. I gave Pap back his bracelet but kept his house key. He always left the house by the back door and returned through the front door. I asked my family not to lock the front door when they left. With our dogs, who greeted everyone, including us, with loud barking, I thought it would be safe to leave the house unlocked.

Our other children had attended college in Chicago but Sue wanted to go away. She applied and was accepted at a college in Missouri. School was starting and the time had come to drive her down. We didn't want to take my father on the trip but he couldn't stay home alone, either. I asked Terri to take Pap for the weekend. Bill offered to pick him up on Sunday.

We loaded the car, barely leaving room for Sue, and left for a long weekend. It was a nice drive, but long, made longer due to the flooding of the Mississippi River. The water was receding but bridges were still out and roads were flooded. We had to drive further south to get across. Water marks reached up to the second floor on many of the houses in the flood plain. Driving through the area—seeing the devastation—made the disaster very real.

We spent the night in a motel, then moved Sue into the dorm the following morning. She unpacked while we attended an orientation lecture designed for parents. Then we stopped at the local discount store to pick up all the things that she had forgotten or didn't have room for, plus snacks for late night studying. I was sad that my youngest daughter was going to college so far from home. Rather than spend the night at the motel, we headed back home via the camper.

It was strange and lonely there. Most of the college kids had returned to school…the volley ball courts and beach were deserted. Many of the birds had already gone South…the air was quiet. Tom and I were the only ones at the camper—no Sue, no Pap.

When we returned home, we discovered that Pap had only spent one night at Terri's house. Here is her story of the weekend:

Second Time He Stayed.

I picked Pap up from his house and the car ride was quite nice. Again he was having a good day. We sang church songs: "Peace is Flowing Like a River", "Be Not Afraid" and "Amazing Grace". These seemed to be his three favorite songs. We talked about religion.

We also talked about how Mom treated him like a child on his good days, trying to help with things he was capable of doing himself. He understood why she did it but it just seemed to upset him when he was actually feeling like himself. Which wasn't very often anymore. I couldn't understand what my family, who lived with him every day, was trying to tell me about how the illness affected him. He seemed so capable. So alive. So in his right mind. Like I said, it was a good day.

We got to my house and went for a walk to the park. While Brittany played, he told me about when he was young. He was a runner. He enjoyed being on track and being in full control of his assets. He told me about how sometimes, now, when he was sick he would just forget everything. Or he would forget the here and now and remember when he was young like it was happening now. And that this was not good. He got kind of quiet at times and stared into space, then he apologized and said he was okay now. I thought maybe we should go home. That way if he wasn't going to want to walk or be up to doing anything he wouldn't have to.

On the way home he told me all about his brother Alvin. He had some good stories, but I don't know if they were all true or not. He just wasn't acting like himself anymore.

When we got home, we talked for a while but then he just wanted to stare at whatever it was off in space that had his undivided attention. He just sat there quiet and still. I thought he looked a little confused like he was trying to solve some great puzzle of the mind and just couldn't find a solution. He was deep in thought but his face had a child-like innocence as if he didn't know what was going on.

After a long while he started coming back to himself and went in search of the kitchen that he was right next to but couldn't find. I have a small step between my family room and kitchen, which is all that separates the two and a small counter. I kept reminding him of the stair but this time he fell and gave himself a nice little scratch. We cleaned it up, but that was it. My weekend became a day. He wanted to go home to his own house.

I called my brother to see if he planned to be home and told him what was going on. That the day that started off so well had taken a nasty turn. Bill said he'd be home and would even come pick him up.

We had dinner and then sat waiting for Bill. Pap was starting to do better. He apologized again and again for how he had been earlier. I told him it didn't matter, as long as he was with me and I could be with him, he could feel free to act anyway he wanted.

Bill had fun with Pap while we were gone. Pap tried to be helpful. Bill looked for the coffee pot to make coffee and found it in the refrigerator in the basement. For some reason Pap cleared off the dining room table and rolled up the tablecloth. Then Pap gave the tomato plants a crew cut, a few leaves on stubs were all that remained. But Bill found the mail and everything was back in order when we arrived home.

The next day Pap asked if there was anything that he could do for me. He always wanted to help and I really didn't know what to say.

Sue came home for Labor Day. We usually spend the holiday weekend at the camper but she wanted to stay in Chicago. The day before she returned to school, the whole family decided to go bowling. I defrosted a turkey breast and put it in the oven to bake while we were gone. We figured it was safe to leave Pap home.

We bowled a few more games than we planned. It was fun to have everyone together; we teased, joked and laughed. I started to worry about my turkey and left early to check on it.

When I entered the kitchen, Pap was standing at the sink and the oven light was on. This was not a good sign. I opened the oven door and looked into an empty cavern, the former occupant had vanished. Looking around the kitchen, I saw my bird swimming in the sink. It was almost completely covered with water and Pap stood next to it, dunking it up and down.

"What in the world are you doing?" I asked.

He had a silly grin on his face and was very pleased with himself as he replied, "Look what I found! I'm cooling it off so I can eat it."

I told Pap that I would finish supper and rescued the bird from its water bath. At first I was worried that it hadn't finished cooking. I cut a test piece and was relieved to discover that the meat was white, not pink.

I planned to send Sue two letters a week while she was away at college. But I didn't want them to be dull, boring…How are you? We are fine…letters. In one of her first letters I wrote:

> Your brother got into a lengthy discussion with Pap. For some reason Bill told Pap that he was 83. Pap thought that he was only 73 and wanted Bill to prove that he was older.

Pap's antics will give me something to write about. This way you won't feel like you are missing out on everything; it might even bring a smile to your face. And you will understand when you receive the tall box with air holes.

A friend asked me how I found something interesting to write about—so often. I told her that it was no problem, I had Pap. Without those letters, many of these events would have been forgotten.

The fall term at my college began. I wasn't happy attending school on Saturday, but this year, my Saturday class was a benefit for my family. I kept an eye on Pap in the morning while Tom worked and made Pap's lunch before I went to school. Pap was only alone for a short time before Tom came home. If the weather was going to be nice, I drove to the camper after school. I still had Sunday to spend outside.

When I came home from work, I never knew what I would find, especially when Pap was home by himself. This time I noticed a little bit of milk on the pantry floor. I cleaned it up and opened the refrigerator door, the sliced ham was on a shelf instead of in the meat bin. I opened the meat bin to put the ham away and found a bowl of cat food in milk. I disposed of it in the downstairs toilet which promptly overflowed. In the bathroom was a very long wooden pole. Why? Where did the pole come from? What was going to be done with it? Too many questions, no answers.

We tried to stop asking questions. We tried to deal with the situation, clean up, fix, put away, and move onto the next. But questions always popped up. Why? When? What? Never any answer, but sometimes a good guess.

I often saw Pap walking toward his girlfriend's house or returning from the direction of her house. One day I commented on his walk, asked him some question about her. He confided that I talked to her more than he did. He thought I called her before we went to the camper.

Sometimes Pap was upset with himself when I came home from work. When I inquired, he said he had screwed up and forgot to meet his girlfriend. He was supposed to meet her, but he must have gotten the time wrong. No one was home. Or he was going to help her with the yard work, but he forgot. Sometimes he was so upset, he went for a walk to her house to apologize. He always quickly returned, commenting that she wasn't home.

Gazing at Pap, I realized he needed a shave. I hooked up his electric shaver in the upstairs bathroom and sent him up to shave. Before long he came back downstairs with the shaver in his hand. He complained it wasn't working. When I opened the shaver, I noticed one of the disks was missing and the rest were clogged with very long, reddish hair? What was he cutting? I operated on the shaver so it would work. I didn't look for the missing disk, there didn't seem to be any point, I didn't know when it was lost. To be on the safe side, I cut Pap's hair. At 83, he only had gray hair at his temples; the rest was blonde.

I received a free radio when I made a credit card purchase and left it on the dining room table in its box. When Bill came downstairs, Pap was standing at the table, screwdriver in hand, trying to pry open the radio. Did he think it was a box of candy? Bill rescued the radio and put it away.

When Tom came home from work, Pap told him that he didn't know what he was doing there. Two men in uniform had told him to stay. We don't know if Pap knew that he was at home, if he was dreaming or if the police brought him home again. There wasn't a message on the answering machine and I didn't receive any messages at work. Pap was the only one home. ???

I hadn't heard from the case worker so I left a message requesting that she call me. When she phoned, she said she hadn't received the signed form from the doctor and Pap could not go to the senior day center without it. She phoned the doctor's office…left messages…but her phone calls were not returned. I asked her to send me the form and I would personally take it to the doctor's office.

I phoned the Clinic to find out the best time to accomplish my mission and was told to come in on Wednesday between 12:00 and 2:00

P.M. I arrived about 12:30—expecting no problems. I thought the doctor would sign the paper and I would be on my way. Wrong! I gave the form to the nurse and explained that I needed it signed. "Oh, yes, I remember seeing this," she said after looking at it. "I gave it to the Doctor and he refused to sign it."

Lovely!

So I waited for Dr. D., caught him on the fly, explained briefly, and ran into major opposition. Dr. D. refused to sign the form—he didn't want to waste the HMO's money. I told him we were paying for this service, not the insurance company. I just needed his permission for my father to go. He said we would have to talk more about it. I sat down to wait.

Finally, Dr. D. called me into his office and asked many questions that I couldn't answer. "What will your father do at day care? What kind of activities do they have? Do they have an exercise program?" I hadn't thought about what Pap would do at the Day Care Center. I just knew it wasn't safe for him to stay home alone. I tried calling Pap's case worker or her supervisor, but both were out to lunch. Dr. D. was steadfast in his refusal to sign the paper. "What if he falls? I will be responsible."

"He can fall at home, no one is there!" I replied. I couldn't believe it. I had found a safe place for Pap to go during the day and the doctor would not sign the paper. I never thought I would be arguing with a doctor. I reminded Dr. D. that my father had wandered away from home and spent the night at the lake front. He had flooded our house—twice. Who knew what he would do next. Because of the aggravation, I completely fell apart, tears streamed down my cheeks and my hands were shaking. When Dr. D. saw the distress he had caused, he relented, and signed the paper, noting that Pap was senile. (I probably would still be in the doctor's office if I hadn't disintegrated.)

I didn't want to take a chance the form would be lost in the mail. I decided to deliver it personally. Northwest Case Management was located in a senior housing complex and was not easy to find. After driving around the whole complex and asking many questions, I finally found Pap's case worker, gave her the signed paper and explained the problem with the doctor. She told me that the day care center she had in mind was set up for Alzheimer's patients. The fact that the doctor noted that Pap was senile was a benefit, not a liability as I had feared. Pap would not be able to go if his mental condition was normal.

Pap's case worker described the Center—it was run by the Council for the Jewish Elderly, located on the border of Chicago and Evanston. They had bus service but we lived outside of their district. While I was there, she called to see if they had an opening.

THE CENTER HAD ROOM FOR HIM!

The caseworker advised me to arrange for a visit, and if we liked it, to call her and she would send over the paperwork.

PROGRESS!!!!! FINALLY!

When I returned to work, I called the Center but didn't receive an answer. Nor was there an answer the next day, nor the next. I wondered if I had the right phone number. Then I looked at my calendar and noticed that it was Rosh Hashanah—the Center was closed for the Jewish holidays.

When I finally reached the Center, I spoke to their director. She said they had a waiting list, but she would add my father's name. When I told her where we lived, she suggested that we visit the Japanese Center which was closer to our home. I explained that my father was losing his current memory, had already wandered from home and needed to be in a Senior Day Care Center for his safety. She realized that my father needed to be in Asher's, their unit for those with mental dementia. There was an opening in the unit and we scheduled an appointment for a visit.

During the drive to the Center on the afternoon of our visit, Pap and I talked about where we were going. I explained that I was concerned about his safety—he had gotten lost. I told him that they had things to do at the Center so he wouldn't be so bored. I mentioned that they would give him a hot lunch. The Center is staffed by very caring people, which was apparent as soon as we entered. Pap was taken for the tour—I tagged along. The outside door is locked and can only be opened by a buzzer. The clients can't decide to leave whenever they want. The Center was designed to include a separate section for people with mental dementia. They spend their day in a very comfortable room, complete with a small kitchen and bathroom facilities. Every day, activities are scheduled to help their coordination, mental as well as physical. They join the more mentally competent group of seniors for various activities: concerts, dances, parties. Field trips are scheduled throughout the month. They go shopping at the mall, out to eat, or for ice cream. The Center maintained an account in each client's name to pay for the outings so I wouldn't have to worry about providing money for each trip. I would receive a notice when his fund was getting low.

A nurse was on staff at the Center and psychological counseling was available for the clients. Each client was evaluated every 90 days. I would receive a card informing me of the date and time of the evaluation, if I wanted to attend. In addition, a support group met in the afternoon, once a month.

Pap passed their preliminary test, or qualified for the program, which might be a better way of stating it. The Center was open from 8:30 until 4:30. They had bus service but Pap was out of their district. I said that I would drive him, it wouldn't be a problem. I liked the place and thought it would be very good for my father. He would be safe...in the hands of caring people. He wouldn't be getting into trouble or sitting in front of the television, sleeping his life away. When the director asked if he would like to attend, Pap said he would give it a try.

Thank you, Lord! I hadn't considered the possibility that my father wouldn't want to go. I don't know what I would have done if he'd said no.

Before Pap could start, he needed to be evaluated by the Center's nurse. We scheduled a visit for the following week. After the nurse's visit, Pap's starting day would be decided.

Life continued to be interesting. Tom stayed home from work because he wasn't feeling well. Pap wanted to give him some tomatoes to take with him. "Where am I going?" Tom asked. "I'm home…I live here." Such fun.

I left Pap home and went to the camper by myself. I had car trouble and called home to talk to Tom or to leave a message on the answering machine. Pap answered the phone, "Tom isn't home and Di went to the country. Do you want to leave a message?"

"I don't think so. I'll call back." Pap hadn't recognized my voice. I couldn't figure out a way to leave a message that wouldn't get screwed up, and didn't know what to do. I got lucky, as I hung up the phone, a man in an old car pulled into the gas station. He was able to fix my car.

The following week, Pap's youngest sister, Shirley, came from California to visit. She was recovering from a stroke and walked with a cane. When she stopped at our house to see her brother, I warned her Pap might not know her because of his memory loss. As she was leaving, she remarked that she was happy—Pap recognized her voice.

A note in a letter to Sue after the visit mentioned that because of Aunt Shirley's visit and our granddaughter's birthday, all kinds of things were in different places yesterday and today. (The note didn't elaborate, and I don't remember.) Pap told Tom he didn't know how to make coffee. GOOD, may he not remember.

Bill called work to tell me that Pap had not come home from church. He had driven around the neighborhood looking for him but didn't see him. I suggested that if Pap wasn't home before Bill had to leave for school, he should call me. We had our missing person message on the answering machine.

Bill called back a few hours later. An hour before he had to leave, he received a phone call from a man who found my father sitting on his porch. Pap admitted that he was lost and asked the man to call us to pick him up. Pap remembered our phone number. This time he was four miles west of our house.

The Center's nurse came to visit Pap, spending more than two hours with him. She gave him a couple of tests, including a test that measured his psychological mood. Once again I joined them at the table but refrained from joining in the conversation. She agreed that the Center would be good for Pap. The nurse remarked, "I was very surprised that your father is able to go to the Center so quickly, normally there is a long waiting list."

I replied, "The Lord meant for Pap to go. He pointed me in the right direction and He has cleared the way."

After the nurse left, Pap asked me why he had to go to the Center if he was doing so well. I told him that it was the Lord's will. I would repeat that phrase many times in the coming weeks when Pap protested about going to the Center.

It was too late to go to work when the nurse left, so I ran a few errands. When I returned, the dirty dishes that were in the drainer were gone, nowhere to be found. Pap had put them away. I searched the house, looking for Pap and found him in the basement investigating the contents of the freezer. The day before I found egg shells in the microwave. Leaving Pap at home alone was like playing with explosives—you never knew what was going to happen.

I stopped on my way to work to tell Angel, our crossing guard, that Pap would soon be going to a Day Care Center. She was happy to get the good news. One day she had watched Pap walk past the church, down the block past the grammar school and then he turned around and came back. She asked him where he was going. He didn't know. She calmed him down by asking him to tell her where the church was. She said, "Don't move. Look at the buildings. What's behind you? What's across the street? Where are you going to go?"

Pap successfully answered: the restaurant, the church, and he was going home. Now he knew in which direction to walk.

Angel said that on a different morning she watched Pap try to open the door of the school. He told her that he couldn't get into church. She pointed him in the right direction that time too.

She had asked various people in the neighborhood to help Pap if he seemed confused. She told them where he lived and explained, "He won't hurt you. If you could just talk to him…ask him where he was going…help him…point him in the right direction…he'd be okay." She told Pap, "Don't worry. Angels are always watching over you."

We both were very glad that Pap would soon be going to the Center, even if it was only three days a week. At least he would be safe and out of harm's way for part of the time.

One night when I was at school, Pap became concerned with my absence and asked Bill where I was. Bill replied that I was out with friends. Pap commented, "It is good that Di has friends. She needs to spend some time with them, without me."

Tom was going to the country for a week of fishing. I knew we would have fun with Pap while he was gone. Before Tom could leave on his vacation, he had to finish something at work. Then he stopped to pick up something at our house before leaving for the country. On the way he passed Pap walking to church. Entering our house, Tom found the garden hose stretched from the radiator in the dining room through the little room into the front room, resting on the floor by the couch. ???

I received the best possible birthday present—Pap was going to spend his day in a safe place. He would have started attending the Center on my birthday but the Center was closed in celebration of the harvest. He started two days later.

I explained to my boss that I had to drive Pap to the Center in the morning and pick him up at night. Three times a week I would arrive an hour later in the morning and have to leave work earlier. My boss said that they would work with me, he often talked to his aging mother on the phone and understood the problems that we were having.

6

Center

I had to change my morning routine in order to drive Pap to the Center in the morning. I knew I had to get up early to stop Pap from going to Mass. That was the only way I would get to work at a decent time. The Center opened at 8:30. If we left the house by 8:15, I could drop Pap off and still get to work by 9:00. If Pap went to church, he wouldn't get home until 9:30.

My drive to work would take longer but gaining peace of mind would be worth it. I planned to take Lake Shore Drive, it was faster—sometimes—and I could watch the lake. I have always liked Chicago's lakefront. I like watching the moods of Lake Michigan, the waves and the colors of the water.

Since I was getting up earlier, I intended to exercise. I'd have a reason to be up when Pap came downstairs, he wouldn't think I was watching him. I hoped we would be able to start the day on a gentle note.

On the morning of Pap's first day at the Center, I had just finished exercising when Pap came downstairs. I explained that he couldn't go to Mass, he needed to go with me instead. He was going to spend the day at the Center, the place we had visited, and I would pick him up after work. Pap agreed. I was happy he agreed and very relieved that I didn't have to persuade him.

When we arrived at the Center, a staff member came out to greet Pap. She told him they had just made a pot of coffee and invited him to join her for a cup. She walked with him to the unit where everyone with mental dementia was gathering. I stayed in the lobby to talk to the nurse. She suggested I bring a change of clothes for Pap to keep at the Center. If he spilled something, he would have clean clothes to change into. Then she asked me to call a couple of times during the day to check on Pap, to make sure he was adjusting.

I was surprised by my feelings…I had stepped back in time…left one of my children at the kindergarten door. I felt sad. As I left my children, I told myself that school would teach things they needed for life; my children were growing up, it was time. Leaving Pap at the Center gave me a feeling of sadness at his decline, balanced by relief. He was safe—the house was safe.

The first time I phoned, Pap was involved in a discussion on Indian Summer. (Pap always liked discussions.) The second time, they were listening to music. The staff reported that he was adjusting well and seemed to be enjoying himself.

When I arrived to get Pap, a little after 4:00 P.M., he was sitting in the lobby talking to a man who was also waiting for his daughter. Pap had already forgotten what he did during the day. He asked if I had gotten the message. What message? He had called the house to tell me he was working late at the railroad. In the car, on the way home, he continued to talk about his job at the railroad. I started to worry about his regression into the past. I was glad he was going to the Center but I didn't want him to get stuck in the past. I hoped that we would strike a balance. Then Pap asked if he had to go back again and I told him that he did. He was going to the Center three days a week.

Pap didn't get into as much mischief during the week of Tom's vacation. Going to the Center gave him mental as well as physical stimulation. He didn't nap as much, he was tired when I picked him up and went to bed earlier. But I still didn't want to leave him home alone when I went to school. Bill wasn't going to be home the night I had class; I called Kathy and asked her to Pap-sit.

Pap was becoming more and more forgetful. He didn't remember where we kept basic items: dishes, silverware, cereal. Since he was having trouble finding things, each morning I got out his cereal, bowl, spoon, and the milk. I put them on the table along with his cup of coffee.

One morning I put a bowl of oatmeal in the microwave to cook while I got dressed. I asked Pap if he wanted some. "No, I don't want any," he answered. "I'll have what I always have." So I poured a generous bowl of Raisin Bran. After he had his cereal, he ate a banana. I poured his cup of coffee and went upstairs to get dressed. When I returned, Pap was eating a bowl of oatmeal that he found in the microwave.

I became more aware of Pap's appearance—what he was wearing, how often he changed clothes. If he wore the same thing too many days in a row, I gave him a clean shirt or pants and asked him to change. He returned to the attic and often came back wearing the same clothes he wore upstairs. We tried replacing his clothes after he went to bed at night. But it was hard to find his clothes in the dark; sometimes we could, many times we couldn't. We didn't want to wake him.

As time passed and his memory slipped, I wouldn't let him go upstairs to change. I insisted he change in either the downstairs bathroom or the dining room. He didn't understand why he couldn't go upstairs, why I insisted he get dressed downstairs. I reminded him that when he reached the attic, he forgot he was going to change clothes. He confided, "Sometimes I remember, but I don't think you are right. So I don't do it." Sometimes he changed clothes without a disagreement but more often the battle of wills lasted too long. It wasn't a good way to start the morning.

Showers were another adventure. The Center's visiting nurse told me older people only had to bathe once or twice a week because their skin was very dry and thin. Pap's showers took forever. When they lengthened to an hour, I moved the shower date to the weekend when I wasn't so rushed. I didn't look forward to the weekend.

I discovered the best time for Pap's shower was after he had breakfast, sometime before noon. If we waited too long, he was tired and had a harder time getting dressed. His modesty prevented us from helping. When I asked him through the door if he was okay, he didn't always answer me. Then I became concerned. Was he all right? Did he hear me or was he just being stubborn? Once Pap told me, "I heard you, but I didn't want to answer."

Pap didn't remember that he went to the Center. Three mornings a week, we discussed that he couldn't go to Mass—he had to go to the Center. I always told him that I would drive him there and pick him up. I never told him that it was a day care center. I always emphasized the social aspect…people to talk to…having something to do…and he would get a hot lunch and a snack. Sometimes that was enough to convince him and he agreed to go, sometimes our debate continued. If Pap countered that he had something he had to do, I replied that he would be home the next day and could do it then. If he still didn't want to go, I brought up his forgetfulness. I assured him it wasn't his fault that he couldn't remember. I knew it was very frustrating for him, but his loss of memory was hard on the family too. He had gotten lost, twice. We were concerned about his safety.

Pap insisted that he was working on his memory, it was getting better. He didn't need to go to the Center. Often he declared, "They told me not to come back. My job is finished."

I always walked with Pap into the Center but I didn't walk with him to the unit. I stopped at the reception desk and talked to the receptionist. In the beginning a staff member came out to walk with him, but after a few weeks, he knew the way by himself. Since we arrived at the Center before the buses brought most of the clients, he joined the staff and other early arrivals for a morning cup of coffee.

If he protested when I walked in with him, I said I wanted to say good morning to my friends. I never gave him the impression that he wasn't capable of entering by himself. "All things work together for good," he remarked in the car or as he entered the Center, especially if I had won the point in our debate. As I left, he advised, "Have a good day, take care of yourself, be good to yourself." Sometimes, he kissed my hand.

In spite of all of our daily discussions and the extra driving, I was very happy that Pap went to the Center three days a week. But that still left two days for Pap to be home—alone. He still had time to be "helpful" which gave me an opportunity to sharpen my detective skills.

Pap washed his clothes and the towels. I tried to wash them before Pap did but didn't always succeed. Sometimes when I took the towels or Pap's clothes out of the drier, they felt funny, sort of sticky. One day I found towels in the drier, they were dry—except for spots that were wet and sticky. I sniffed the wet spots and smelled liquid laundry detergent. Pap thought the drier was a washing machine? Later I found wet clothes spread all over the basement. Pap forgot we had a drier?

When I came home from work I continued my practice of checking the basement refrigerator and freezer along with the shelves. One day I found a can of tuna on the shelf with four or five holes in the lid, but not enough to open it. It looked like it had been operated on with a screwdriver. I took possession.

After work one evening, I opened the upstairs refrigerator and was surprised to see a red and white box full of fried chicken. Where did it come from? Did Pap find it somewhere? I asked my family. No one bought it. It tasted all right, so we ate it. (A year later I learned Aunt Connie brought it. She asked if we enjoyed the chicken that she and Aunt Edna brought when they came to visit. She wasn't sure that Pap knew them, but he enjoyed the chicken. Mystery solved.)

Tom called me at work to ask, "What did you do to the new VCR movie that I just bought?" His question puzzled me so I asked him to explain. He said he came home from work and looked for his new movie and finally found the tape, pulled out of it's case and thrown away in the garbage. Pap was nowhere to be found. ???

A half hour later, Tom knew where Pap was. The owner of an ice cream parlor phoned with the story. Pap had walked in, said he was lost, and asked the man to call us. This time he was four miles north.

We guessed Pap found the tape, thought it was something to eat and took it apart. When he discovered it wasn't edible, he realized he was in trouble and ran away from home. After he walked awhile, he forgot he was running away. (Tom was able to fix the tape.)

Sue, away at college, continued to receive two letters a week but I warned her that they might soon become cards as my homework increased. We continued to hint of things to come in her letters and in our phone conversations. We told her to watch out for a tall box with air holes. We knew she missed Pap and we were going to send him to her so she wouldn't be lonely.

I read someplace that a person's eyes are the windows to their mind. Often, when I looked into Pap's eyes it was like looking through the windows of an abandoned house, the resident was gone, no one was home. All that was left was a flat blue pool, without life, without the sparkle.

My discussions with Pap in the morning continued. Now I added to my list of reasons for his going to the Center that he got lost three times, flooded out our house twice. I told him we couldn't afford to have someone come to the house to stay with him. When I was a child, he made decisions for me that I didn't like, now I had to make decisions for him. Pap remarked, "I didn't say that I'm not going to go, I just thought you ought to know that I'm not getting anything out of it."

Our discussions in the evening continued when I picked him up. He never remembered what he did that day. If he had gone on a trip, sang songs, danced, played bingo, it was all the same—gone. Most of the clients had already left via the Center's buses before I arrived. Pap sat in the lobby waiting for me. When he had someone to talk to, it wasn't too bad. When he was alone, he thought he was in a doctor's office, waiting for his appointment. He informed me that the tests were finished. They told him not to come back.

I was afraid to allow Pap to keep the idea that he didn't need to go to the Center, that he was finished. He forgot 95 percent of the time, but that left the 5 percent he remembered. I always explained that the Center wasn't a doctor's office, he didn't go there for an examination or tests. He went to the Center to be with other people, to have something to do.

I knew from which parent I had received my logical mind. I was beginning to regret my father's ability to debate. It was always a challenge to keep my patience and win. I didn't look forward to our drives back and forth.

Tom and I planned to visit Sue at school. We wanted to make the trip before winter, while the roads were still clear. We asked Kathy and Bill to watch Pap. Terri was expecting another child and taking care of Pap would be too much for her.

We drove to the camper on Friday night and left from there in the morning. It was a beautiful day for a drive, sunny, cool and clear. Many of the trees were still wearing their fall colors. The Mississippi River had returned to normal depth, bridges and roads were open so the drive wasn't as long. Sue took us on a tour of the town and a neighboring State Park. We went bowling and to a movie. I didn't miss Pap because Tom did a very good Pap imitation, missing memory and all. Late Sunday morning, the birds were the only ones awake on the campus when we dropped Sue off before heading home. Bill was happy to see us when we arrived late Sunday night. The weekend went well, but he was glad that we were home.

Monday morning, about 2:00 A.M., smoke or the smoke alarm woke us. When I opened my eyes, our bedroom was very hazy, smoke drifted in from the upstairs hallway. As Tom hurried downstairs, he told me to wake Bill and Pap. I called Bill, grabbed a fire extinguisher from the hallway and followed Tom. The downstairs was filled with dark, black smoke. The smoke came from the kitchen.

Entering the kitchen, Tom saw Pap standing next to the stove, watching something burn. The fire had spread to the hood over the stove and flames climbed the kitchen cabinet. After Tom extinguished the fire, Pap said, "I'm glad you did that."

We chased the dogs outside, opened doors and windows and tried to clear the smoke from the house. A plastic thermal pitcher that I used for coffee had melted on the stove. We surmised Pap wanted a cup of coffee and instead of heating a cup in the microwave, he heated the pitcher on the stove. We were lucky. No one was hurt. The only major damage was the scorched hood over the stove, a charred spot on the counter top and a charred cabinet door. Everything else was smoke damage. Thank You, Lord.

After the house cleared of smoke, Pap didn't want to go to bed and we weren't going to let him stay up by himself. He sat at his place at the dining room table and declared he wasn't tired, he would go to bed when he was ready. Then he informed us he was going to leave…he wasn't staying here anymore…this was not his home.

I was too tired to debate. Tom dealt with Pap. When Pap finally went to bed, we did the same after removing the knobs from the stove. I couldn't get the picture of Pap—standing at the stove, watching the fire, not trying to put it out—out of my mind. We didn't want to think about what might have happened if Pap had been home alone.

Monday morning, I drove Pap to the Center and explained what had happened that morning. I asked if they had room for Pap every day…it was dangerous for him to remain home alone. Pap had already forgotten the fire.

Then I returned home to clean up. We decided to lock the door between the kitchen and the dining room when we went to bed at night. We went to the hardware store and bought a sliding bolt lock for the door. We bought a new hood for the stove. We bought white paint for the kitchen. I washed everything—dishes, pans, glasses, silverware, shelves, boxes, cans. The smoke had entered all of the cabinets. Tom washed the ceiling, cabinets, walls and windows in the kitchen. Then he painted the walls before moving into the dining room to do the same. The kitchen was the worst but sooty smoke was everywhere.

Tom went to the Center to pick up Pap. He received the good news—they had room for Pap every day. Thank you, Lord.

When Pap walked into the house, he noticed we were painting the kitchen and remarked, "It must be nice to redecorate whenever you want."

Before going to bed, I put a couple of boxes of cereal on the dining room table along with a bowl and spoon. I found an old thermos and filled it with coffee and put that on the table too. I made sure there were bananas in the fruit bowl, then I locked the door going into the kitchen. If Pap got up during the night, he would have cereal and fruit to eat, coffee to drink.

I phoned Pap's case worker Tuesday morning. I informed her that I had requested that Pap be allowed to attend the Center five days a week for his safety and described the fire. I confided how happy we were that the Center had room for him. She said she would put through the paperwork approving his attendance five days a week.

Our discussions about going to the Center continued. Every day. Why did he have to go? He didn't remember going there. He was going to Mass! He would walk; I didn't have to drive him. He would walk home after Mass. (One of the staff at the Center attended our church. I wondered if sometimes he thought the Center was our church.) What did I want him to make for dinner? Did I want him to do anything while he was home?

It was very hard to keep my patience. If I got upset, so would he. If my voice started to get tense, we would argue. If my voice stayed calm, our discussion was friendly. I always explained that he couldn't stay home alone, it wasn't safe. Occasionally I remarked that I had already raised my children. If I was desperate, I reminded him that he got lost three times, flooded the house twice, and set fire to the kitchen. He never liked to hear about those things. Sometimes I had to pull out the heavy artillery—threaten him with a nursing home. I assured him that we didn't want him to go to a nursing home but we might not have a choice. Many times I just said I wasn't discussing it anymore, we each needed to do what we had to do. He had to go to the Center, I had to go to work. If we were in the car, to end the discussion, I turned up the radio.

Pap had become well liked at the Center. He kept his harmonica in his pocket and played it when the spirit moved him. Unlike many people whose personality picks up more vinegar than sugar as they get older, Pap remained good natured unless he was upset. The Center's visiting nurse told me that my father had an uncanny knack of giving a compliment to the person who needed it the most.

Pap slept later in the mornings and so did I. I set my alarm so that I would be up before he was, but I no longer exercised. I called Pap before I went downstairs to unlock the door and start the coffee. Sometimes he answered me right away. Sometimes I had to call him a couple of times. Once he confided, "I heard you but I didn't want to answer. My mother was always calling me." After that statement, I never knew whether he heard me and was playing possum or was still sleeping. I decided to go up into the attic to check whenever he didn't answer after my third call.

One morning I woke up with more stress than usual, my shoulders were so tight they ached. I decided to exercise before going to work. My timing was good, Pap came downstairs as I finished. I got the milk for his cereal and poured his coffee. I explained that I was going upstairs to change for work, then I would eat breakfast and we would leave. (I told him the same thing every morning.)

When I returned, Pap was gone, and so was his jacket. Blast! Where did he go? I looked in the basement…I looked in the attic…I looked in the alley…I couldn't find him. I grabbed my jacket and quickly walked to our church. He wasn't there, but Angel was. I asked if she had seen Pap. She hadn't, and I didn't linger to talk. But before continuing my search, I told her that Pap was going to the Center five days a week. I didn't want her to worry when she didn't see him.

I turned around and walked at top speed to the other church Pap sometimes attended. As I walked, I wondered where Pap was. I asked myself how we were going to prevent this from happening…again. I couldn't stay with him all the time. What could I do to prevent his leaving? Get dressed downstairs? Hide his coat? Lock the door? Always questions, but no answers. For each solution, I thought of a reason why it wouldn't work.

As I opened the door of the church, I expected to find my father. The church contained many things, a beautiful altar with carved wooden statues, flowers and lighted candles, colorful banners, people kneeling in the pews...but it didn't contain my father. Where did he go? All I could do was return home and wait for him to arrive.

When I walked into the house, Pap was sitting at his place at the dining room table drinking a cup of coffee. I asked where he went. He said he was in the basement getting milk. Wrong! He said he was taking out the garbage. He was tossing out something that I had given him in the car. We hadn't been in the car that morning and I didn't see him in the alley. He said he was looking for me, my car was gone. No it wasn't. I don't know where he went but I was thankful he was back. I decided the Lord knew I needed more exercise for stress and arranged a walk. It was a beautiful morning...now that I knew where Pap was, I could enjoy it.

On the way to the Center, Pap asked me to drop him off at church. I said I couldn't do that. I was going to work, he was going to the Center, and I would pick him up after work. When we arrived at the Center, he asked where I wanted him to be when I got off work.

My car had a personality quirk, it had to warm up for five minutes before it would move. We tried to solve the problem, many mechanics had looked at it, nothing worked, so we lived with it. One morning, frost covered the windows of my car. I started the car and began to scrap the frost off. For some reason I kept my purse slung over my shoulder. When I was almost done, Pap locked the doors of the car, with him inside and me out. Luckily I had an extra set of car keys in my purse. Good Morning!

A few days later, after I picked Pap up from the Center, I stopped at the grocery store to do the week's shopping. When we finally arrived home, I unlocked the front door for Pap before unloading my car. Our dogs greeted us at the door and wanted to go out so I unlocked the back door and let them out before going to empty my trunk. I asked Pap to leave the doors alone. When I came up the stairs with my arms weighed down by groceries, I couldn't get in, Pap had locked the door. Our front door bell didn't work and I couldn't get Pap's attention. I was glad I had let the dogs out.

I went to the hardware store and had duplicate keys made for my car and the house. I attached them to the zipper of the battle jacket I wore. As long as I had my jacket on, I would have a spare key. I jingled as I walked but many times that simple step kept us out of trouble. When summer came I would have to come up with a new idea.

One afternoon, I phoned our insurance agent to discuss our policy. After she answered my question, we spent a short time chatting about life—the stress caused by my father. She had cared for her elderly mother and understood the challenges I was facing. She confided that she often poured a glass of Scotch to help her unwind before going to bed at night. She also mentioned she kept a rosary in her car and said a decade while driving.

I didn't want to get into the habit of having a drink at night to unwind. I was afraid I would become dependent on it. But since I was spending more time in my car, I liked the idea of saying the rosary. It might help me to calm down, not worry as much. I knew I needed all the help that I could get.

I went to Alverno, a religious store near our house, and bought a couple of musical tapes along with a chaplet, 25 beads on a chain with a medal instead of a cross. I thought it would be easier to say than the rosary, I wouldn't have to remember which decade I was on. I kept it in the car and got into the habit of saying a chaplet after I dropped Pap off at the Center on my way to work. I always prayed for patience and strength. If I got stuck in traffic, I might say two chaplets. If the day was particularly stressful, I would say another one on the way to pick up Pap.

Every week, the Center had a dance. Pap loved to dance and since men were in short supply, he was never without a partner. The nurse called me at work after one of the dances, she was concerned about his breathing. When he was dancing, he seemed to run out of air, and had to sit down to catch his breath. She explained how emphysema affected the lungs, they lost their elasticity and didn't push out all of the old air. She suggested that I ask his doctor to test his lung capacity and to prescribe a bronchial aid for his shortness of breath.

I called the Clinic for an appointment. The day of our visit, I explained to Dr. D. what I had been told by the nurse at the Center. Before ordering the lung capacity test, he ordered an x-ray of Pap's lungs. When he had the new x-ray, Dr. D. stated that my father's lungs hadn't changed in three years, he didn't need a lung capacity test. To prove his point he showed me the earlier x-rays. I acknowledged that Pap had emphysema, but, I argued, he was more active now that he was at the Center, he was dancing, he was running out of air. Whether his lungs had or had not changed in three years was not the issue. The nurse at the Center, a qualified professional, advised he have his lung capacity checked. After considerable discussion, Dr. D. finally agreed to order the test. When he received the results, the doctor prescribed the bronchial aid and wrote a note authorizing the nurse to administer it.

Before we left the Clinic, I asked for a referral for Pap's eye appointment. I discovered that Pap's ophthalmologist was no longer with the HMO. Pap would have to see their new doctor in his office downtown. The nurse gave me the phone number to make an appointment.

◆　　◆　　◆

Sue came home often. She missed her boyfriend, her home, and my cooking. She made friends with some students from Chicago and hitched a ride. When they drove in, I met them at various places—throughout the city and suburbs—at all hours of the evening. Then we rendezvoused for the return trip.

Late one evening when I met Sue, I warned her that Pap might not know who she was. Sue thought that since she was home so often, he would remember her. I told her not to be upset if he didn't. He forgot my name and her dad's—and he saw us daily.

◆   ◆   ◆

Driving to work on a Friday morning in December I reflected on how lucky I was. I counted my blessings. Living outside of the Center's boundaries for bus service was to our benefit. How would Pap remember to get on the bus in the morning if no one was home? Arriving home at night would be another interesting event. What if he beat us home? It was so nice to find our mail. It was wonderful to have everything in the house the way we left it in the morning. I didn't miss the surprises.

Even though my job was located in a place that was very cold and had become more demanding, I was thankful my boss understood the reason for my reduced hours. By taking a shorter lunch, I was able to keep up with my responsibilities.

When I arrived at work, I was the first person in the office and the phone was ringing. My boss, who was out of town, was on the phone and he was livid. Why hadn't I answered the phone? They didn't have the material that they needed for the show. Where was it? I reminded him that I had to drive my father to the Center before I could go to work. I explained that I didn't know anything about the material he was looking for, but I would see what I could do. He continued to rant and rave…it was my responsibility to know everything that went on in the office. I hung up the phone, determined to quit. I called Tom and told him I was quitting. Next I tried to solve the problem that was upsetting my boss. When he called back later, he apologized. I didn't quit, but I was determined to pay off as many of our bills as I could so I wouldn't be stuck there.

Pap and I talked about many things on the way to and from the Center. Often he talked about the job he had working at the railroad as a young man. All winter, he remembered how he had to work outside when it was very cold. (When summer came, he described working outside on the box cars in the heat.) He never talked about any other job.

Often, our conversation was about the traffic. Each sentence was repeated many times during the drive as if it hadn't been spoken before.

"Where did all the cars come from?"

"There are a lot of cars on the street, aren't there?"

"There isn't going to be any room if they continue to make cars."

Sometimes we talked about the weather:

"It looks like rain."

"It has been raining for days."

"We haven't had any rain in a long time."

"This is a new kind of snow, the old kind was red or brown. The new kind melts slower."

"They used to put black stuff on the snow to melt it faster."

Dinnertime was always interesting. Like Mikey, the boy in the cereal ad, Pap ate everything. He had a harder time cutting his food so before I gave him his plate, I cut whatever needed cutting and removed the bones. Pap became so completely engrossed in his food that he didn't hear anything that was going on around him. Our dogs were able to visit the rest of the family and then station themselves next to Pap. He always gave them something. It didn't matter that I told him we fed the dogs. Sometimes he even poured coffee for them. They didn't like coffee.

After one meal he told me, "Dinner was good. I'll pay you tomorrow for Kathy and me."

Where did he think he was? I reminded him that he was at home, he didn't need to pay for his food. Kathy? ???

As I did my Christmas shopping, I bought gifts for Pap to give to others. The previous year he had forgotten Christmas and I didn't want him to be embarrassed again. When he remembered that Christmas was coming, I mentioned that I had already bought his presents. I thought it would be easier for him if I did his shopping. He was happy I thought of it.

On Christmas Eve our family gathered at our house. Pap enjoyed visiting with his grandchildren and watching his great granddaughter. Pap enjoyed drinking the punch and eating the cookies. We exchanged presents and sang Christmas carols. We missed Aunt Ruth; this was the first Christmas that she wasn't able to join us. We missed my uncle too. He had declined my invitation; he thought our gathering might be too hard.

The week between Christmas and New Year's was traditionally slow at work. Many of our customers were closed for the week and we operated with a skeleton crew—me. I was elected to run the office and take care of any customer requests and problems. The day after Christmas, I returned to work to a very frigid atmosphere—the temperature on the thermostat was set to 58 degrees and there was a note on my desk stating that I, along with another person, would be responsible for cleaning the kitchen. I didn't think so. This was not the way to come back to work after the holiday. When my boss phoned, two days later, we discussed the note. I was firm—cleaning the kitchen was not part of my job description.

It became more noticeable that Pap's vision was deteriorating. After I took down the miniature lights on the stairway after Christmas, Pap couldn't find the stairs at night if the hall light wasn't on. Coming downstairs, he didn't know he was on the first floor and he wanted to keep going. I was worried. I called the Clinic to arrange for an appointment with the new ophthalmologist and discovered that Dr. D. had transferred to a new location, Pap had a new primary care doctor.

Before Dr. S. could request a referral, he had to examine Pap. I made the appointment.

The day of our appointment, I updated Dr. S. on Pap's condition. I told him Pap was having trouble with his memory, he had gotten lost more than once and now attended a day care center for his safety. Dr. S. recommended we try a new drug, Cognex, that had been used to treat people with Parkinson's disease. The drug was given to people with mental dementia and the results were promising. As with all drugs, there were side effects. Pap would have to have regular blood tests to monitor the function of his liver because it could be damaged by the medicine. Dr. S. prescribed a low dosage to see how Pap reacted and authorized the eye appointment.

I noticed an immediate improvement in Pap's memory when he started taking the pill—he knew our names. Before he started taking Cognex, he didn't know who we were. The change wasn't large, but we were grateful for any improvement.

We had to go downtown to see Pap's eye doctor. I hated to drive downtown and always took the train. But I wasn't going downtown by myself, Pap would be with me and his pace had slowed and he shuffled his feet. I didn't have confidence in his ability to get on or off of the train quickly. I was afraid Pap would get crushed by the doors or stay on the train when I got off. I decided it would be safer to drive—and less stressful.

Dr. E. had a winning personality and put all of his patients at ease. I liked him right away and told him about the ultrasound on Pap's right eye. Pap added, "My right eye is getting better, it's as good as my left eye." I soon understood why Pap said that. Dr. E's examination revealed Pap's cataract had grown over his good eye so that he was almost blind. His right eye wasn't getting better, his left eye was getting worse—I hadn't thought of that. We made an appointment for preliminary eye tests to be conducted at Dr. E's office in the suburbs. If everything went well, the operation would be on my father's 84th birthday. What a marvelous birthday present.

At the end of January, our grandson was born. The night of his birth, Terri invited us to come to the hospital to see the baby. It had been snowing all day, and was getting worse. Tom was very tired, he didn't want to drive through a snow storm to the South side. I wanted to see my daughter and new grandson—I wasn't going to let a little thing like snow stop me. Tom stayed with Pap and I braved the weather. Because of the snow, travel was very slow. I was afraid visiting hours would end before I reached the hospital.

I arrived at the hospital a half-hour before visiting hours ended and received a nice surprise. Our grandson shared his mother's room, so I was able to hold him. Just to see him would have made me happy, holding him was ten times better. It made the trip through the snow worthwhile. When Brittany was born, I was able to take time off from work and help my daughter. Now I had Pap to take care of, I wouldn't be able to help my daughter with Benjamin.

My boss planned to add my name to the company checking account so that I could sign checks in his absence. I mentioned his idea to a person at school who advised me that I might be liable. When my boss phoned from out of town, I made the mistake of telling him that I was concerned about my liability and asked if I could talk to our company lawyer to make sure I wouldn't be held personally responsible for checks I signed.

My boss lost his temper, his voice became louder and his tone changed to one of authority as he said I couldn't talk to our lawyer and emphasized he was the owner of the company and he made the rules. I didn't argue back, having learned from previous experience that it wouldn't do any good. I decided to wait until he calmed down before I broached the subject again.

But his attitude made me furious. How dare he talk to me that way? How dare he involve me in something that might be hazardous to the financial welfare of myself and family? My husband and I were members of a legal service—I called their lawyer and asked his opinion. He informed me that I could be liable for unpaid taxes; he would do some research and send me his findings.

The verbal exchange with my boss occurred on Friday afternoon. I remained angry all weekend and went on a shopping spree trying to vent some of my frustration. I spent more than two hundred dollars, and then felt guilty about spending the money. I was so angry I wanted to punch someone.

I sat myself down in a corner and had a heart-to-heart talk with myself. I couldn't continue the way I was going—I had to take care of myself. My attitude wasn't fair to Tom, Pap, or myself. I remembered that exercising had helped me with stress before. Sick, tired, or healthy, I was going to have to exercise regularly if I was going to survive.

At noon on a frigid Saturday, our dogs dashed from the windows to the front door and back again, barking. It was too early for the mailman, who were they barking at? Since our doorbell didn't work, I looked out the window and was surprised to see Uncle Alvin. He had taken the bus from Wisconsin and was staying at Aunt Connie's. He had walked from her house, more than four miles, in very cold weather, to see his brother.

I was impressed with my uncle's ability. He traveled alone from Wisconsin by bus and navigated miles of streets on foot to get to our house. I thought that was an accomplishment for a young person, let alone someone who was 87 and I commented on his long walk. "I'm used to walking," Uncle Alvin replied. "I've walked sixteen miles every day for years when I was a mailman and I still walk every day." We discussed my father's worsening condition. He didn't understand why his younger brother was losing his memory.

Pap enjoyed visiting with his brother, and I think he even knew who he was. A couple of days later, I watched Pap search through everything in the house. I asked what he was looking for. Pap chuckled at the humor of the situation. Alvin had given him some pills to help his memory and he had lost them. ???

I received a call from the visiting nurse at the Center inquiring into Pap's bathing habits. I confided the problems I was having: he was taking a hour or longer in the shower; he had a hard time changing clothes. I heard water running but I didn't know if he was actually taking a shower. If I gave him clean clothes, he often was confused and put on the dirty clothes instead. Pap wouldn't allow me to help him. The nurse confirmed that some things were very difficult for a family member to accept from their family. Sometimes it was easier for the person to accept help from a caregiver who was specially trained. She mentioned that personal care was available at the Center for a nominal fee. If I brought clean clothes for him, he could change after taking a shower. She said that I didn't need to decide right away, I should give it some thought and call her if I wanted to take advantage of the service.

It was hard for me to admit I couldn't take care of my father. I felt guilty that I wasn't doing a better job, but I didn't know how to improve on what I was doing. I thought about how much I dreaded Pap's showers and the reduced stress that we would have if Pap had personal care at the Center. I made my decision, then called the nurse. I knew for Pap's good and my sanity, personal care at the Center was the way to go.

I bought a sports bag and loaded it—washcloth, towel, soap, shampoo, deodorant, razor, comb, toothbrush and paste, and added a change of clothes. I brought the bag with me to the Center on the day of Pap's first shower. I expected to pick the bag up with Pap. It was a relief when I discovered that his bag would remain at the Center. They would wash his towel and clothes. One less thing for me to worry about—or forget.

Pap didn't take to the shower at the Center very well. I didn't mention it when I picked him up but the next day he didn't want to go back. It took a while before he got used to taking a shower at the Center and having someone help him and the staff figured out the best way to work with him. I found out Pap remembered some of the things I told him. A staff member remarked that after his shower Pap told her that his daughter told him to always wear his ID bracelet. Progress!

I took Pap to the Clinic for the preliminary blood tests and EKG before his cataract operation. I told Dr. S. that the Cognex seemed to be helping my father. After taking the medicine, Pap knew who I was, and the staff at the Center said he was more alert, more willing to participate. The blood test didn't show signs of liver damage so Dr. S. increased the dosage to two pills a day, one in the morning and one in the evening.

Next we visited Pap's eye doctor at his office in the suburbs. After the eye tests were completed, Dr. E. scheduled the cataract's removal. The time was set for eleven in the morning. We received instructions for the day of his operation—Pap had to fast after Midnight, nothing to eat or drink. I knew that was going to be very difficult.

My family and I discussed how we were going to care for Pap after the operation. I was concerned about his sleeping in the attic. Climbing the stairs was hard enough with his limited vision, after the operation his vision would be further reduced. How would he safely get to the attic? We decided to move his bed downstairs into the little room. Bill volunteered to spend the night on the couch to keep Pap company. Tom and Bill agreed that I had the most patience, I needed my sleep for the next day.

The day of Pap's operation, I hid the coffee pot. Pap hadn't used the thermos, he didn't know what it was. I moved the thermos into the kitchen and used it for coffee. I put the cereal back in the pantry and hid the fruit. When Pap got up, I told him that his eye was going to be operated on and he couldn't have anything to eat or drink. Of course, he didn't remember.

All morning, I had to keep reminding him that he couldn't have anything to eat or drink. By nine o'clock my patience was gone, I stood in the living room talking to my Friend in a loud, exasperated voice, "You are going to have to help me with him. I can't do this by myself." After this outburst Pap behaved for about five minutes and then he started up again. I decided we needed to leave for the hospital. NOW! Staying home was not working.

The wait at the hospital wasn't too bad. Pap was undressed, and in a bed with no food or coffee in sight. I stayed by his bedside until they came to fetch him for the operation. I mentioned that he must be hungry since he hadn't eaten that morning. Pap bragged, "Yes, I did. I found something in my pocket to eat, so I ate it."

I debated going to a restaurant or eating at the hospital, and the hospital cafeteria won. My New Year's resolution had been to cut back on fat, to eat healthier meals, and I was doing fairly well. I made a nice salad at the salad bar and ordered a cup of soup and a piece of fish to go with it. I was proud of myself. I was fine until I saw a piece of chocolate cream pie—it called my name. I figured that for everything I had been through that morning, I deserved it...it was delicious.

Dr. E. came to see me after the operation. Pap was in recovery; the operation was a success. The cataract was removed and a lens was implanted into Pap's eye. He would have to wear a protective covering for a few weeks until the lens was firmly attached. It would be a few days before Dr. E. knew just how much vision Pap had.

Before Pap was released from the hospital in the late afternoon, I received instructions and medicine for his eye. Two different drops were to be put in three times a day. I should replace the bandage after putting the drops in. The nurse said to give him Tylenol for the pain.

Pap had minimal vision out of his lazy right eye. His good eye was completely bandaged to allow it to heal. Getting Pap into the car was next to impossible. He could barely see and he didn't know how to duck. He was still groggy from the operation and I couldn't make him bend and I couldn't pick him up. If he could stand up all the way home, it would be no problem. It took a while, but I finally got him into the car.

On the way home we discussed how important it was to leave the bandage over his eye. I told him a cataract had been removed, that was why his eye was bandaged. He had to leave the bandage alone.

Getting into the house was more fun, Pap didn't want my help. He insisted he could find and climb the stairs by himself. When Pap was finally settled in his chair at the dining room table, I gave him a cup of coffee and started dinner. Pap took off his bandage and rubbed his eye. I reminded him of the importance of leaving his eye alone as I replaced the bandage. Between five and nine o'clock, Pap took the bandage off of his eye five times. He took it off as soon as I put it back on. He forgot. By nine o'clock, any patience I had left was gone. I stood by his chair slapping his hand, yelling, "No, no, no, no, no." My action worried my family—I had finally lost it.

I left Pap in my family's care and escaped to the drug store for more supplies. I wanted mittens for Pap's hands or a straight jacket. I couldn't find anything at the store that would work. How was his eye going to heal if he didn't leave it alone? I bought more gauze and bandages.

When I returned home, we decided it was time for Pap to go to bed and showed him where it was. It was just a short distance from the downstairs bathroom. Before he fell asleep, we replaced his bandages a few more times. Tom and Bill decided I should go to bed. I needed a good night's sleep, so I could continue the battle tomorrow. I didn't argue, I went to bed.

We were scheduled to visit Dr. E. at his downtown office the next morning. During the night, we had another record snowfall and travel advisories were issued. I didn't know how I would get Pap into or out of the car, in good weather, let alone in snow. We couldn't take the train. I called the doctor's office and explained my problem. Pap's appointment was changed to the suburban office the next day. Dr. E. told me to remove most of Pap's bandages, leave the metal protective cover over his eye and use tape at the edges to keep it on. Since Pap would be able to see out of the holes in the cover, he might leave it on.

Pap continued to take off his eye covering and rub his eye. He explained he wasn't rubbing it, he was wiping it. As I replaced the cover, I repeated that he needed to leave it on, his eye had been operated on and he had to keep his hands off of it. Then I reminded him again and again and again. I sounded like a broken record. I could have used a tape recorder repeating the same message over and over and over.

When we arrived at the doctor's office the next morning, I was encouraged to learn that Pap hadn't damaged his eye. His vision would be better than it had been. We should keep the protective eye covering on and continue with the drops. I asked Dr. E. to write instructions for the nurse at the Center, without which she would not be allowed to put in his drops. He knew the staff at the Center and was familiar with their procedures. We set up the next appointment for his office in the suburbs.

When we returned to the Center, I had a conference with the nurse. I gave her the doctor's written instructions and a bag containing Pap's eye drops and tape. I told her Pap was going to have to be reminded to keep the cover on his eye. He was getting better but still took it off to rub his eye.

After a week, we moved Pap's bed back up to the attic. He wasn't taking his bandage off at night as often and since his vision through his metal protector was good, we thought he could safely go up and down the stairs. Bill was glad to get back to his own bed, even if he still had a noisy roommate.

I was worried that I would forget to drop off the bag with Pap's eye supplies in the morning when I took Pap to the Center or I'd forget to pick it up at night. I made a sign on cardboard, REMEMBER DROPS, and hung it from the rear view mirror in my car. If Tom was going to pick up Pap, I alerted the nurse and the receptionist. I asked them to make sure my husband took Pap's medicine home with him.

The message to leave the covering on was finally starting to get through to Pap, at least at the Center. When the nurse removed the covering to put the drops in Pap's eye, Pap told her his daughter told him to keep the covering on. The nurse assured him she would replace the covering after she put in the drops.

I arranged Pap's visits to the doctor so I would lose the least amount of time off from work. When I made a morning appointment, I would drop Pap off at the Center an hour later, at the same time the buses brought the other clients. On this particular day, I had already escorted Pap inside, exchanged greetings and information with the staff, and was ready to leave. A bus pulled up at the door and the clients disembarked. I held the door for them as they entered. A short, tiny, elderly woman descended from the bus. Glaring at me, she complained, "You are in my way." I was very glad that despite all of our problems, Pap had a good disposition.

Many times I arrived at work sputtering from something Pap had done. My co-workers listened as I related my current tale, letting off steam. After one such outburst, a co-worker remarked, "Now you know what your mission in life is…to take care of your father." I was so glad he had shared that.

One evening, Pap stayed in the downstairs bathroom for over half an hour. At first I didn't notice his absence, I was busy. After a while, I realized he had been in the bathroom a very long time. That was unusual for my father. He rarely spent more than 15 minutes in the bathroom and that included shaving. I was getting worried. What was he doing? I called him a couple of times. He answered that he was fine and would be right out. When he came out, the protective covering was off of his eye. What did he do?

Replacing the covering, I explained once again that he had to leave his eye covered. They had removed a cataract and inserted a lens so he could see better. It was important to leave his eye alone. It was necessary for the eye's healing.

He declared, "My eye is getting better because of the care I'm giving it."

What care?

On our next visit, I told Dr. E. that I was worried. Pap was constantly rubbing his eye and he had been in the bathroom for over 30 minutes, taking care of his eye. Dr. E. said that Pap's eye was past the danger point and his vision was very good. We could stop the drops, leave off the covering, and return for a checkup in a month.

Thank you, Lord.

7

Passover

Ash Wednesday was approaching, heralding the beginning of Lent. I didn't know what to give up for Lent—I had already quit smoking and I didn't drink. I couldn't give up chocolate. After much contemplation, I decided that this year I wasn't going to give up anything—I was under enough stress. I would try to keep my patience with my father and survive.

Pap's eye was past the danger point, but I was still concerned since he rubbed them continually. I worried Pap would damage his eye by scratching his lens. On our next visit to the ophthalmologist, I voiced my concern, "Pap isn't leaving his eyes alone, he is constantly rubbing them. As soon as we get in the car, he takes out his handkerchief and wipes his eyes, again and again. I still sound like a broken record as I repeat the same thing over and over—Pap, leave your eyes alone. Pap, don't wipe your eyes."

Dr. E. replied, "It isn't unusual for a person's eyes to water more as they get older. Your father's eyes are producing an abundant supply of water. You shouldn't be concerned that he wipes them often…his vision is still improving. Start using the eye drops again, they relieve the irritation as the eye adjusts to the lens."

I hadn't realized how much Pap's vision had deteriorated—how much the operation expanded his world. Now he could read signs on the buildings. He enjoyed looking at the flags flying at the car lot. He recognized the park where he played as a child. He read the names of businesses as we drove by. He was reading the newspaper again. How many of our problems were caused because he couldn't see? Many questions, no answers.

The mail was missing, again. Pap could see better, he could get into mischief.

"No, you can't have that, it's not yours." This phrase was back in our vocabulary as Pap regularly took possession of things that weren't his.

Both Bill and I had become light sleepers. Since only a curtain separated Bill's part of the attic from Pap's, he heard Pap get up in the middle of the night. He listened for Pap to go downstairs to the bathroom and come back to bed. Now that Pap could see better, he didn't always go back to sleep. He sat on the bed playing with paper: rattling, folding, putting down, picking back up. He sat on his bed clearing his throat and spitting, over and over. Bill got tired of listening to the noises and commanded, "Go back to sleep."

Instead of sitting on his bed, Pap got dressed or organized his clothes in the middle of the night. "Turn off the light," Bill protested. "Go back to sleep. It's not time to get up."

Sometimes Pap didn't listen when Bill told him to turn off the light and go back to sleep. Bill tried a different approach and said, "Pap, you have to get up early in the morning to go to work. You'd better go back to sleep."

Our male dog became Pap's guardian. If neither Bill nor I woke when Pap was up during the night, Cuyler came into our bedroom to get me.

Two months after Pap's operation, Bill asked if we could put Pap's cataract back. Pap's mischief was getting to him.

Tom and I took advantage of a nice weekend and escaped to the county. We took Pap with us. Pap got up on Saturday at 9:00 A.M. He had a bowl of cereal and a banana. At 9:30, I made breakfast for Tom, Pap ate too—3 pancakes and 2 sausages. At noon, I was hungry. Pap joined me, eating a tuna fish salad sandwich on toast. A couple of hours later, Pap joined Tom, eating a bologna sandwich. At 4:00 P.M., we had supper of fish, fried potatoes, and corn. That night I realized how much Pap had eaten. He was never full.

On Monday, I discussed Pap's diet with the staff at the Center. At first, they thought I was worried about the food he ate at the Center. They understood my concern when I listed everything Pap had to eat on Saturday. I learned what time they had morning and afternoon snacks and what food was served. I decided to keep cheese, crackers, sardines, and fruit on hand for morning and afternoon snacks. If Pap didn't know he was full, I would have to regulate his eating.

Regulating Pap's eating was easier said than done. Before leaving for school, I made mashed potatoes, baked beans, and ham for Pap and Tom. I was running late and didn't have time to eat. I decided to eat after class. An hour and a half later I was back, sitting at the dining room table, eating my dinner. Pap saw me and asked if there was something for him to eat. I reminded him that he had just finished supper. "I'll make something for myself," he announced. He was hurt that I wasn't feeding him.

The day I was dreading arrived. Ever since my father started living in the past, I was worried that he would get stuck in the years of my childhood—the fire, and the death of my mother and brother. That was a very painful time for us—living through it once was enough. When I arrived at the Center, a staff member told me, "Your father is very concerned about his daughter. He's afraid they are coming to take her away. I don't know who 'they' are, but Bill has been agitated all day." On the drive home I reassured my father that I was fine. I was older now and no one was going to take me away. That time had passed.

There must be a part of the brain that protects a person from painful experiences. My father never talked about my mother or brother, never remembered the fire, and never mentioned someone taking me away, again.

Tom enjoyed talking with Pap and often asked what he did at the Center. Pap described his job—he packed up things and mailed them.

He told Tom that he always gave his paycheck to me. When I came home from school, Tom asked what I did with the money. "What money?" I asked. Tom teased for a little while before he told me about Pap's job and his weekly paycheck.

Tom and Pap talked about driving. Pap confided that he was waiting for his driver's license. He ordered it through the mail, and when it arrived, he would be able to drive the car.

Pap and Tom sat in the front room watching television together. Pap sat on the couch with a cat asleep on his lap and Tom sat in the swing chair. (Pap loved to sit in the swing chair but he always got out of it when Tom came home.) They both liked to watch the same programs. Sometimes a favorite program was a repeat of a repeat. When Pap protested when Tom changed the channel, Tom explained that he had just watched the program a few days ago. "That's okay," Pap replied, "It's always new to me."

Pap got into the habit of going into the kitchen after supper, over and over again. If I wasn't home and Tom was tired, he locked the kitchen door to keep Pap from getting into trouble. Pap became frustrated when he couldn't open the kitchen door and complained to Tom, "I built this house—I don't know who changed the lock."

Tom explained that it was our house and he lived with us. "I didn't know you were married," Pap answered. "Don't tell Diane. A parent should remember some of the important things."

My father subscribed to *Guidepost* magazine. I enjoyed reading their stories, they were short and there was always something in the issue to help boost my spirits. I had considered writing about the day I was guided to be of help to my neighbor when she collapsed at the camper, then sending the story to the magazine. Before Passover, I received the current issue and opened it to an invitation—"Would You Like To Tell a Story?" They issued an invitation and I responded.

I wrote my story and tried to compose a letter, at their request, describing my writing ambitions. I didn't have any—I didn't know what I was going to say. Then I remembered Sue's idea…that I write about our experiences living with my father as his memory deteriorated and her reason, it might help others.

I didn't know if I would attempt to write our story, it would be a lot of work. I didn't know if I had the time, let alone the talent, to write something that someone else would want to read. After much internal debate, I decided to make an outline of the events that had already happened, just in case I changed my mind. I was surprised that I had already forgotten much of what had occurred. So much was happening daily, that yesterday was already dim and the day before was gone. In what order did things happen? I remembered the big things, but what about the small ones? All gone.

I realized I needed to take detailed notes. I found a letter I wrote to Sue that mentioned a smoke-filled house. I said I wasn't going to tell her about it because she was home when it happened. I wished that I had written about it anyway, because now I didn't remember and when I asked Sue, she didn't either. All I knew from the letter was the date. The smoky house occurred over Labor Day weekend, before the fire in the kitchen. If I decided to write our story, I would need a lot of help—I couldn't depend on my memory.

After spending years in the basement at school taking business classes, I was now on the second floor, enrolled in biology, the last course I needed for my degree. I was glad I was finishing, but I was also sad. I enjoyed going to school. I didn't enjoy studying for tests but I enjoyed learning and meeting people from various cultures. I enjoyed meeting a friend for a cup of coffee before class, she lent an ear to my grumbling. She had an aging mother living with her; I had a father who was growing younger. We had other things in common besides school.

I didn't know if I wanted to transfer to a four-year college. I didn't even know if my father's condition would allow me to continue to go to school. What would I do with a Bachelors degree after I got it? At the rate I was going, I would be retired before I finished. I decided to continue taking classes that interested me at the community college.

Just because I had my Associates degree didn't mean I had to stop going to school.

My friend needed a speech course for her degree, and I thought it would be an interesting class to take. I hadn't given a formal talk in a very long time and could use practice in speaking before a group. I signed up for the Fall class too.

While waiting in the hallway for our biology class to begin, my friend talked to a comrade from another semester. She was currently enrolled in a creative writing course. She told us the class met once a week, lasted for three hours and required a two-to-three page paper written for each session. Since they had a good teacher, she really enjoyed it. I didn't know creative writing was available at our school, and decided to keep it in mind.

My story was not among those picked for the magazine. Over 6,000 people responded to their invitation to tell a story, I was in very good company. I pictured all the guardian angels shuffling their person's story to the top of the stack.

Interesting events continued to happen on the home front. Our downstairs toilet wouldn't flush. What had Pap done? It was working perfectly before he went in. Once again we needed to "operate." The plunger didn't do any good, so I bought Drano and the bowl emptied very slowly. Finally in desperation, I dumped a pail of water down, hoping the force of the water would clear whatever was in there. It seemed to help. Many buckets of water later, we were back in business.

Pap kept his electric razor in the upstairs bathroom. He had a Norelco that had three heads for smooth shaving. As his memory declined, I plugged in his razor so he could shave. When he was finished, I cleaned it and put it away. Keeping the razor in the upstairs bathroom no longer seemed like a good idea. I sent Pap up to shave and he forgot why he was upstairs. I moved his razor to the downstairs bathroom.

Pap always closed the door while he was shaving. One evening, I heard tinkling, like wind chimes or glass breaking while Pap was behind the closed door. Now that his vision had improved, he could see to clean his razor. When he opened the door, I went to investigate.

Pap's shaver was in pieces. I found two of the three heads, and two of the three circular blades that fit on the heads. The other set was missing. I replaced what I found and asked Pap not to clean his razor. He said he didn't.

Sunday morning Pap shaved downstairs…twice…at my request. He forgot to shave the hair under his chin and the front of his neck. I reminded Pap that we had to leave if we were going to be on time for church. "Don't worry about it!" he said as he went upstairs. He got Bill's shaver from the upstairs bathroom and climbed the stairs to the attic and proceeded to shave for the third time, waking Bill up in the process. When he came downstairs, he still hadn't shaved the hair under his chin. "I don't shave my neck," he declared. Then he lingered to finish his coffee and stopped to pet the dogs before he was ready to go…we were late for church.

Pap cleaned his razor again. This time he lost all of the pieces. I searched our small bathroom thoroughly, but the pieces had disappeared. I went to the store hoping to buy replacement blades but Pap's razor was obsolete, no blades were stocked. I didn't want to spend $70 for a new razor that might be broken the next time Pap used it. I called Norelco, explained my problem and was assured that they would send out new blades for $36, including shipping and handling. It would take a few days to process the order.

In the meantime, Pap had to shave. We still had Muscle's electric razor. I plugged it in for Pap. He could shave with it but he didn't know how to open it to clean it. When the replacement blades arrived, I gave Pap's razor to Bill.

On the way home from the Center, I discovered Pap was stashing food. He didn't finish his lunch or snack at the Center and saved pieces in his shirt pocket, pants pocket or in the waistband of his pants. He sat in the car or at the dining room table, reached in some place, retrieved something, and ate it.

One morning, Pap came downstairs without his ID bracelet. I climbed the stairs to the attic to search for it. I didn't find the bracelet but I found a can of partially opened sardines. How long had they been sitting there? I didn't know but I took possession. I gave Pap his second ID bracelet.

"My left eye is fine. Put the drops in my right eye," Pap said as we went through the daily task of pills and drops. "I want to get my right eye taken care of."

I discussed Pap's right eye with his eye doctor. I confided that I didn't think I was up to another operation. We had too much fun with his left eye and the returns were worth it—Pap could see. Pap wouldn't receive as much benefit from operating on his lazy right eye. We decided not to operate.

Next, we discussed glasses. Pap didn't do as well on the eye tests; he wasn't able to read some of the letters. Dr. E. recommended glasses for reading and glasses for distance, bifocals were out. He said a person with normal memory would need six months to adjust to bifocals, but each day would be a new day for Pap. I knew Pap would lose his glasses before a day passed. I told Dr. E. that I didn't think Pap had trouble seeing, he was always pointing out something new on the drive to and from the Center. I suggested that I talk to the staff at the Center to find out how well Pap did there. Then I would be able to decide if glasses were the answer. Dr. E. gave me prescriptions for two pairs of glasses, just in case.

I talked to the staff at the Center and they confirmed that Pap was able to see well. He read the newspaper every day. He complimented a staff member on a pair of small earrings that she was wearing. He carefully cut out rain drops to decorate a window for their party. They agreed Pap would lose his glasses. I decided not to fill the prescriptions.

At our next appointment, I informed Dr. E. of my decision not to fill the prescriptions. When Pap took the eye test, he could read each letter separately, but when the letters were together, he couldn't read them. We thought he might be trying to make a word. Dr. E. agreed that Pap could see well enough for his purposes. No glasses.

Before we bought our park-model trailer, we traditionally started our camping season on Easter weekend. Now we went to the camper year round, but we still spent Easter at the campground. That year, spring arrived early and Easter weekend was beautiful. It was warm enough to be outside, so we raked and burned last year's leaves. We gave Pap a rake and he really enjoyed what he was doing, and didn't want to come inside when we finished.

Pap enjoyed raking the leaves so much, the next weekend he raked the leaves at home. He made two big piles in the alley and then came inside. He was finished, but I wasn't. We couldn't burn the leaves in the city like we did at the camper, and I couldn't leave the piles just sitting in the alley. I went to the store to see if I could buy brown bags to put them in.

Our porches were in sad shape. The steps were loose and I was afraid someone would get hurt. Every day we found cards from contractors offering to give us an estimate. The condition of our porch bothered Pap. As we left for the Center in the morning, he mentioned he would paint the porch the next day. Over the years he had replaced the steps and painted the porches many times, but those days were gone.

My co-workers did carpentry work in their spare time. I knew they had high standards of workmanship and asked if they would be interested in replacing our porch. When we received their estimate, we decided to replace both our front and our back porches.

Pap watched the tearing down of the old and building of the new with great interest. As the work progressed, all of the old lumber was dumped in the back yard to be disposed of later. Pap sat at the dining room window staring at the growing mountain. He wanted to stack the wood, put it in piles, make it neat. We told him many times, each morning and every evening, that the workers would take care of the old wood when they were finished.

Pap liked the new porches. He admired the front porch as he sat in the car before we left in the morning. He no longer felt that he needed to stay home to fix the stairs or paint the porch. I bought a couple of plastic chairs so he could sit on the back porch and enjoy a cup of coffee in nice weather.

My uncle phoned to tell us that he had decided to sell his house, it was becoming too much work for him to cut the grass, clean the house. He knew Aunt Ruth's condition would never allow her to return home—she was paralyzed, could barely talk, and was on a liquid diet. He found a retirement/nursing home where they both could live.

Early on a Saturday morning, Pap and I drove to their house to help sort out their things for an estate sale. Aunt Connie and my cousins were already there. The house was crowded with packed boxes. In a house that was normally uncluttered, we had to clear a spot on the couch for Pap to sit. My cousin mentioned that it felt very sad in their house without Aunt Ruth and with everything torn up, waiting for new homes. I felt bad because I didn't feel the sadness.

After reflecting on her statement for a while, I told her that she was able to feel the sadness because she was leading a normal life—mine was no longer normal. I no longer spent time contemplating a situation; most of them were too complex or sad. My life had become a time of dealing with a problem, cleaning up, finding or putting away, and going on to the next challenge.

Pap didn't understand what was happening. He didn't remember that his sister, Ruth, had had a stroke. I had made the decision not to take him to visit his sister at the nursing home. I didn't think that it would do either of them any good. She didn't look at all like the well groomed person we were used to seeing. Her stroke had aged her and she had trouble speaking and moving. If he remembered the visit, he might worry about her—or himself.

For my aunt to see her brother in his condition wouldn't be good for her either. She didn't know that my father was gradually drifting away, as if he was on a raft, slowly being tugged by the currents out to sea. Occasionally the wind changed and he would come back to shore for a little while, or the wind would stop and he would remain in the same waters until the winds picked up, stirring the current to draw him further away.

On Tuesday, when I picked Pap up from the Center, the nurse was waiting for me. Pap didn't want to dance that afternoon, he said his foot hurt. But when she offered to look at it, he told her not to bother, it was fine. She thought that I should know. Was his sore foot an excuse? Was he too tired to dance or was something else wrong?

I looked at Pap's toenails. They weren't too long, but I cut them anyway. Then I looked at his shoes. They were worn on the sides of the heels. Was that why his feet hurt? I didn't want to take Pap shoe shopping. I went hunting for a pair of shoes similar to what he had. I was very fortunate and found a pair that fit him perfectly.

Now that Pap could see better, he was more mobile. I came downstairs dressed for work to find Pap standing by the table finishing his coffee, with his coat on. I asked where he was going. He replied he was going to Mass like he did every morning.

Here we go again. It had been a while since he got up early and remembered going to Mass. I enjoyed not having to argue with him every morning. I really didn't want to start again.

Mother's Day, Pap came downstairs at 6:00 A.M. Since he was up, we went to the early Sunday Mass—it was a beautiful day.

My children thought we should do something as a family. They knew I loved Lincoln Park Zoo, so we decided to go there. At first Pap enjoyed the walk, looked at everything and commented on what he saw. Then he stopped talking...his pace quickened and a frightened expression appeared on his face. "Where are we going?" he asked.

After we told him, he moved quickly...couldn't stop and grabbed onto a water fountain to stop himself and almost fell down. Something was wrong! I sent the kids into the new primate house, took Pap's arm and slowly walked to a bench. We sat and rested awhile. He seemed normal. When we got up, he had trouble walking again. He didn't have his balance and leaned to the side and staggered toward a railing. Something was definitely wrong!

We didn't know what was causing his problem. Was it caused by the unevenness of the sidewalk or by the small hills? I wondered if something had shut down in his brain? He was okay when we left. We tried to rent a wheelchair but they were all in use. We walked over to the sea lions where Kathy spent a portion of the day sitting with Pap. The other kids each took a turn. When I wanted to take a turn, they wouldn't let me. They insisted, "You have Pap all the time, it's your day and we will sit with Pap. You love the zoo, you should enjoy it, that was why we came." For a change I didn't argue. Pap enjoyed sitting, watching the sea lions and the children playing.

I was worried about Pap's balance and his trouble walking. I made an appointment with Pap's primary care doctor, and reported what happened at the zoo. Pap's blood pressure and pulse were normal, and so were his heart and lungs. He had good balance. Dr. S. didn't know what caused the problems Pap had on Sunday. We discussed Pap's medication. I explained to Dr. S. that the pills seemed to be helping Pap, now he knew who we were. He increased the dosage to three pills a day and wrote a letter to the nurse at the Center authorizing her to give the pills to Pap. I made a new sign for my car: **REMEMBER PILLS**. I hung it from my rear view mirror as a reminder to pick the pills up with Pap. After a couple of weeks, I decided that remembering to pick up the pills—everyday—was one thing that I didn't need to do. I made a separate bottle for the nurse at the Center and asked her to let me know when she needed more.

Pap's style of walking changed. Now he walked with his right hand in his pocket. (Very debonair?) His step became more of a shuffle than a step and his pace slowed even more. Instead of walking beside me, he walked ten spaces behind and to the right. If I slowed down...so did he. If I stopped to wait for him...he stopped too.

The long school year was drawing to a close. Sue was coming home for the summer. She missed her family, her boyfriend, and Chicago, and decided to transfer to a college in the city rather than return to Missouri. Tom drove down to get her in my car, it was newer and a hatchback—they could put more stuff in it.

While at work, I received a phone call from a nurse in a hospital in Missouri. My daughter and husband were involved in a car accident. They were in separate hospitals. The nurse didn't know the extent of their injuries but they were both talking and concerned about the other. Sue had asked her to call me. The nurse would have my daughter call after she was examined.

I didn't know what to do. I finally called my son, told him what had happened and asked him to try to get more information. He found out Sue had been treated and released. The hospital said she was very shaken up and had needed stitches, but was otherwise all right.

Sue finally called me. It was very good to hear her voice. She waited until she found out her father's condition before phoning. She told me what happened. "It was a beautiful day as we loaded the car and left school. We were in no hurry as we drove out of town, discussing where to stop for breakfast. Suddenly, a truck crossed the median directly in front of us to turn into a store and cut us off. Dad tried to stop but he couldn't, we hit the truck head on…Yes, we were wearing our seatbelts. I wasn't able to open my door, but Dad got it open. I've got a long cut on my leg and I'm sore, but I'm okay. Dad was squashed by the steering wheel of the car. His chest and back hurt but nothing is broken—his blood pressure is high. They are keeping him in the hospital overnight for observation."

The accident was on the evening news and the front page of the paper. Looking at the pictures of my car later, it was a miracle anyone walked away from it. Thank You, Lord.

They were bruised, Sue needed stitches, Tom spent the night in the hospital. But they were all right. My car was totaled, but it could be replaced—they couldn't. We were lucky. Thank You, Lord.

I was very proud of my children and their mates. All of them called to see how I was doing, expressed concern, and asked when they should leave to get their dad and sister. I told them to wait. If I knew their father, he would want to drive home himself.

I was right. The insurance company arranged for a loaner car. (It would have to be driven back to Missouri, they didn't have one-way rentals.) Sue and Tom repacked the car and drove home.

We had to replace my car, but I didn't want to buy a new one. I didn't want car payments since I didn't have confidence in the longevity of my job. My car was only five years old and in good condition, but it had more than 120,000 miles. I knew we wouldn't receive much money for it.

Tom had wanted to trade in my car for a long time. The mileage was high and things were continually going wrong. We were always spending money on repairs. I joked with him that he didn't need to go to such extremes to get me to replace my car.

Tom's mission was to find a car for me. My requests were based on my trips with Pap. I wanted a four-door vehicle with automatic transmission, power windows, and automatic door locks. After much searching, he found an older car that had everything I required. It even had a sun roof and a tape player. It only had 76,000 miles.

Pap didn't know how to open the door of my new car, he couldn't find the handle. That made me happy. In my old car, he often opened the door before I finished parking. (He only opened the door of the new car twice, once in July and the second time in September.) He was very frustrated when he couldn't open the door and always wanted me to show him where the handle was. Sometimes I joked about it and told him that since I was his chauffeur, it was my job to open his door.

Then he locked me out of the car. Twice. Time to get more keys made.

While Tom was home from work recovering from the accident, he became aware of our daily routine. He asked if I had to go through this every morning, and I replied that I did. Each day was a new day. Sometimes, Pap remembered something from the day before but not often. I got out the milk for Pap's cereal and poured his cup of coffee. Sometimes I got out his shaver after he had breakfast so he could shave. Then I reminded him a couple of times to shave. We found his jacket and hat and made sure he had a handkerchief.

We often discussed that he had to go to the Center and why he needed to go. Sometimes it was enough just to tell him he would be with people and have something to do. Sometimes he argued the point. He didn't like being reminded of the floods, the times he was lost, or the fire in the kitchen. I didn't like reminding him, but when I needed to use heavy artillery, I did. It was all part of our morning routine.

One morning I asked Pap to put on his coat…a couple of times. He either didn't hear me or was ignoring me. I stopped what I was doing and looked at him. He stood in the dining room with his hands over his ears. I had to laugh. He didn't want to hear me.

It was almost time to register for my graduation. My family thought I should go through with the formal ceremony instead of having my diploma sent to me. I had worked very hard for my diploma—they wanted to watch me get it.

We discussed taking Pap to the ceremony. I knew if he had his memory, he would be proud of me. I was graduating—with honors. But Pap no longer remembered most things and the graduation was held in the evening, past his bedtime. Sue's boyfriend offered to Pap-sit so the rest of my family could go.

8

Summer

I t was very nice to have Sue back in the city, even though she was seldom home. She led a normal teenager's life—continually in motion. She was like a gentle breeze that blew through the house from time to time.

With the arrival of warm weather, Pap and I went to the country almost every weekend. About an hour before we were ready to leave, I alerted Pap, "I'm going to the camper tonight and you're coming with me. We'll be leaving soon."

This year Pap seemed to enjoy the country and didn't protest when I told him he was going. At the camper, we kept the knobs off of the stove when it wasn't in use. I left the night lights on in the bunkroom and the bathroom. I left a bowl, boxes of cereal, and a spoon on the table at night.

Pap and I were the only ones at the camper on a beautiful spring weekend. On Saturday night, he slept in three different beds. He slept in both of the bottom bunks in the bunkroom and then spent the rest of the night in the bed in Sue's room. Having guests stay overnight at the camper would be interesting.

Pap always wanted to help, but I didn't know what to give him to do—there were no more leaves to rake. After pondering the possibilities, I decided to ask him to water the pine trees. We had planted four as windbreaks and they could use extra water. Pap enjoyed watering the trees and the plants and the grass.

We didn't always understand what or who Pap was talking about. Some things remained a mystery. Pap became obsessed with the children, except we didn't know who he was referring to. Was he thinking of a young daughter, his four grandchildren or his great-grandchildren? Terri's family had increased; now they had a son and a daughter. The children had just spent the weekend with us. Was he thinking of them? Always questions, no answers.

When Bill walked into the kitchen at home, Pap was standing by the sink, placing slices of bread on the counter. When Bill asked what he was doing, Pap replied, "I'm making lunches for the kids to take to school." Bill stopped him and told him to put the bread away. "The kids are going to starve and it'll be all your fault," Pap declared as he stormed out of the kitchen. Later, Pap announced that the kids were coming home after dark and turned the porch light on. We didn't know who he was expecting but we humored him and left the light on until he went to bed.

Monday morning, Pap started the day without his upper teeth. I climbed the stairs to the attic to search for his teeth and discovered his charge cards spread out on his bed. Where did his charge cards come from? Where were his teeth? I lifted his pillow and found his teeth wrapped in a tissue. I took possession of the charge cards and gave Pap his teeth.

Wednesday morning, Pap walked into the dining room with a wad of bills in his hand. "Look what I found!" he exclaimed. When I asked where he got the money, he said he found it in the attic. I asked to see it. He had two twenty's, one five, and six one's. He shared with me—he kept the singles and gave me the rest. It had been a long time since he had any money. I wondered if he had more stashed.

The next morning, when I came downstairs dressed for work, Pap was putting on my jacket. I asked where he was going in my jacket. He said he was going to the bank. I told him that my jacket was to small for him. After he took off my jacket, I convinced him that it was too early to go to the bank. The bank wasn't open yet; we would stop on the way home from the Center.

I was becoming concerned with Pap's preoccupation with money. First I found the credit cards on his bed, then he came downstairs with money he had hidden, now he wanted to go to the bank. I didn't like the direction we were going. I didn't want a repeat…to the bank…to the bank…every day. We did this already.

Everyday, after exercising, before I got dressed for work, I reminded Pap that I was going upstairs to change and then I would eat breakfast and we would leave. I said this mostly so he would know what the plans were and not leave without me. It also helped to ease him out the door. He didn't feel rushed because he had advance warning that we were leaving.

Friday morning, I came downstairs and Pap was gone, so was his coat. Blast! Where did he go? I grabbed my jacket and went for a fast walk. I spotted Pap two blocks away, on the side street, turning the corner on the way to church. After I caught up to him, I asked where he was going. "I always go to church every morning," he answered.

I wished that he could go to church in the morning. I knew it meant a lot to him. But I had to go to work. My boss wasn't happy with all of the hours that I was taking off. I convinced Pap we had someplace to go that morning. He could go to church tomorrow—I would drive him.

Monday evening, Pap sat at the dining room table eating. I asked Sue to watch Pap while her dad and I sat out on the front porch, drinking coffee, and enjoying the nice weather. Sue had to get something from upstairs, when she returned, Pap was gone.

As soon as Sue told me, I hurried through the house and out the kitchen door to the alley. I was relieved when I recognized a familiar back, shuffling down the alley, two blocks away. After I caught up to him, I asked where he was going. "To the bank to get money for you and me," he answered. I reminded him that he didn't have the necessary papers. "I don't need them," he confided, "I've done this before." So I told him the bank was already closed, but we would go to the bank tomorrow. He turned around and slowly walked back home.

Bill suggested that we lock the back door when we were sitting on the front porch. Since we had replaced the lock, Pap wouldn't know how to work the new one and wouldn't be able to leave the house without our knowledge.

The Center closed for a day to observe Shavuot. Sue offered to stay home with Pap so I wouldn't have to miss work. The day passed peacefully until late in the morning when Pap sat at the dining room table, staring at the tangle of wood in the backyard that was left over from the porch repair. He wanted to move it, straighten it out, put it away. Sue had a hard time convincing Pap to leave the wood alone. She told him the workmen would take care of it but he still wanted to move it. Nothing worked until Sue declared, "Mom will be mad."

When I arrived home, I got a hug and kiss from Pap. "I love you," he said.

I was surprised. My father wasn't a person who showed his feelings, he seldom hugged, let alone kissed someone. He was very reserved. I wasn't sure who he thought I was. Wife? Daughter? Girlfriend? I didn't want to take a chance, so I told him that I was his daughter.

Now that Pap had better vision, he was interested in everyone's mail. He read it and put it in a safe place or tore it up. He didn't stop with Bill's mail; he took ours, Sue's, anything that wasn't put away.

When I walked into the dining room, Pap had an envelope in his hand. To be safe, I asked to see it. When he handed it to me, I saw that it was addressed to Sue. I told him that the letter wasn't his. He replied, "We are running out of room!"

Running out of room for what? Room in the envelope? Room to store the envelope? If he wanted to confuse me, he succeeded. I was confused.

Then he asked, "Has anyone been bringing the milk in from the porch? We are almost out."

We had our milk delivered when we first bought our house. But it had been more than twenty years since milk was delivered. What did that have to do with the envelope? So many questions. No answers.

The Center's nurse phoned me at work. Pap sat down between two chairs, missed both of them and ended up on the floor. He wasn't hurt and joked about falling. She was concerned that he was losing his depth perception and thought I should know.

During our next visit with Pap's ophthalmologist, I discussed Pap's recent fall and asked if Pap was losing his depth perception. Was that why he had trouble walking? Dr. E. explained that two working eyes are needed to distinguish depth. Pap never had good depth perception because of his lazy right eye, but he had learned to compensate for his disability. The disease was probably affecting the portion of Pap's brain that made those adjustments.

Memorial Day officially starts the summer season at the campground. The pools open, line dancing lessons start on Saturday mornings and entertainment is scheduled for Saturday nights. There is a variety of scheduled activities in which to participate. Pap would have more to do, more people to watch.

In all the years we owned our property, I never spent much time at our camper. I was always outside—somewhere—at the lakes, the pool, parks, trails, dances, walking, visiting friends, or riding my scooter or bike. This year my activities would have to change. Pap needed more supervision. I would have to spend more time at our camper, leaving him alone for long periods of time was risky.

I noticed that many of the small towns surrounding our campground sponsored festivals throughout the summer. Parades or open air concerts were often a part of their celebration. If I watched the paper, I could find things to do that both Pap and I would enjoy. He wouldn't be watching television all of the time.

At the camper, I found wet Kleenex on Pap's pillow in the bunkroom. Was he washing the tissue to reuse it? I hid the box of Kleenex and confirmed that he had a handkerchief.

Next, I discovered brown stains on the towel in the bathroom. What was Pap using the towel for? That same weekend, Pap told me that on Monday he was hitting the road—he was going to get a job. We discussed his new idea.

I was always afraid to agree with Pap on something that involved his activity. I worried he would remember and do it. His short term memory was gone, but at times he remembered. I didn't want him to retain something that was dangerous to his well being nor did I want him to recall something painful.

I stopped correcting Pap on the little things that didn't matter. If he thought it had been raining for a long time, even if it was the first rainfall in a month, I agreed. If he said it was Tuesday and it was only Monday, I didn't correct him. If he stated we were going North and we were headed South, I didn't argue. If Pap wanted me to enter while he held the door, I didn't protest. As long as his ideas weren't hazardous to his health or dangerous, I didn't correct or argue with him.

After we returned home on Monday night, Pap wanted a kiss. "Or is it verboten?" he asked. I answered that a daughter always gives a kiss to her father and I was his daughter. I didn't want to take a chance that Pap thought I was his girlfriend or wife, so I added that I had a husband and it wasn't him. Pap must have been hurt by my statement and remembered it, because everyday for a week he wanted to argue.

I was in the backyard, when the phone rang and Pap answered it. A friend asked if Tom was home and Pap replied, "I don't know, does he live here?" After talking to Pap for a few minutes, Tom's friend decided to call back at another time.

At the camper on Saturday morning, Pap was worried, "I want to go home, the dogs are all alone." I told him Bill was home with the dogs. "I have to go home, my daughter doesn't know where I am!" Pap said. I explained I was his daughter—he was with me. My answer didn't sink in, he kept talking about going home—insisting "she is worried".

In the city Sunday night, Pap unplugged the microwave—it was running, he could see the clock. I insisted the microwave remain plugged in. Next he reset the thermostat on the furnace to 78. Pap declared, "I would go anywhere with you." I'm not sure who he thought I was—daughter, lover, wife?

Monday morning, I noticed Pap's pills were almost gone and the druggist couldn't refill his prescription. I made an appointment for Pap at the Clinic. Dr. S. had rotated—Pap had another new doctor. This doctor wasn't familiar with Cognex and didn't want to authorize the medication without doing some study. Once again I needed to plead my father's case. I explained how much the pill helped Pap, how necessary it was to the survival of our family. I managed to get a new prescription, but the doctor stressed that he would review the medicine before our next visit.

The next morning was an ordinary morning, no worse than any others. Pap had a hard time getting up and we were late leaving for the Center but he didn't argue about going. Our ride to the Center was peaceful until Pap asked if I was going to work. I replied I was and that I would pick him up on the way home. He erupted when I mentioned that he needed to wait for me to pick him up. The veins in his neck popped out as he exploded, "What makes you think that you are my boss? My boss is the Guy upstairs." His anger caught me off guard...I wasn't expecting it...I hadn't said anything new. I often told him that I would pick him up after work, almost every day in fact.

I was so frustrated...so angry...I wanted to punch something...and I did. The steering wheel of the car took the brunt of my feelings as I pounded my clenched fists on it, beating the wheel until my hands hurt. I didn't know where Pap's anger came from...so suddenly...or why he was angry. Did his anger stem from his doctor's appointment the day before or from getting to bed after 10:00 P.M.? I had a hard time waking him that morning, he didn't want to get up. Was that the reason he was angry? Because I insisted he get up? I felt bad that I had lost my temper and apologized.

"You're always angry with me," Pap snapped.

I not only walked Pap into the Center, but back to the unit. I wanted to warn the staff that Pap was in a belligerent mood. A staff member advised me not to worry about it, they knew how to handle him. He was often like that. Her statement surprised me—Pap was seldom angry at home.

She remarked, "Bill just dotes on his daughter."

"Is that good or bad?" I asked.

"He is always talking about you," she replied. "He often goes to the front to look for you." Does he miss me or does he just want to leave the Center? Pap was always happy to see Tom or me, especially when he was leaving the Center early.

As I drove to work, I pleaded my case to my Friend in a loud voice. I felt guilty that I had exploded. I didn't want Pap to think I was always angry with him. I demanded of God, "You have to help me with this. If Pap's mission is to teach me patience—it isn't working! I don't have any!" I asked for patience and strength and said an extra chaplet.

When I picked Pap up that night, he had forgotten his anger of the morning. I wished I could forget that easily.

That evening, my comrades from a previous job were getting together for dinner. We had become good friends during the years we worked together and continued to meet occasionally. Sue said I needed a break, she would stay with Pap.

Pap gave Sue a hard time. He wanted to do things and she kept stopping him. She reminded him that mom wouldn't like it. "She's not here," Pap replied, "I can do what I want." Bill told his sister that Pap was testing her authority like kids test a substitute teacher at school.

I wanted a statue of St. Francis of Assisi, the patron saint of animals, for the camper. We had many things in common. My birthday is on his feast day, I love animals, and had spent my school years taught by Franciscan's.

A vendor at the crossroads outside of our campground had a tall painted statue of the Virgin Mary that I saw regularly. I often apologized to Her when I stopped at the junction. I explained that I was sorry I wasn't buying Her but I didn't have any extra money and I really wanted a statue of St. Francis.

My neighbor had an all white, small statue of the Virgin Mary in the front of their lot. She had found the statue laying by the side of the road at a cemetery. When no one claimed it after a month, the caretaker gave her the statue.

My neighbor really liked the tall, painted statue of Mary at the corner stand, so her sister bought it as a birthday present. They asked if I would like to have their small, white statue. With the help of a wheelbarrow and a friend, the very heavy, small statue moved to a place where I could see Her whenever I looked out the door of our room addition.

The bottom of the statue was very uneven. We had to bury the base in the ground and build up the broken areas with dirt before She stood straight. After a few weeks passed, I noticed dirt was accumulating on the bottom of Mary's gown. On closer examination, I realized that part of Her gown had been damaged and I decided to try to fix it. After the repairs were made, Mary was grey and white. That would never do—She looked worse than before I had fixed Her. At my family's suggestion, I painted Her in natural colors. My father enjoyed watching as I crawled around on my knees and belly applying the primer and then a week later, repeated the process painting the colors. I was very pleased with the finished statue, the colors brought out details that had been hidden. I joked with my neighbors, "Mary needed a tailor, that's why She came to visit me."

After supper at the camper, I watched as Pap searched his pockets. When I asked what he was looking for, he replied, "I always pay for my meals." I reminded him that we were at our camper and he didn't need to pay. Then he decided he was going home. "I'll walk, I've done it before." I told him it would be a long walk, we were a hundred miles from home. He looked surprised and said, "Thank you for telling me."

On the way back to the city, Pap was very upset that he didn't have any money. He searched his pockets...continually. Nothing I said stopped him. I explained that since we were going home, he didn't need money. Besides, he could get money at home. Nothing worked. He kept saying, "we have to go back." His searching and comments continued for the rest of the trip...over 45 minutes...until we arrived home.

This behavior became a regular part of our trips home from the camper. If Tom was in the car, Pap sat in the back seat and behaved. If Pap was in the front seat, about half way home he started searching for money, saying we had to go back. It made the long trip...longer.

In the spring, I had planted a garden in our back yard. It was very small, just a few tomatoes, green peppers and spinach. The tomatoes and green peppers were safe, I had placed wire cages around them. The spinach wasn't safe, Pap trampled on it.

As the tomato plants became larger, nothing gave Pap greater pleasure than to look for tomatoes. He peered over and through the fence surrounding the garden, looking for blossoms, looking for growing fruit. He went in regularly to straighten the plants in their baskets. In the process, he stomped all over the spinach. When I asked him to move, he was very hurt, he wanted to help. I explained I wanted the spinach to grow so that he could enjoy eating it. Then he felt better, but he still didn't realize he was smashing the plants. I decided to forget about the spinach.

Pap watched the tomatoes grow with interest and picked them when they were still very green. Then he brought them inside to ripen on the window sill. Nothing I said made any difference, Pap would not let them ripen on the vine.

My throat was always sore. It hurt to swallow, sometimes it hurt to talk, and sometimes I lost my voice. The coolness and dampness at work were contributing factors. I was tired of being sick. I left work early so I could stop at our family doctor's office to see what, if anything, could be done for me. Short of getting a different job, was there any medicine I could take that would clear up my throat? I hoped I would be able to see Dr. T. before it was time to get Pap.

Dr. T. didn't schedule appointments, his office policy was first come, first serve, except for emergencies. The waiting room was crowded when I signed in. I found an empty chair and sat down to wait. I knew my turn wouldn't come before I needed to fetch Pap. Before leaving, I told the nurse where I was going and that I would return.

Pap saw me as I opened the doors of the Center. Before we left, he introduced me to a staff member as his wife. I didn't want Pap to keep the idea in his head that I was his wife—it might lead to more problems. As I opened the car door, I reminded him I was his daughter, not his wife. "That's okay," he remarked, "What they don't know won't hurt them."

We returned to Dr. T's office and sat down to wait. When it was my turn, the nurse took my blood pressure and commented that it was that of a young girl—eight points lower than it had been. I explained that it must be due to the daily exercise; it surely wasn't because of less stress.

I told Pap I needed to see the doctor about my sore throat. He was relieved it was me instead of him. I asked Pap to wait for me, then asked the nurse to keep an eye on Pap. Dr. T. prescribed a medicine that he thought would clear up the infection in my throat. While I was there, I asked him to prescribe a strong tranquilizer. He looked up my records and discovered that the last time he prescribed them was when my father was hospitalized with pneumonia. I agreed, but reminded him that I was under a lot of stress and I wanted to have them available if my world started falling apart. We discussed my father's worsening condition, and Dr. T. advised me to be careful, to watch out for my health.

When I came out of the doctor's office, I was happy to see Pap in the waiting room, engrossed in a conversation with another patient. On the way home, Pap asked about my health, over and over. I kept reassuring him that it was just a sore throat, my doctor had given me medicine and I would be better soon.

After we arrived home, I realized Pap's shirt was bulging, like he had grown a big breast overnight. When I investigated, I found an empty Styrofoam cup stuck inside his shirt. ???

Every once in a while, Tom got off early and picked up Pap. This time, Pap was very happy to see Tom, he wanted to go home. The staff warned Tom that Pap was more hyper than usual and had refused to take a shower. They didn't know why he refused, but they didn't think we needed to worry about it. The staff advised us to wait and see what happened on the next shower day.

When they got home, Pap went out into the yard. He did some "weeding"—pulled out all of the flowering plants. After he had made the place tidy, he went into the garden, stomped on the rest of the spinach, and straightened the tomato plants. For a change I kept my big mouth shut. Pap had had a rough day.

On Friday, Pap took his shower at the Center. That evening, when we arrived at the camper, I went into the bunkroom to turn on the light for Pap. He followed and stretched out his arms, blocking the door. I didn't know what he was up to so I ducked underneath and escaped into the bigger room. I didn't ask questions. Instead, I ignored his action and continued the routine of unpacking. Then I reminded him that it was late and time for him to go to bed.

Saturday night, a country band played at the campground. Pap and I went to the dance. The band played some of the songs that I had learned at line dance lessons. It was quite crowded, but I was able to keep on eye on Pap while I was dancing.

The next time I checked, Pap was no longer in his chair. I quickly spotted him in the crowd, he appeared to be looking for something. When I caught up to him, he told me that he was looking for the bathroom. (I always suggested Pap stop in the bathroom before we left the camper. I was concerned he would get lost in a strange bathroom, that he wouldn't know how to get out. I couldn't go into a man's bathroom to rescue him.)

I walked with Pap to the bathroom and opened the door, then I waited outside. The band played a song, and then another. Still Pap didn't come out. I finally asked a friend to go in, see if he was okay, and show him the way out.

After the dance, I watched as Pap searched through his pockets. When I asked what he was looking for, he replied, "My car keys, I always drive home." With that he went to the driver's side of the car and asked for my keys. I opened the door on the passenger side of the car and waited for him to get in. As soon as he was seated, he started to scoot over to the driver's side. When I asked where he was going, Pap answered, "I always drive when we're together." Opening the door on the driver's side, I insisted that I would drive this time since it was late and I knew where we were going.

Monday, the nurse from the Center called me at work. Pap had diarrhea and couldn't remain at the Center. There was a possibility that he would transmit it to the rest of the clients. They had already cleaned him up four times.

When I picked Pap up, he didn't know that anything was wrong. He felt fine. I called the Clinic, but Pap's primary doctor wasn't on call. Fortunately, another doctor was there and I told her about Pap's problems. She advised me to give him Kaopectate after every bowel movement and keep him away from coffee and milk. He could have clear broth only, no solid food.

I gave Pap a dose of Kaopectate right away. Whenever he came out of the bathroom, I asked him if he had a bowel movement. He didn't remember. How are you supposed to help someone when he doesn't remember what just happened?

It wasn't a problem to keep Pap from drinking coffee or eating solid food on Monday night. Pap ate a bowl of chicken broth and went to bed.

Tuesday morning was another story. I removed the cereal and fruit from the table. When Pap came downstairs, I made a bowl of chicken broth and placed it on the dining room table for him. I didn't lock the kitchen door but slid the bolt closed. Then I went into the basement to wash a load of clothes. Some sixth sense sent me back upstairs. Pap had a bowl of cereal with milk in his hands—he was very happy. He had managed to open the kitchen door, had found a bowl, the cereal, milk, and a spoon, and was sitting at the table ready to eat.

I took the cereal away and dumped it down the toilet. Pap became very angry. He threw his spoon down onto the table so that it skipped across the table top. I explained that he just finished a bowl of soup, he shouldn't be hungry. I was following his doctor's instructions. I was instructed not to give him cereal. It didn't help. He wasn't sick…hadn't been sick…wanted his cereal.

I knew it was going to be a long day. I phoned the Center and informed them that I was keeping Pap home. I talked to the nurse and told her what the doctor had said.

Again I used a thermos for coffee and left the coffee pot dry. Pap continually went to the pot all day long. Sometimes I reminded him that he wasn't supposed to have coffee; sometimes I said I would make a new pot of coffee soon. We made it through the day. I didn't know if he still had diarrhea. He didn't remember and I couldn't tell.

When my children were babies, it was very hard to take care of them when they were sick because they couldn't tell me what was wrong. Taking care of Pap was even harder at times; he couldn't tell me because he didn't remember and I couldn't look.

Tuesday evening Pap said he was cold. I shut the windows and gave him a flannel shirt to put on. He must have had the chills because a little later, he took the shirt off and wanted to open the windows.

Wednesday morning, I drove Pap to the Center. I told the nurse that as far as I could tell, his system was back to normal and asked her to call me at work if he was still sick.

Thursday morning, Pap was very pleased with himself. "Look what I found," he beamed as he showed me a bowl of cereal. He had found something to eat. Of course, I had left a bowl, spoon, and cereal on the table for him. I had to laugh, I was glad he had found it.

That evening, when we returned from the Center, Pap stood on the porch, searching through his pockets. He declared, "You'll have to unlock the door, I don't have my key." I replied that it would be no problem, I had mine. He hadn't carried house keys in over a year.

Pap was almost out of his pills, again. In order to get a new prescription, he had to be examined by his doctor. I made an appointment at the Clinic and found out that he had another new doctor—they had rotated again.

I had a new problem when I drove Pap to the Clinic for his examination. Parking had always been a problem. The Clinic was located on the corner of a main street and a side street. Parking was prohibited on the main street, but I had always found a spot on the side street. Now the side street had signs restricting parking to residents displaying a sticker. The few spaces assigned to the Clinic were filled. I knew I couldn't drop Pap off and ask him to wait for me. He would forget he was waiting and wander away. I found parking two blocks away, and we walked back to the Clinic. I was glad the weather was good and the sidewalks were dry. I didn't know what we would do once winter came.

I had to start from square one and familiarize the new doctor with Cognex. Once again I needed to plead my case, tell the doctor how important it was that my father receive the medication. The new doctor noticed that Pap had never visited a neurologist, he hadn't had any tests for his mental condition. She prescribed the necessary medicine and authorized a visit to a neurologist.

Unfortunately, Pap's new doctor was only at the Clinic for a short period of time. By the time her request was approved, the appointment made, and the paperwork filled out, she had rotated, and I would have to break in another new doctor.

Conditions at work continued to worsen. The head of our shipping department resigned and rather than replace him, my boss proposed that his workload be divided among the remaining personnel. I was tired of assuming more responsibilities. My boss and I had a heated discussion during which I became so upset I couldn't talk. I took a tranquilizer, just to calm down. I decided that enough was enough. After my vacation and the Jewish High Holy days in the fall when the Center was closed, I would look for a new job.

I was eligible for two weeks vacation and decided to save one week for the fall when the Center was closed. I asked for the other week in August when Tom was on vacation. Tom wanted to travel to the East coast to visit his family but I couldn't picture taking Pap on the trip. It would be more fun than any of us wanted. Just the thought of it sent chills up and down my spine. I felt it was asking too much to have our children watch Pap for a week and we didn't have the money to take advantage of short term care at a nursing home. Besides, I didn't feel it would be good for Pap. Tom changed his mind about the trip, instead we took Pap with us to the camper.

The land where we camp is not flat, the terrain includes gently rolling hills. The moles are very busy digging tunnels everywhere. The streets are paved but there are no sidewalks; pathways are sometimes gravel or woodchips. Pap didn't seem to have difficulty with the unevenness of the ground in the past but now I noticed he was having trouble walking. He didn't like to use my arm for balance; I had a cane in the car, but he didn't want to use it either. I often asked my Friend to help my stubborn father get around safely, without falling and breaking his bones.

The property owner's association at the campground had scheduled its annual meeting for Sunday and I wanted to attend. Everyone must have wanted to attend because the parking lot was full. I had to park further away, on the other side of a steep hill. Pap had trouble with the climb. When I offered my arm, he refused. Rather than antagonize him, I left him to his own devises. He made it up safely and we found a place to sit. Pap enjoyed listening to the speakers. When Tom arrived, he treated us to ice cream. Pap didn't want ice cream. He was busy, he was listening. I realized he could no longer do two things at the same time. Something we take for granted, a little thing like eating while listening, was no longer possible for him. For quite some time, I had noticed Pap was becoming more and more absorbed in his food and less aware of the events going on around him. I just hadn't realized what his total concentration meant.

While we were on vacation, we made an appointment with the local car dealer to give my car a checkup. At the dealer's, we left Pap waiting in my car while we talked to the repairman. It took longer than we expected to go over the checklist of what they were going to do. Tom was concerned that Pap was uncomfortable in the hot car. He went outside and brought Pap into the air conditioned waiting room, found him a comfortable chair, and gave him a cup of coffee before he rejoined me.

Because Pap was on vacation with us, we decided to rent a car—Tom's motorcycle wouldn't get the three of us around. They had a van we could use but Pap would have trouble climbing in and out. They didn't have a four-door car available so we settled for a small two-door.

When we returned to the waiting room, Pap was angry. "I'm never doing this again," he fumed. We think he was frightened, afraid that we had abandoned him. My car was his security blanket. He often waited for me in the car while I went into a store to pick up some needed item. We had taken him out of a secure environment and left him in a strange place with strange people. Even though we were in the same building, he didn't know we were there—he couldn't see us. We told him that we were getting my car fixed, but he didn't remember. I realized I would have to be more careful where I left him alone.

The last day of our vacation, a crowd of people gathered on the road near our camper. Tom and I wandered over to see what was going on. A large fish hawk, an Osprey, had landed with a big bass in its talons. He stood on the road, daring anyone to come close, devouring his meal while stopping traffic. I still had film left in my camera. I didn't have a zoom lens so I inched my way close to the bird and sat down nearby, observing and taking pictures. While I watched the bird, Tom returned to the camper to watch Pap.

The following Tuesday, when I picked Pap up from the Center, I mentioned that I was way behind at work because of our vacation. He was surprised and asked me how I enjoyed my vacation. I replied that he should know, he went with us. Nothing of the week at the camper remained; he had completely forgotten.

Summer would soon be over, the festivals in the towns and the scheduled weekend activities at the camper would end. Pap wouldn't have as much to do and I wouldn't have as many people to talk with. We continued to go to parades and concerts in the neighboring towns, taking advantage of the remaining time.

The Nature Club traditionally held a chili supper at the end of summer. Before we ate, we always worked on a club project. I decided to take Pap to the supper but I told our president that we would be late, we were going to Mass first. I explained it was easier to take Pap to afternoon Mass on Saturday than to try to get him moving early on Sunday morning.

Pap enjoyed the chili supper, both the chili and the desserts. After supper, we sat around a campfire. Pap loved to sing and the group started singing *I've Been Working On The Railroad*. The song was one of his favorites so he sang with confidence and at an accelerated speed, way ahead of the rest.

I was glad that the members were aware of Pap's memory loss. At the beginning of summer I had warned them that my involvement with the club would be limited. During the evening, they talked to Pap and made him feel welcome. At the end of the evening, they watched him while I got the car.

I finally received the Center's schedule for September. Labor Day, Rosh Hashanah, Yom Kippur, and Succoth all fell in the same month. The Center would be closed for eight weekdays, spread over three weeks. Sue offered to stay with Pap a couple of the days and I had five days of vacation left. I gave my boss a schedule of the dates that I would be gone. He wasn't happy, but I reminded him that I was taking vacation time.

When I realized how many days Pap would be home, I ordered a book from the local Alzheimer's chapter: *Failure-Free Activities For The Alzheimer's Patient.* I hoped I would get a few new ideas to help occupy Pap's time.

The Saturday before Labor Day we were still in the city. I wanted to get a few things done in the house before we left for the camper. Since Tom had to stay in the city because of work, he decided to visit our grandchildren and made me an offer I couldn't refuse. "You'll have Pap all weekend. I'll take him with me to Terri's and you can have some time to yourself. You can pick Pap up when you're ready to go."

I enjoyed having the house to myself. I was able to work at my own pace. It was very nice not to have to worry about what Pap was doing. When I finished, I didn't really want to leave.

When I arrived at Terri's, I only stayed for a little while before Pap and I left for the camper. On the drive, Pap asked me how I enjoyed being alone. I said that I enjoyed it. Then he asked me again, and again, and again. Each time I told him that I enjoyed being by myself. Was he worried that I had been alone?

A big band was playing at the camper on Saturday night. I knew it would be very crowded but we went, since I knew Pap enjoyed the big band music. Pap asked me to dance when they played a slow tune. I agreed and we shuffled in place for a while. (Since my father had gotten older, the only dance he did was a box step, except he left off most of the box.) He had more trouble than usual keeping with the beat of the music. When the music stopped, Pap said that he didn't like the way the band played the song, it was too hard to dance to. A couple of songs later, the band played a polka. Pap asked if I wanted to dance with him. Slow, shuffle-in-place step to a polka? I didn't think so. So as not to hurt his feelings, I said I was tired.

9

Fall

The pace at the campground slowed in September. The pools closed, line dance lessons ended, and fewer activities were scheduled. Frost warnings became a part of the weather report, the feeling of fall was in the air. Soon the leaves would change color and drop from the trees. Pap could rake leaves, he would have something to do on weekends.

Already acorns were falling from the trees at the camper. We had two very big oak trees and the nuts were plentiful. For an able-bodied person, walking on acorns was like walking on marbles, the foot slipped without warning. I didn't know how hazardous the acorns would be for Pap. He didn't have good balance and he wouldn't hold onto my arm. I tried to push the acorns off of the stairs with my foot, I swept them up with a broom, but the more I swept, the more they fell.

Classes started at my school. I was glad that I had decided to sign up for Speech; I needed to be able to put my life aside and be a student for a little while every week.

I also enjoyed meeting my friend before class. Besides school, we had another problem in common, the responsibility of caring for a parent. Her mother, who lived with her, didn't have mental dementia but had health problems when she forgot or refused to take her medicine. This combined with personality conflicts between them enabled my friend to understand some of the things that I was going through; she lent a sympathetic ear to my grousing (grumbling with enthusiasm).

One evening, my friend had had a particularly bad day—she woke up late, her mother was impossible, she made an error at work, and her boss was unhappy. I listened to her story and then shared mine. She remarked that listening to me always made her feel better. As bad as her day was, mine was always worse.

I was glad that I made her feel better.

Speech wasn't as demanding as some of the courses I had taken. Each student was required to present three speeches throughout the term. I decided to give one speech on living with a person with mental dementia and another on the prairie at Nachusa—conserving our natural resources. I wasn't sure what to choose for the third.

The idea for my third speech was given to me by my classmates when we were discussing subjects for our first speech. I commented that I used to be shy and no one believed me. Their disbelief made me realize how much I had changed, the paths that I had walked, how I had been guided to become the person I am. Someone who never returned anything to the store because she was afraid was now arguing with doctors. I had come a long way. My first speech was on *Overcoming Shyness*, followed by *Living With Mental Dementia,* and finally *Nachusa.*

The Jewish Holy Days disrupted Pap's routine. I tried to find safe things for him to do since I didn't think it would be good for either of us if he sat and watched television all day. I gave him towels to fold. I asked him to stack the old newspapers for recycling. One day in desperation, I gave Pap a jar of pennies. I asked him to count them. He was occupied for hours. He made stacks of ten, recounted the stacks of ten, arranged them in rows, and then rearranged the rows. He enjoyed playing with the money.

I loaded the record player with some of Pap's favorite music. I played big bands, swing or dixieland alternating with old gospel songs or contemporary church music. Pap enjoyed listening to the music, and sometimes he sang along. I enjoyed listening to Pap sing, and I especially enjoyed not listening to the television.

I scheduled a visit with Pap's caseworker for a day the Center was closed. The morning of her visit, I had to hide the cereal after Pap had two bowls and a coffee cup full. Pap became angry when I removed the cereal and argued with me for the rest of the morning. Then he took the new *Readers Digest*, put it in his pocket, insisted that he printed it, and strode upstairs.

The caseworker's visit was short since Pap's case was a review. She asked Pap a few questions, verified his financial status, and updated her records. This time I answered more questions than Pap did. I was so upset with Pap that I asked her for information on nursing homes.

After the caseworker left, I informed Pap that we were going to stop at my school so I could get an I.D. card, then we would visit his sister. He was still angry and wanted to know why I was planning his day.

At school, the waiting line for I.D. cards was very long. I knew Pap would get tired standing in line waiting with me, but I had to remain in his sight. I couldn't leave him sitting at a table in the cafeteria with a cup of coffee, he might wander away. Once again I got lucky. The waiting line was close to the counselor's office. Pap sat in a chair in their waiting room while I waited in line. The glass window allowed him to keep his eye on me so he wouldn't panic. He watched the long line of waiting students and their children and I kept an eye on Pap.

When I called Aunt Connie that morning, she had invited us for lunch. We sat around her kitchen table eating pizza, drinking coffee, and talking. It was hard to draw Pap into the conversation, most of the time he just listened. But on the way home he remarked that he enjoyed the visit.

Making the most of my time off from work, I took Pap for his first visit to the neurologist. Her office hours were like that of our family doctor, first come, first serve. After a couple of hours wait, we were ushered into a room to wait some more.

Dr. K. was a tall, slender woman with an European accent. She had a stern manner, just one glance in my direction was all that was needed to keep me silent. She asked Pap many questions to test his mental condition. Pap knew the date of his birth and his telephone number but he didn't know how old he was. He knew it was the fall but he didn't know the month, or the year, or the name of the president of the United States.

When I explained the difference Cognex made to Pap's memory, Dr. K. asked Pap to walk across the room. After observing his gait, she prescribed a medicine to balance the Cognex. She explained that Cognex was originally designed for people with Parkinson's disease so it stiffened their muscles. That was why Pap was having trouble walking. The new medicine would give Pap back his flexibility so he wouldn't fall. She also ordered an MRI (Magnetic Resinous Image) of Pap's brain so she could see what was happening. I was impressed by her compassion and skill. Progress!

Every year my family asked what I wanted for my birthday. This year I had an answer, I asked for a special birthday present, I wanted to go to the camper without Pap. I wanted to go to "Autumn on the Prairie" at Nachusa. My family arranged their schedules so I could have my weekend. It was the first weekend in a very long time that I didn't have Pap. Both days were beautiful and I made the most of them. On Saturday I stayed at Nachusa until dusk. Sunday I was only at the camper to sleep, eat, cleanup, and leave. The rest of the time I was outside: walking, riding my scooter, visiting friends. Freedom!

I ran into one of my friends while I was wandering on Sunday. She commented that she hadn't seen me in a long time and asked about Pap. I described some of Pap's current adventures and shared my escapades of the weekend.

She had her own tale to tell. Her mother-in-law, who lived with her other son, was affected by a form of mental dementia. The son had installed a phone in his mom's room so she could talk to her friends whenever she wanted. Very early one morning, the family's sleep was disturbed by a loud voice that commanded, "This is the police. Throw down your weapons and surrender, we have the house surrounded." When her son opened the door, the police told him that his mom had called 911 and asked for help, she was being held hostage. Needless to say, the telephone was removed from his mom's room.

The mother also had a habit of getting up in the middle of the night. She wasn't content with wandering inside the house—she opened the door and went out. They had to install a bolt at the top of their outside doors to keep his mom inside at night. She couldn't open the door and didn't think to look at the top.

I often met people who had their own stories to share about living with someone with memory loss. Our stories were different but similar. I knew many people were facing the same challenges. I wasn't alone.

We survived the days that the Center was closed. It wasn't easy for Pap, nor for us. Pap was impossible. At the Center he received mental stimulation, interacted with others, and engaged in physical activity designed for his capabilities. We didn't have the staff's intervention skills, nor did we have their patience.

Pap got used to staying home. After the Jewish Holy Days, he didn't want to go back to the Center. I brought out the heavy artillery: fire, two floods, lost three times. "Why do you always bring up those things?" Pap wanted to know. "I've changed and you won't give me a chance. I'm better now. I'm not going to make the same mistake again."

"It isn't safe for you to stay home alone," I replied. Two floods were one too many, one fire was one too many. I can't take a chance that it will happen again. For your safety and ours, you have to go to the Center."

Pap reluctantly got ready to leave for the Center. He finished his coffee and reached for his jacket and had a hard time putting it on. He held the jacket upside down and couldn't find the sleeves. As he became frustrated, I provided a helping hand.

I discussed Pap's belligerent behavior with the Center's staff. Were more of the clients impossible, or was Pap the only one? They assured me that Pap was reacting normally; the change in routine caused his erratic behavior. Once things were back to normal, Pap should be better. I hoped they were right.

After we came home from the Center, I remembered that I needed to buy birthday cards for Brittany and invited Pap to go with me to the store. It was a straight, short walk from our house. I thought the exercise would be good for him. We bought our cards and started walking home. On the way, I met an old friend. I stopped to chat with her and Pap continued on, around the corner and down the street. Cutting the visit short, I caught up to Pap. When I joined him he remarked that he liked to walk. I was glad he was enjoying himself and managed to turn him around and guide him home.

After we arrived home, I went into the kitchen to prepare dinner and Pap sat down to watch television with Tom. Before ten minutes passed, Pap came into the kitchen. He said he had something to tell me. (He often did that. It was usually a problem—it could be anything from the toilet is stopped up to we're out of toilet paper.) This time Pap said, "The man next to me is holding a gun on us."

I went into the front room and asked Tom what they were watching. "Bill Crosby," he replied. That show wasn't violent, where did Pap see a man with a gun? I walked back into the kitchen and told Pap that the man was gone.

"Good," he said, "but I'm sorry the police didn't get him."

We had a marvelous time at our granddaughter's birthday party on Saturday. Pap enjoyed talking with Brittany. He enjoyed playing with Benjamin and making faces at him and giving him blocks and watching him play. Pap enjoyed the festivities. Pap enjoyed the cake.

As soon as we found a solution to one problem, another developed. We never replaced the overhead door of our garage after the fire; we couldn't use the garage for our cars so Tom kept his motorcycle in it. Normally, parking our car wasn't a problem. We didn't have a driveway but we always found a place on the main street we lived on. While there wasn't a steady stream of cars, the street was seldom free of traffic unless it was late at night. Sue often used my car, parking it wherever there was an empty space. One night, when she returned home parking was at a premium. She couldn't find a spot on our side of the street so she parked my car across the street.

I spotted my car as soon as I walked out of the door in the morning. When the traffic cleared, I started across the street with Pap following ten steps behind. I cautioned him to hurry up and he slowed down. He was almost hit by a truck.

That evening, I told Sue about my morning's scare and asked her not to park my car on the other side of the street. I thought it would be safer for Pap if she parked on a side street, even if it was a longer walk. If she had to park across the street, I asked her to leave a note in my coffee cup so I could move my car before going outside with Pap. Watching Pap get run over wasn't the way I wanted to start the day.

I realized that I had found a solution to another problem. I always parked my car on the north side of the street when we went to Mass even though our church was located on the south side. We crossed at a traffic light, but my father's slow pace made me nervous since the light started to change before I was on the other side. I decided to heed my own council, I would park on the south side when we went to Mass.

Pap didn't want to go to the Center, instead he wanted to argue. He asked, "Who decided that I should go?"

I didn't want to argue again. That was what we were doing every morning, and I was tired of the daily battle. I calmly said, "You go to the Center, I go to work, that is what we do."

He said, "You're bossy."

"That's my job," I replied. He surprised me—he didn't argue. He put on his coat and hat, finished his coffee, and got ready to go.

The weather forecast for the weekend was beautiful. Tom had to work and I didn't want to stay in the city. I decided that it was better to be at the camper with Pap than to be inside in the city. As usual, Friday night I showed Pap where he was sleeping in the bunkroom. He never remembered. I turned the television on in the room addition and sat down to watch the news. Then I heard noises coming from the camper. When I went to investigate, Pap was in the bathroom, sitting on the toilet, taking off his shoes. A towel lay across the bottom of the tub, like a blanket. Did he think he was sleeping in the tub? I pointed him in the right direction, back to his bed in the bunkroom.

A short time later Pap wandered into the room addition, he couldn't sleep. When I asked why, he replied, "Connie is home alone to do all of the work. I want to go home to help her." I explained that Connie's son was with her, she wasn't alone. We would go home on Sunday.

Sunday, as we were getting ready to leave, Pap couldn't zip his jacket. Once in the car, he couldn't put on his seat belt. On the drive home, I thought about our weekend. I didn't know what I was going to do. Sitting by himself, watching television wasn't good for Pap. It was hard enough to find activities he could participate in at the camper during the summer. In the fall, it was quiet, no formal activities were scheduled, but I didn't want to stay in Chicago, either.

When I returned from school on Monday night, Sue's boyfriend warned that he had good news and bad news. I asked for the bad news first. He said, "There is pooh on the toilet and the bathroom floor. The good news is that I didn't get it on me."

Bill told me that we had a new problem. He discovered that Pap was using a glass by his bed or a bucket in the back of the attic for a toilet. Bill heard Pap urinating at night. Many times he woke to the sound, many times he told Pap to go downstairs to the bathroom. Bill said that he did not like to be awakened by the sound of "rushing water", we had to do something.

Pap had installed a dividing door to keep the cats out of his workshop. Since he was going into the workshop part of the attic to use a bucket, we decided to close and latch the door. If he couldn't get into the back, maybe he would use the bathroom downstairs. I thought that going to the camper, where everything was on one level, might be confusing Pap, he might not know where he was when he woke up.

The next night, Bill woke to the sound of the door rattling, Pap was trying to get into the back of the attic. Bill said, "Pap, there isn't a bathroom back there, you have to go downstairs." This time, Pap did.

I had a talk with Pap. I told him that someone was using a bucket in the attic as a bathroom. Using a bucket was not acceptable. It needed to stop; we had a bathroom. Surprisingly, Pap stopped using the bucket or the glass. He returned to going to the bathroom, in the bathroom.

Saturday at the camper, Pap decided to go out for a walk. (He often did that. He walked to the street to look up and down or walked around the camper looking at the birds, the trees, and the flowers. I didn't always follow him outside but I always monitored his actions.) I looked outside, Pap was watching the birds at the feeder behind our trailer. A couple of minutes later, I looked again. At first I didn't see him. Blast! Where had he gone so quickly? Then I saw his back disappear around the side of a trailer four lots away. I walked over to find out where he was going. He was happy to see me—he had lost our camper. I was glad that I had looked when I did. Pap lost at the campground would not have been fun.

When we returned to the city, Pap didn't want to go to bed, he wasn't tired. I finally shagged him to bed after 9:00 P.M.; at 11:30 he was back downstairs. He couldn't sleep, he was hungry. I gave him a bowl of cereal.

Monday morning, I called Pap at 7:00 and he answered me. A little later I called him again, and again, he answered. "Is everything alright?" I called when he still didn't come down. He replied that he was getting up. At 8:00, he still wasn't downstairs. I had called him a total of four times. He finally came down at 8:25. We should have already left.

Tuesday morning, Pap was up on time, but he came downstairs without a shirt.

Thursday, Pap was downstairs by 7:30, fully dressed. I told him that I was going to have breakfast and then we would leave. Pap went back upstairs. I went up to check on him when he didn't answer me. He had taken one shoe off. Was he going back to bed?

I didn't want to keep the job I had. I wanted to get a new one but I realized that wish was a pipe dream. Looking for a job was stressful; learning a new job was stressful; and I was already under enough stress. Moreover, it wasn't fair to ask a new company to put up with the erratic schedule I was forced to keep living with Pap. For the time being I would have to stay where I was. That thought did not make me happy.

I stopped at the grocery store on the way home from work to pick up a few things while Pap waited for me in the car. As soon as I entered the store, I was greeted by a bucket of beautiful flowers—bouquets of mixed flowers were on sale. I decided to treat myself and took a bouquet home. The flowers looked so nice on the dining room table—Pap enjoyed them; I enjoyed them. I decided to splurge and buy a fresh bouquet every week that I continued to work.

We went to the Clinic for the necessary blood tests before Pap's MRI. After the blood tests were taken, I was informed that the test the neurologist ordered wasn't approved. The nurse explained that a CAT (Computerized Axial Tomography) scan was approved and if the results of that test called for the more expensive test, it would be approved at that time.

The CAT scan was scheduled for the morning. Pap could have coffee and breakfast when he woke up; he didn't have to fast before the test. That would be easier on both of us. The nurse at the hospital understood when I explained Pap's memory loss and the test proceeded without any problems. They hooked Pap up to an I.V. and he had a nice rest. He wasn't upset when we left the hospital. The nurse said his doctor would have the results in a few weeks.

Indian summer arrived. I wanted to spend as much time outside as I could and that meant going to the camper. Tom had to work, so Pap and I went. It wasn't wise to leave Pap alone for a long period of time but at the same time, I needed to take a break from him. I decided that I would take my camera, ride around the campground on my scooter, and take pictures of the beautiful colors of fall. I put a movie on the

VCR for Pap and disappeared for an hour. It was only an hour and one roll of film, but my mini-vacation was worth it.

The Nature Club scheduled a Stone Soup supper for the last meeting of the year. As we arrived, groups of people were leaving for the nature trails to paint bluebird boxes, while others gathered around the big soup pot suspended over the open fire. I knew that it wasn't a good idea to take Pap out on a trail but I wanted to help and offered to paint a box that hadn't been placed yet. Pap watched as I assembled the materials to do the job. I had to return to our camper to pick up something I forgot and took Pap with me. When we returned, he didn't want to get out of the car. I thought that he was tired, so I didn't argue and left him sitting in the car watching the activity. As the members returned from the trails and sat down to eat, I convinced Pap to join us. After we returned to the camper, Pap said that he never wanted to go by my friends again. I realized too late that he hadn't been tired, he was hurt because he didn't have a job to do, he wasn't included in the activity.

A new problem was developing when I drove Pap home from the Center. The first time, Pap put his finger into the top of the window as I closed it. Luckily no damage was done because the car was running and I released him at the first yelp. He quickly forgot that his finger was caught and did the same thing again. Twice, I had closed the window on his finger. Next I smashed his finger in the car door. He put his hand on the top of the door to steady himself as I was closing it, getting stuck in the locked door. I unlocked the door as quickly as I could but the damage was done. I looked at his finger, the nail was already turning blue but nothing seemed to be broken.

I made a mental note to close Pap's window before I parked the car, maybe then he wouldn't put his finger in the window. I made a second mental note to wait until Pap had moved completely away from the car before shutting the door.

Pap was always hungry when he returned from the Center. He wanted to eat right away. At first he was satisfied with a piece of fruit, but recently he was eating handfuls of cereal from the boxes that were always on the dining room table. He had so many handfuls that he didn't eat all of his supper. He gave half of it to the dogs, which upset Tom.

"If you keep the cereal off of the table," Tom said, "Pap will learn to eat his supper." I reminded Tom that Pap wouldn't remember, that he was past the point where he could learn anything. But, I agreed that Pap needed to eat more than cereal so I put the boxes of cereal away. I decided to place the boxes on the table after Pap went to bed, so he would have cereal to snack on if he got up during the night, then put them away after he had eaten his breakfast.

Pap was very angry that the cereal wasn't on the table anymore. He argued with me daily...about everything...all week. Friday night, Pap and I drove to the camper for the weekend. He was still angry with me. I told him to take his anger, put it in a bag, and throw it away. I didn't want to deal with it.

(Most of the time Pap didn't remember good or bad things or if he did remember, he pretended that he didn't. I never knew when he was going to remember something. Sometimes when his feelings were hurt or if he got angry, he remembered; at other times he quickly forgot.)

I wanted to give Tom something special for Christmas. He had given me a very unique birthday card with a special message: "God grant you the strength of eagles' wings, the faith and courage to fly to new heights, and the wisdom to rely on His Spirit to carry you there." The picture on the front was of an eagle flying through the clouds, high above the trees. I decided to use that eagle as a model and paint a picture for Tom. I didn't have the necessary skill to paint the scene on the front of the card so I designed my own. I worked on a sketch and tried to plan the scenery for the painting. I decided on distant mountains with the eagle flying over tree tops in the foreground.

I knew the number of weekends that I was going to spend at the camper were limited. As the weather became colder, it would be easier to keep Pap in the city. This was the weekend to paint Tom's eagle.

I hadn't painted mountains in many years. By the time I was done...instead of the small, very far away mountains that I had planned, I had huge, giant, nearby peaks. The small eagle I had sketched needed to be enlarged. As I worked on the painting, I felt that I was the eagle...flying free, high above the trees.

I hoped that Tom would like his present.

Following our custom, Pap and I went to Saturday afternoon Mass. As usual, I let Pap go into the pew ahead of me. I always sat so that I could be the leader—Pap followed me to communion and I always walked slowly so that he could follow me on the return to our pew. Then I remained standing until he returned. I was very surprised when upon returning to the pew after receiving communion, Pap took the Host out of his mouth and put it in his pocket to save for later.

Saturday evening, I showed Pap where he was sleeping and returned to the family room to watch television. I heard a noise in the bunk-room and went to investigate. Pap was opening and closing the closet doors. What was he looking for? Was he going to sleep in the closet? I showed Pap where he was sleeping. Again.

After we returned home on Sunday, Pap announced that he wanted to go to his house in the country—two dogs were waiting for him. Was he talking about our dogs in the city, our neighbor's dogs in the country, or had he regressed in time, to his early years of marriage when we lived in the country? I didn't know. Always questions, no answers. I told Pap that the dogs were fine and he lived with us in our house in the city.

Monday, the temperature dropped 20 degrees while I was at work. When I picked Pap up from the Center, he had on a short sleeved summer shirt. Even though he said that he was warm enough in the car, I knew he had to be chilled. When we arrived home, before going to fetch a flannel shirt for him, I started a pot of coffee. When I returned, Pap had taken the coffee pot off of the burner and was standing there, holding his cup under the dripping coffee. I was afraid that he would get burned and I erupted. "What in the Sam Hill do you think you're doing? I can't leave you alone for five minutes without your getting into trouble."

I was so glad to see Tom when he came home—I quickly left for school.

Pap was still up when I returned. He remembered that I had gotten angry and tried to patch things up. "I really like spending time with you. I wish we could spend more time together."

We visited the neurologist to get the results of Pap's CAT scan. While we were waiting, a salesperson from Cognex stopped by with literature. The manufacturer of Cognex had created an Alzheimer's Family Care program for the persons afflicted by Alzheimer's disease and their caregivers. The salesman explained the program and gave me an information packet. I asked for a few extra copies. I thought the information might be helpful for other clients at the Center and I could also use the information for my speech on aging.

Dr. K. asked Pap some questions to test his mental state. His mental condition seemed to be about the same as on our last visit. Pap knew his birthday and his telephone number. He thought he had a couple of children but forgot their names. He didn't know the month, the year or the president. We discussed the results of the CAT scan and the blood tests. Dr. K. said Pap didn't have a tumor, he had an advanced case of hardening of the arteries, which affected his cranial area. His brain had shrunk more than was normal for a person of his age.

Pap appeared to be doing well on the Cognex. We were to continue using it since the blood tests hadn't shown any adverse effects. The Cogentin that she had prescribed for his rigidity seemed to be helping so she increased the dosage. We should return after Christmas for the next visit. She gave me a prescription that would last until January. I was relieved that I wouldn't have to fight with a doctor to get Pap's medicine.

While we were waiting, I had noticed Pap picking at the finger that been smashed in the car door. It looked like he had removed part of the blackened nail, and I was afraid his finger would become infected. Before we left her office, I asked Dr. K. to look at Pap's fingernail.

After Dr. K. examined Pap's finger, she asked her nurse to remove the nail and bandage the finger. I told the nurse that Pap would take the bandage off, he wouldn't remember. After removing the nail, the nurse applied a disinfectant before using more tape than normal to bandage his finger. She said he might leave the bandage on but I had my doubts.

I was in for a surprise. Pap left the bandage on for more than a week allowing his finger to heal.

I gave my speech, *When A Relative Becomes A Stranger,* in class. I decided to make it a positive speech. I wanted it to be meaningful for everyone, not only those with family members suffering from mental dementia. I listed various steps that could be taken in advance to make intervention easier: direct deposit of Social Security and pension checks, direct payment of bills from a bank account, joint checking and saving accounts, a living will, a will, and power of attorney. I mentioned that we should exercise our mind as well as our body as we age; research had shown that it was possible to exercise the brain through mental activity. I shared the information I had gathered on Alzheimer's and Cognex. One of my classmates had personal experience with the disease, her forty year old sister-in-law had Alzheimer's. I gave her an information packet from Cognex.

When early registration came at school, I signed up for Creative Writing. I still wasn't ready to stop going to school. I tried to convince my friend that she wanted to take the class but she decided to take the semester off. I looked forward to meeting her for coffee before class and I would miss her support.

A few weeks later, when I picked Pap up from the Center, he asked how I knew where he was. That night he didn't go to bed at his normal time of 7:00. He came into the kitchen to tell me that he was worried, "I opened the door and the dogs got out."

I replied, "Don't worry, I will get the dogs back in." Listening to me, he was relieved. He had given the problem to someone else, it wasn't his anymore. I would fix what was wrong. He went to bed about 9:00.

The next morning, Pap had more trouble than usual getting in motion for the day. His shoes weren't tied. When I told him to tie his shoes, he only tied one and left the other shoelace hanging. I tied his other shoelace for him. As we were getting ready to leave, he wanted to put his coat on, inside out. Then he couldn't put on his gloves.

When we arrived at the Center, a group of students were sitting in the hallway—on the chairs and on the floor. Pap started to take a seat rather than walk back to the unit. I could see he was confused so I walked him back. I mentioned his confusion to one of the staff. She had noticed that he was confused the previous afternoon and asked if there had been a change in his schedule. I didn't know of any change. After we talked for a little while, she mentioned that a client had a stroke at the Center on the preceding afternoon and they had to call an ambulance. When I inquired further, I learned that the person was a lady with whom Pap drank morning coffee every day. No wonder he was upset.

Pap was confused for the rest of the day. By the next morning, Saturday, he was back to normal, except I noticed one shoelace trailing on the ground when he walked into the kitchen. He wanted to go to church but Tom stopped him and explained that we would go later.

It was a nice day, so I decided to rake leaves. Before I started, I needed to buy yard bags. I left Pap home and walked to the store. When I returned, Pap was upset that I had gone without him. He was still pouting when I went out to rake. I announced that he could stay inside or come out and help me. It didn't matter, I was going outside. A short time later Pap came out to help.

On Sunday I left Pap home watching a football game with Tom while I went Christmas shopping. Four hours later I returned. Pap asked me over, and over, and over again if I had a good time without him. He finally stopped when I asked him if he had a good time with Tom watching the football game.

Snow and ice were more of a problem for Pap this year. Even with the medicine to counteract the stiffness in his joints, Pap's walking was a slow shuffle. He wouldn't take my arm and didn't like it when I helped him over the icy sidewalks. I explained that I didn't want him to fall and break something. Sometimes he reluctantly allowed me to help, but most of the time he pulled away, insisting on walking by himself.

In order to start the day in a gentle mood, I looked out the window every morning when I woke up. If it had snowed during the night, I substituted shoveling for exercising. I tried to keep pathways clear to the street at strategic places where I parked my car. I spread salt if it was icy.

Our neighbor, across the street, got into the habit of parking in front of our house. She arrived before us and parked by my shoveled walkway, every day. I had to find another place to park. There were many empty places, but they didn't have cleared paths to the sidewalk. Pap wouldn't allow me to help him across the snowy, icy parkway to the sidewalk, insisting that he was capable of walking by himself over the ice and snow. He insisted, "I have always done this—without your help!"

After our neighbor parked in front of our house for more than a week, I watched for her. "Please don't park in front of our house unless there aren't any other spots available," I requested and explained Pap's problems. She wasn't aware of his deteriorating condition. After that, I was able to park in front of our house. I also asked Sue to take her father's car if she went out so that I could keep my parking place.

One evening when we returned from the Center, Pap went directly upstairs to the bathroom instead of sitting down for coffee at the dining room table. He was in the bathroom for a very long time, over a half hour. What was he doing? His shaving gear was downstairs. When I asked him if he was all right, he said he would be right out. (He wasn't locked in, we had put tape over the door so that it couldn't be locked. He never used the bathroom as a library. He never spent a long time in the bathroom unless he was taking a shower. What was he doing?) When he came downstairs, I went up to look around. The First Aid kit was laying out on the sink, so I put it away.

At dinner I noticed that Pap's thumb was bleeding—it was fresh blood. Even though he protested, complaining that it hurt, I washed the cut and put on a band-aid. I saw a couple of cuts on his thumb while I was washing it and asked how he had cut himself. He didn't remember. He had been sitting on the couch watching television with Tom. I searched the couch for something sharp. Nothing. I couldn't figure out how he had cut himself.

Bill looked in the upstairs bathroom. He didn't find anything. I remembered the half hour Pap had spent upstairs. I went back up to investigate. I didn't see anything either. Then I remembered the First Aid kit. When I opened it, everything was in its place, nothing was open. Questions, questions. How? Where? The questions kept me looking. I noticed that Tom's grooming kit was open. The cover for a disposable razor was laying inside it. I went downstairs and looked in Pap's shirt pocket. I found a single edge, disposable razor without its cover, blade up. Every time Pap put his hand in his pocket, he sliced his thumb. I took possession. Mystery solved.

Tom was tired, he had had a hard day and decided to go to bed early. Entering our bedroom, he discovered that his bed was already occupied. Someone was sleeping in his bed, and that someone was Pap. When Tom woke Pap and told him to go to bed, Pap protested, "I am in bed."

"I know and it's my bed," Tom replied. "You need to go to your bed."

After some discussion, Pap sat up, looked around and agreed that he wasn't in his bed. He got dressed and came downstairs for something to eat before going up to his bed.

Saturday was the designated day at our church for Market Day pickup. When we were out of town, I asked Kathy to retrieve my order. Since I was in town, I decided to take Pap with me to pick up our order, then run a couple of errands. Pap could walk around the stores with me and get some exercise. He would have something to do.

The morning progressed normally. When Pap came downstairs, he was fully dressed and his shoes were tied. He ate breakfast, finished his coffee, put on his coat—no problems. As he was getting into my car, I saw bare ankles. He wasn't wearing socks!

I was already late to pick up our order. I didn't want to go back into the house, get his socks, convince him to put them on, wait for him to put his shoes back on, and leave again. That was too much work. Since it was a cool day, I decided to get our order, and return home. I would run the errands later, after Tom came home. I made a mental note to check that Pap was wearing socks from now on.

Tom and I discussed our options when his company offered more than one type of health insurance. We decided that an HMO would be good for our family because all tests would be covered. We decided to keep our family doctor for fevers, sore throats, and advice.

I was experiencing severe pains in my shoulders, elbows, and wrists. I didn't know what was causing them but I was tired of the pain. I made an appointment to see our HMO doctor.

The day of my appointment, I told Dr. L. that I was falling apart, and described my various pains. She replied that I was evenly balanced since it affected both sides and only my joints. What else was wrong with me? I told her about my father, my job, and my chronic sore throat. I explained that I exercised daily and took vitamins.

During our conversation, she mentioned that our bodies are very selfish; they take care of themselves. While we were talking, I expressed either anger or frustration. Watching me, Dr. L. said I was the cause of some of my pain. How? I had no idea what I had done, so she told me to repeat what I had said. When I did so, I noticed that I was clenching my fists, tensing my arms and shoulders. No wonder they hurt.

Dr. L. gave me medicine to try in case the cause of my pain was arthritis. She suggested that I investigate a nursing home for Pap. She also suggested that I think about working part time or taking a leave of absence. She recommended that I read *The Dance Of Anger,* which was written for women by a psychologist, Harriet G. Lerner. This doctor helped her patients use their anger positively instead of letting it control or destroy them.

I replied that I had set boundaries. I had decided that if Pap couldn't walk or take care of his bathroom needs, I was going to put him in a nursing home. As long as Pap could function, walk, and feed himself, I was going to try to do the best that I could while he lived at home.

Dr. L. suggested I have a talk with my father. I should tell him all the things he had done that had hurt me, then I would have closure. I told her that I couldn't see any value in doing that. What good would it do? Pap was past the point where he could engage in meaningful conversation. He didn't remember the actions that caused me pain. Why should I hurt him? I told her about my beautician's experience. Her father lived with them for a short time while he recovered from a heart attack. While he was in her care, she told him the things he had done that hurt her when she was a child. Later, she felt guilty and regretted telling him. I didn't want to have regret added to the load that I was carrying.

I left her office and stopped at a bookstore to buy the book she had recommended. I knew I needed help with my anger.

Later that week, Tom woke up during the middle of the night to go to the bathroom. As he got out of bed, Pap walked into our bedroom. Tom asked, "Where are you going Pap?"

"I don't know, I was going somewhere," Pap replied.

Tom pointed Pap in the direction of his bed. That's all we needed, Pap wandering around during the night, climbing into a bed that was already occupied.

Christmas was quickly approaching. Terri asked what I thought about celebrating Christmas Eve at their house. If everyone came to her house, they wouldn't have to leave early because of their children. I told her that we would have to leave early because of Pap. We decided to keep the Christmas celebration at our house.

Christmas Eve, I was busy in the kitchen cooking, getting ready for the family gathering that evening. Pap came into the kitchen, opened the back door and let the dogs out. Instead of closing the door, he stood there...holding the door open...watching the dogs outside. Since I was working in the path of the subzero wind as it rushed through the open door, I asked him to close the door. Pap stepped outside and closed the door. I couldn't believe it. Opening the door, I asked, "What in the world are you doing? Come inside, it's cold out there, you don't have a coat on." Pap just stood there. I tried to keep my patience as I explained, "The gates are closed, the dogs will stay in the yard. The dogs have coats on, you don't. The dogs will be okay, I'll leave them in...Come inside...Close the door!"

Pap got mad at me. He was leaving...going home. I told him that he was home, this was his home. "No, it's not!" he replied and proceeded to put on his coat. As he zipped his coat, the zipper got stuck half way up. Coming to his aid, I operated on it. Once the zipper was free, Pap took off his coat and went into the front room to watch television.

Merry Christmas!

The gathering was fun—Pap played with our grandson; our granddaughter led him to the table for supper. Pap enjoyed the extra attention he received and he enjoyed the food. He was with us in body, but his mind was somewhere else. He opened his presents but he seemed to be confused, he didn't know which presents were his or why he was receiving them. He went to bed earlier than usual.

Tom liked the painting of the eagle. He was surprised and asked when I had painted it. I confided that he almost caught me working on it a couple of times, when he returned early while I was fixing something in the painting that bothered me. (Bill had said that the eagle looked like a road-kill…squashed.) I was glad that I had changed the proportions on the bird and got it into the air, since Tom hung the painting in the hallway where he could see it while sitting in the swinging chair.

The day after Christmas the temperature was 58 degrees in my office, but this time there wasn't a note to make me angry. Once again I was the only person there but this time I had dressed for the cold. I wrote a note to my boss, asking him to get an energy conserving thermostat. I tried to use my anger constructively.

Pap seemed to be more confused than normal during the week between Christmas and New Year's. When I picked him up from the Center, he said he couldn't go with me. He was waiting for Kathy or Sue. Another time he told me that he had two daughters—Kathy and someone else. The staff warned that he was very restless, he was wandering a lot.

Friday morning we were ready to go to the Center, so I told Pap to put on his coat. He put on one of his new shirts instead. I explained that the shirt wouldn't do, he needed his coat, it was cold outside. He looked at me and asked, "How would you like a year's vacation?"

"I would love it," I replied. "When can I leave?"

On New Year's Eve, I gave Pap a load of towels to fold. He folded three or four washcloths, two towels and then stopped.

That evening I gave Pap his pill. While I watched, he said, "Down the hatch," and put the pill into his mouth. Then I went into the kitchen to get his supper. When I returned, I noticed that his hand was green. I investigated and discovered that he was holding the pill that I had watched him put in his mouth. I took his dinner away until he took his pill. I explained the benefits of taking his pills, not hiding them.

We received a gift on New Years day—a couple of inches of fresh snow. After I got dressed, I went outside to shovel. I always tried to get it done before Pap saw it, I didn't want to discuss why he shouldn't shovel. When I came inside, Bill told me that Pap came downstairs with his shirt tucked into his underwear, socks and shoes on—but no pants.

Happy New Year!

The following Monday, our office was closed for the holiday but the Center was open. I took Pap to the Center and returned home to enjoy a day without Pap. As I looked at our Nativity set in the dining room window, I noticed a green and yellow shape by the manger. I thought it was one of the miniature lights, but they didn't come in mixed colors. On closer examination I discovered that it was one of Pap's pills. ???

I wanted to do something special with the day. Should I go shopping or stay home? I realized that it was very rare to have the house all to myself and chose to stay home. To further take advantage of my freedom, I turned on the water supply to the upstairs bathtub. (We had shut off the water after the second flood.) I enjoyed my first leisurely, uninterrupted bubble bath since the summer.

The next morning, I heard noises at 5:00 and got up. Pap was fully dressed and going downstairs. When I complained that it was too early to be up and told him that he should still be sleeping, he replied he was hungry. So I made a cheese sandwich for him and laid down on the couch. I was tired and wanted to go back to bed, but I was afraid that he might go for a walk if I left him alone. Pap finally went back to bed at 6:00.

On Saturday, Pap was able to fold the towels.

Sunday, Terri and her children came to our house to visit. Pap enjoyed talking with her and watching the children play. I felt bad, I wanted to spend more time with the kids; they were growing up quickly. But it was impossible with Pap. It didn't matter if we were at their house or ours, Pap always wanted my attention.

After Terri and her children left, I went into the kitchen to prepare supper. Pap made many trips into the kitchen to visit me. I heard his feet as he wore out a path between the kitchen and the front room. At first I thought he was hungry, supper was late. I explained that it would soon be ready to eat. Shuffle…shuffle…shuffle. After he had been back and forth a few times, I realized that the problem wasn't hunger, Pap was confused—he wanted to go home. I assured him that he was home. Shuffle…shuffle…shuffle. Back and forth…Back and forth. "How long have I lived here?" he asked. Over thirty years, I answered. Shuffle…shuffle…shuffle. Pap said, "I'm not a two-timer." ??? I replied that I was his daughter and he lived with my husband and me in our house. Shuffle…shuffle…shuffle. "How long have I known that you're my daughter?" he asked. Fifty years, I answered.

I was trying to keep my patience, but I wasn't succeeding very well. Finally, dinner was ready and we sat down to eat. Before long, Pap went to bed.

Less than an hour passed before Bill came downstairs to get me. We had a problem. Bill didn't have a good sense of smell but he could smell something. Either Pap had diarrhea or ? Bill had noticed that there was brown stuff smeared all over the upstairs bathroom floor. I went up to check on Pap. He was a mess and so was his bed. I took Pap downstairs to the first floor bathroom, washed off his legs and feet and gave him new underwear. I stripped his bed, found more blankets and sheets, remade it, and sent Pap back to bed. I washed the bathroom floor; put the clothing, sheets, pillow cases, blankets, underwear in the washing machine; took a shower, and collapsed in bed. It had been a long day.

The next morning, I overslept. I called Pap at 7:15, then again at 7:45. He was having trouble getting up, getting dressed. Finally, he came downstairs without his teeth. It was after 8:30. We left the house at 9:00. I would be late for work again.

When I picked Pap up that afternoon, he was back to normal.

The next evening Tom and I sat around the dining room table talking before supper. After he finished eating, Tom went into the front room to watch television. While I was clearing the table, Pap told me that my friend was interested in our building. He confided, "Don't ask me how I know, I just do."

I asked Pap which friend was interested in the building. When he pointed to Tom, I explained that Tom was my husband and he owned the building.

"Forget I said anything," Pap replied.

The next evening, I made hamburgers and pea soup for dinner. Pap gave most of his soup to the dogs. He was very restless and made many trips to the bathroom. I asked him if something was wrong. He answered that he had a problem but he had fixed it. What problem? There was water all over the upstairs bathroom floor. ???

The following morning Pap was up at 6:00. This time, Bill got up with him and gave him some cereal. He stayed up with him until I came downstairs. At 7:00 Pap wanted to go back to bed, but I wouldn't let him.

When I dropped Pap off at the Center, he didn't know where to go. He started to sit down in one of the chairs and wait, so I walked him back to the unit.

When I got to work, I called the social worker. I asked her for a list of nursing homes. I felt drained, all of my patience was gone.

The next morning, I gave Pap one of his new shirts to put on. He put it on and took it off, more than five times. He buttoned it, then unbuttoned it. When I asked him what was wrong, he said the shirt wasn't his. I took the new shirt away and gave him one of his old ones. He put on the shirt and left it on. I decided to wash all of his new shirts before he wore them.

While at work, I noticed that one of my checks was missing. I had written a check and forgot to enter it in my checkbook. That night at home, I looked through our paid bills; everything was recorded in the checkbook. I searched my memory. I couldn't remember what the check was for. What had I done? It really bothered me. Before going to bed, I remembered writing a $10 check to the Chicago chapter of the

Alzheimer's Association. I ordered a book: *How to Choose a Nursing Home.*

On Monday, January 16, I left work early to pick Pap up for his appointment with Dr. K., his neurologist. When we entered the office at 1:20, a patient suggested that I talk to the nurse because Dr. K. wasn't taking any more appointments that day. I informed the nurse that the Clinic had made the appointment for Pap. She said not to worry about it, the Clinic appointments were on another sheet of paper. We sat down to wait.

At 4:15, the nurse finally called Pap's name. Dr. K. saw us walking to the examination room and asked where we were going, she wasn't seeing anyone else. The nurse explained that the Clinic had made the appointment and we had waited a long time.

I explained to Dr. K. that I picked Pap up from the Center after he had his lunch. I thought it would be better for him to eat before we came. That was why we arrived after 1:00.

Dr. K suggested that for our next visit, I should call the office to confirm with the nurse that we were coming so we wouldn't have such a long wait.

Pap wasn't able to answer as many of Dr. K's questions, but he was able to carry on a conversation. When he didn't know something, he said that he never worried about it or he never thought about it. It wasn't important to him.

He did know his phone number and his birth date. He was confused about the name of the day, and the month…the season of the year was gone too. He told Dr. K. that the rest of his children were at home. I'm not sure who he thought I was.

I mentioned some of the problems that we were having at home. Pap's trouble getting dressed and his cut finger, to name a few. Dr. K. reminded me that the disease was progressive, but Pap was doing well.

The Cogentin had helped his rigidity. There was still some stiffness but not as much as there had been. I should continue giving him the medicine. Dr. K. decided to increase his dosage of Cognex. She thought it might help with his memory. I was to increase his remaining pills to four a day. When I got the prescription refilled, I would get a stronger dosage.

At the Center on Tuesday, I discussed Pap's visit with Dr. K. with the nurse. I gave her the note for the new prescription and we decided to double the pills.

That evening, my creative writing class started at school. There were 22 students and many had taken the class before. I thought it spoke well of the teacher that students were returning to his class. We took turns telling our reason for taking the course. Everyone had a specific purpose, except me. The others knew what they wanted to write.

The teacher told us what he expected from his class. When he finished I knew that I was drowning. We had to read six books. I still hadn't finished *The Dance Of Anger*. I'd had the book for over a month and enjoyed reading it and thought it helped me. Even though I was on a break from school, I couldn't finish it. I didn't know how I was going to read six books but I felt that it was important for me to take the class.

When I returned home that night, I groused to Bill. "I have to read six books and write a book report on each one as a writer, not a reader. I have to write 40 pages of stuff and turn it in. Where am I going to get the time? I don't have writing experience. The people in my class are already writers, not beginners. Some of them have work published."

Bill advised, "You're a writer too, Mom. You just don't know it yet."

Wednesday came and went. Maybe it was a good day, maybe it wasn't. I didn't make any notes and I don't remember.

Thursday, January 19, Pap came downstairs in his long johns, shirt, shoes, and socks—no pants. I went to fetch pants. Then I gave Pap his first pill and watched while he took it. I noticed that he put something down on the newspaper. After Pap ate, I checked the newspaper and there was his pill. I gave Pap another pill, explaining how important it was that he took it and how it helped his memory. He went to spit in the kitchen sink. There was his second pill. I didn't want to take a chance and give him another.

After I walked Pap back to the unit at the Center, I stopped in the nurse's office to alert her to the trouble I was having giving Pap his pills. She advised me to open the capsule and mix it with a treat—ice cream or applesauce. She told me that intelligence doesn't leave, just the memory. She wished there was a way to test the IQ of the mentally impaired.

10

Hospital

I t started out as a normal Friday, except that I overslept. Pap came downstairs fully dressed, socks on, shoes tied, before 8:00 A.M. We left for the Center on schedule. Pap was more talkative than usual, commenting on all the cars and people on the street.

Before noon, I received a call from the nurse at the Center. Pap had fallen. He was walking down the hall, holding on to his coat, when he fell. Many people were in the area but no one saw him go down. The staff had him remain on the floor until he was checked by the nurse. He mentioned that his back hurt and said, "I shouldn't have done it, the signs were all wrong." The nurse told me that he was able to get up unaided, but she thought I might want to have his doctor examine him.

I called the Clinic and explained the situation. The nurse said they were completely booked for the day but I could bring him in at 10:30 the next morning. Again I explained that he had lost his current memory and would have forgotten the accident by the time I went to get him. He wouldn't know if anything hurt. She said to come at 3:45 that afternoon—she would squeeze him in. I also learned that Pap would have a new doctor, his doctor had rotated again.

When I arrived at the Center, Pap was walking in the hall. A staff member reported that he'd had a shower and had complained about a pain in his left thigh. They had noticed that his balance had been off for the past few days. The nurse told me that he was cool to the touch and had a blue cast to his nose after he fell. Pap had already forgotten his fall. I found Pap's coat laying across the seats of a couple of chairs, hidden from his sight, underneath a table.

As I drove to the Clinic, I told Pap that we weren't going home; we were going to see his doctor because he had fallen at the Center and I wanted to be sure that he was all right. As Pap's loss of memory became more pronounced, he sang more often. The song he was singing that day was a line from the *Battle Hymn Of the Republic*, "Glory, glory hal-lelujah." As we drove to the Clinic, he serenaded me. He didn't remember the complete verse, so he sang a few lines, with enthusiasm, over and over.

We didn't have a long wait at the Clinic. When the doctor came into the examining room, Pap introduced me as his wife. The doctor asked a few questions to test his mental state. Pap knew it was the first month of the year, but didn't know the name of the month. He also didn't know the year, the president, or the mayor of our city. He knew his birth date but not his age.

The nurse had already taken Pap's pulse, temperature and blood pressure. She had checked his weight. This saved the doctor's time and allowed her to concentrate on the reason for the visit. I repeated what I had been told by the staff at the Center. When she listened to Pap's heart, she didn't like what she heard. Looking through his medical records, she couldn't find a history of erratic heart rhythm, so she ordered an EKG. I thought the test would require a trip to the hospital but they had the equipment available in the room. When she received the results, she ordered an ambulance to take Pap to the hospital for further tests. She said it was possible he'd had a slight heart attack.

While we waited for the ambulance, Pap sat on the examining table swinging his legs like a school boy sitting on a fence. When he tired of that, he tapped out a rhythm with his feet on the step that was attached to the table. He broke into song, "Glory, glory, hallelujah" every few minutes, sometimes accompanied by toe tapping. For variety, he leaned forward and tried to touch his toes. I was afraid he would fall off of the table. He was having a good time.

When the ambulance arrived, I explained to the paramedics what happened at the Center. The doctor ordered an I.V. and instructed them to hook him up to a monitor. I mentioned that I was going to stop for a cup of coffee before going to the hospital. One of the paramedics suggested that I get a sandwich too. I was glad he suggested it, it was a good idea.

Pap left for the hospital, and I phoned my family. My husband offered to go with me to the hospital. I answered with a question. "How long could it take to admit Pap to the hospital? I don't think I'll be there that long. Why should we both go?" I knew Tom was tired so I turned down his offer.

I stopped at a fast food restaurant near the clinic and ordered a sandwich with a small coffee. Then I drove across town, eating my sandwich, drinking my coffee while fighting rush-hour traffic. It was now after 6:00 P.M.

When I bought the sandwich I realized I was low on money. I knew they had a pay parking garage at the hospital but I didn't know how long I would be at the hospital or if I would have enough money to retrieve my car. I didn't know how to access cash from my credit card and I didn't have a cash card. After driving around awhile, I finally found parking on the street. I left Pap's coat in the car and walked the two blocks to the hospital.

The ambulance had already arrived. I found Pap in the Emergency Room. A tiny, Oriental nurse was drawing his blood for tests and checking on his monitor hookups. The ambulance had brought his EKG strip, but they did not have a record of the events that lead to his hospital trip. For the third time that day, I related the story as it was told to me. I explained to the nurse that Pap would not know where he was and that he might try to get up and leave. It wasn't until he introduced me as his wife that she believed me.

I spoke to the doctor-in-charge. He wanted to get the results of the blood test and monitor Pap's heart for a while before deciding if he should be admitted. I informed him that Pap had complained that his back hurt. The doctor said they would x-ray his back and phone me at home when they had the results of the tests.

When I heard that Pap might be released, I was surprised. I expected them to keep him, not release him. Wasn't that why we were there? I decided to wait at the hospital. Our house was more than a half-hour drive away, I didn't want to drive home only to turn around and come back to pick up Pap.

As I stood by Pap's bedside, he grew concerned that I was tired and suggested that I should get some rest. Since it was his bedtime, I figured that he was tired and wanted to sleep. I decided it would be better for him if I waited where he couldn't see me.

I called home to tell my family that I would be staying at the hospital. I wanted to wait for the results of the tests to find out if Pap was going to be admitted.

I returned to my car to get Pap's coat, in case he was released, and a book to read. I found a quiet corner of the hospital and settled down to try to finish *The Dance of Anger*. It was almost 8:00 P.M.

Nine o'clock came and went. Pap was taken up to x-ray where he pulled out his I.V. They called a nurse from Emergency to deal with him. He lost a bit of blood from this stunt. The doctor decided not to put the I.V. back in until they got the results from his tests.

I was watching an ice-dancing program on TV in the waiting room when they brought Pap back from x-ray. Before long, the nurse came to ask for my help. She explained that my father had gotten out of bed, was getting dressed and refused to get back into bed. She said she didn't understand—one minute he was resting comfortably, the next he was up. I was not at all surprised that he was being difficult, I had been expecting it. I had been surprised that he was good for so long.

The nurse decided to allow him to keep his shirt on, since his monitor had not shown anything erratic and we were just waiting for the results of the blood test before he was released. But he had to get back into bed.

Before ten, they had the results of the blood tests and the decision was made to admit him. The blood tests showed raised levels of a subset of a cardiac enzyme—Creatine Phosphokinase (CPK) that increases in the blood 3 to 6 hours after a heart attack and returns to normal levels within 48 hours. They wanted to keep him for observation.

Meanwhile, Pap decided that he was getting out of bed. He declared, "They are all crooks and scoundrels. I am leaving."

I answered that they were doctors who were working in his best interest and he had to stay. Then he announced that he had to go to the bathroom and no one was stopping him. I tried to hold him back, to keep him in bed. He only weighed 130 lbs.; I was younger and stronger but he was very determined. It took all my strength and I was losing the battle. Finally a male nurse came to help and walked Pap to the bathroom.

They wanted Pap to take off his shirt so they could put the gown back on and restart the I.V. Pap was upset and was not about to cooperate. The nurse finally went to the doctor for help. He authorized a sedative and restraints to keep Pap in bed, and to keep the I.V. in place. After the sedative took effect, Pap apologized for giving them a hard time.

Sue phoned from home to see if I wanted company. I told her that the doctors had decided to admit Pap and I would be leaving soon. Sue mentioned that I sounded very tired. I agreed with her, I was.

The nurse took pity on me and asked if I wanted a cup of coffee. I was afraid to go back into the waiting room, afraid Pap would act up again. I sat just out of Pap's sight, drank a cup of coffee and waited for Pap to be admitted.

Two doctors from Intensive Care came to talk to the Emergency Room doctor. They asked me to stay to answer some questions after I met with the admitting personnel. I asked if I could answer their questions now rather than wait. They turned down my request; they wanted to wait until Pap was moved to Intensive Care. I warned them that Pap would not know where he was or why he was there. Even if they told him every five minutes, he would forget because his current memory was gone.

I met with the person from Admitting. I was able to give her my father's insurance card and his social security number. I knew he had been a patient in their hospital and answered most of her medical questions.

It was after 10:30 when Pap was taken up to Intensive Care. The nurse from Emergency asked me to wait in the IC waiting room while they got Pap settled. She explained that they would come for me when they were ready. They would also give me Pap's belongings to take home, they didn't have facilities for storage in IC.

The waiting room was very dark; no lights were on. A few people were already curled up under quilts, asleep on couches in the room. In the far corner, a television was on, with the volume turned down low. A few men sat around a table watching it. A man sat in a yoga position on top of a table, talking on the house phone. He offered the phone to me. I declined and used the other one to call home to tell them why I was delayed. Most of my family were in bed—where I wanted to be.

I found an empty chair and sat down to wait. I talked to the man who sat cross legged on the table. His wife had had a massive stroke and he had to make the decision to operate. She was recovering, but it would be slow. I shared the experience that we had with Aunt Ruth, but I didn't go into the details of her recovery. I knew the difficult decisions that he had made.

After waiting in the dark room for over an hour, I got impatient. I went looking for the doctors. I thought they might not know that I was still there.

At midnight, I finally met with the doctors in Intensive Care and the Irish nurse who was going to take care of Pap. I repeated Pap's story for the last time that day. I could see Pap sitting up in bed, peering out at me from under the side railing. He reminded me of a little, lost boy. I didn't like leaving him there, but I knew that he would be in good hands. I told Pap to behave, kissed the top of his head and left.

The nurse said she would bring Pap's clothes out to the waiting room. When she came out with Pap's belongings, she noticed the book that I had just finished. She said she had read The *Dance Of Anger* and found it to be very helpful. I spent some time talking with her about Pap's loss of memory before leaving for the elevator and my car. I was glad the paramedics suggested that I stop for a sandwich. I had been at the hospital for more than six hours.

It had been a long day, made more difficult because Pap could not tell anyone what happened. He just didn't remember.

Saturday morning I called the hospital to see how Pap was doing and talked to the nurse responsible for his care. She said he was resting comfortably, the monitors weren't showing anything abnormal, and he would probably be transferred to a regular floor later in the day. I confided that I didn't know if it would be good for Pap to see me, he might want to go home. She agreed and suggested that I stay home and get some rest myself. Pap was in good hands.

I called Kathy and Terri to tell them what had happened. Kathy was home but no one answered the phone at Terri's house. I shared what I had been told by the nurse with Kathy and suggested that it might be in Pap's best interest if we didn't visit him. He might get upset, and want to go home. I knew that Pap wouldn't be released until he was moved to a regular floor.

Saturday evening, Pap was moved to the fourth floor. I spoke to the nurse on his new floor and learned that he was doing well. I mentioned that I thought it might be best for him if I didn't visit. She understood and said she would keep me informed.

Early Sunday morning, I called the hospital and spoke to Pap's nurse. She said he had spent a comfortable night and that the doctor hadn't been in to see him yet. I asked when Pap would be released. She replied that patients were seldom released on a Sunday. He would probably be released on Monday.

I took advantage of not having Pap at home and wrote about our experience at the hospital for my writing class. I figured our story would be a good way to make a dent in the forty pages that my teacher expected. If I wrote it while it was still fresh in my mind, some of the details wouldn't be forgotten.

After I finished, Sue and I left to meet the rest of my children who were bowling at a local alley. When we went outside, the snow that had started falling in the morning, was coming down in large, heavy flakes—visibility was poor. I was glad that we weren't going very far. Traveling would be slow.

When Sue and I returned home, I learned that a friend of Aunt Ruth's had called to tell us that she was having trouble breathing. I thought about driving over to see her and wondered how I would feel if she passed away. She was an hour away in good weather, but much further today. I decided that because of her condition, I wouldn't feel bad if I didn't see her before she died. Before her stroke, she had been very active, now she couldn't walk, couldn't eat, and had trouble talking. I knew that her passing was for the best. Soon, she would be able to talk, walk, and sing again—she would be in a better place.

Less than an hour passed when Aunt Ruth's friend called to tell me that my aunt had passed away. I was glad that I had made the decision to stay home, I would have been in transit, I wouldn't have seen her.

I called Kathy and Terri to tell them. I didn't have the details but I thought the wake would be on Tuesday, with the funeral on Wednesday.

Monday morning I called the Center to tell them that Pap was in the hospital for observation, and canceled his lunch. I thought he might be released that day but I would keep them informed.

I also talked to the nurse at the Center. I confided that I wasn't getting very much information from the nurses on duty other than he was resting comfortably or he had a good night. I was getting frustrated. I didn't know if I should call the Clinic and talk to Pap's new doctor or ? She suggested that I call the hospital and ask for the house doctor. If I explained who I was, and my involvement in the case, I might get more information.

I thought that was an excellent idea. I called the fourth floor and asked for the house doctor. She wasn't available so I requested that the doctor return my call.

The house doctor, Dr. B., was as happy to talk to me as I was to her. I explained what happened on Friday, as far as I knew. I told her how Cognex helped Pap's memory—it was important that he receive it. I also told her about our visit to Pap's neurologist, on Monday, the week that he fell. Dr. K. had increased Pap's dosage from 3 to 4 pills a day. I thought the increase might have been the cause of his problems. Dr. B. said that she would call Dr. K. to arrange for a consultation. Pap wouldn't be released on Monday, but if he remained stable, he would be released Tuesday.

On Tuesday morning, I talked to Dr. B. about Pap's condition. Since Pap had been confined to bed, I asked if Pap would be able to walk. I told her that I wouldn't be able to take him home if he couldn't walk by himself.

Dr. B. called back and said that she had ordered a Therapist to work with Pap and he was able to walk with assistance. Dr. B. hadn't been aware that I was taking Pap home; she thought he was going back to a nursing home. She seemed to be very concerned.

We spent some time discussing the situation. I explained why my family had not visited Pap while he was in the hospital. I didn't want to upset him, to have him think that he was going home. Dr. B. said that she would sign the release so that I could take him home, but she would note that he was released to a nursing home if that was my decision. She had talked to Dr. K., who would be coming to the hospital after her office hours. Pap would be released after Dr. K. saw him.

I left work about two in the afternoon. I wanted to meet with Dr. K. when she arrived at the hospital.

Pap was in a Catholic hospital. Before I went to his room I stopped in the Chapel and said a prayer that I would make the right decision. I asked for strength.

When I entered my father's room, I saw an old man wearing a mustache, sitting in a chair, with a piece of material in his hands. He ignored everything that was happening in the room as he gathered the material into small folds, like pleats of a fan, over and over, trying to get it right.

Dr. K. was already in the room. She said that my father was unable to follow any of her commands, he had deteriorated since she'd seen him a week ago. He was happy doing his thing. In his mind, he was doing his work and he didn't want to be disturbed. He got upset when anyone talked to him—he was busy. She advised that it would be best if he went to a nursing home. In his condition, home care would be next to impossible for the family.

I agreed with her. I couldn't take care of the man I saw. Dr. K. said she would write the order on his chart.

I wasn't prepared for the person I saw sitting in the chair. My father had been gone for a long time, slowly replaced by a person who kept his gentleness and humor but who had lost his wisdom, his ability to see the answers to a problem. Now that person was gone too. Pap, who had always been clean shaven, was sporting a mustache. It was very hard to see him as a frail, thin, old man, confined to a chair, folding and refolding a gown. I wanted to ask where the man I brought to the hospital was. Where had he gone? Where did they get this substitute? I didn't bring Pap to the hospital to trade him in—I wanted him back.

I could tell that Pap recognized me, but not as his daughter, just as someone he knew.

When I spoke to the nurses, they confided that they were surprised when they heard I was taking him home. They didn't see how I was going to be able to care for him.

Pap had passed the point where I could take care of him. The house doctor had hinted at that fact when I called her Tuesday morning. He had been off his medication, Cognex (for his mind), since Friday. He had been confined to bed; he had forgotten how to walk. He wouldn't be able to learn.

I should have been prepared for this, but I **wasn't**. It was easier to make the decision since the doctors and nurses were advising me that he needed more help than I was able to give. I didn't feel guilty.

I called Tom to tell him that I had made the decision to move Pap to a nursing home. (I had talked to him a few times during the morning, after each talk with the house doctor. He offered to go to the hospital with me. Foolish me, I had refused.) I told him what I had seen, what Dr. K. had said, and what my decision had been. He could tell that I was upset. He said he was leaving work and would soon be at the hospital.

I still had the bottle of tranquilizers in my purse from my summer visit to my family doctor. I took two. I needed to be able to talk, to think rationally; the events of the day weren't allowing me to.

I called Bill at work and told him. He was surprised. We hadn't expected Pap's condition to deteriorate that badly. When he heard that I was on a pay phone, he said he would call his sisters. Sue wasn't home. I didn't want to leave that kind of message on the answering machine. Terri was already upset with me since I had tried to call her on Saturday afternoon and hadn't been able to reach her. She didn't find out about Pap's hospitalization until Sue called her Saturday night. I didn't want that to happen again. I wasn't looking forward to attending Aunt Ruth's wake that evening and telling Pap's brother and sisters either.

I stopped in the Chapel before returning to Pap's room. I said a chaplet; I asked for strength, patience, and guidance. Then I returned to Pap's room to wait for Tom.

Evening Mass was on the television. It was broadcast throughout the hospital as it was celebrated in the chapel. I thought about going back downstairs to attend the Mass in person. But I wanted to talk to the social worker; she would be going home soon and I didn't want to miss her. The nurse had called her office and requested that she stop by Pap's room. I stood in Pap's room, watched a stranger and looked for signs of Pap, watched Mass on TV, and waited for Tom and the social worker.

When Tom saw Pap, he agreed with my decision. Pap was gone. He was replaced by a thin, frail man sporting a ridiculous mustache. Pap didn't recognize Tom either.

We went down to the social worker's office. Two women were in the room, getting ready to leave. After we explained the situation that we were facing, one recommended a nursing home close to our house that was small and had a feeling of home. She said it didn't feel like a nursing home, but since it was so small, she didn't know if they would have an opening. They also gave us a listing of other nursing homes in our area that they worked with and suggested we visit a few before making our decision. After we chose a nursing home, we should call them and they would handle the arrangements.

When we got home, I called the small nursing home that had been recommended. I was able to arrange a visit for that evening. I planned to visit the home and then go to the wake. Then I called another that was close by to arrange a visit for Wednesday after the funeral.

Tom and I visited the nursing home after supper. I liked the place. The social worker was right, it didn't feel like a nursing home. The person we spoke to was understanding. She told us that they had a variety of residents ranging in age from their middle thirties to 97. One person had multiple sclerosis, another diabetes; many of the residents were not able to live alone. They also had some with mental dementia. The door from the first floor day room opened on a large, fenced-in back yard where those with diminished mental capacity could visit freely. Every floor had its own day room, complete with either a parakeet or a canary for the enjoyment of the residents. We were in luck. They had space for him in a two-bed room on the first floor. We met the other occupant and he seemed nice.

I wanted to visit at least one more place before making a decision but the nursing home felt right. When we walked in, the residents weren't lined up in wheel chairs watching the door open and close.

The residents all seemed to be involved somewhere, in their rooms or in the big day room. I felt comfortable with the place.

After visiting the nursing home, we drove to the funeral parlor where I saw the rest of my family. I gathered hugs from all and shared my experiences of the day. Kathy mentioned that I seemed to be holding up well. Tom was surprised when he heard me say that I had taken tranquilizers. (I hadn't thought to tell him and he didn't ask.) I had to tell my father's sisters and brother how my father's condition had deteriorated. I had to explain that I was moving Pap to a nursing home. They hadn't seen him in months. They found it hard to understand.

Wednesday morning, I called the Center to tell them that Pap would not be returning. I explained that Pap's condition had deteriorated in the hospital…he forgot how to walk.

I was told that everyone liked him and he would be missed. The nurse said that it must be time. I agreed. I had been close to putting him in a home two weeks before. This way, I didn't have the guilt. Nor did anyone at the Center have to tell us that he could no longer attend. The decision was taken out of our hands.

I called work. They were surprised to hear from me—they knew I was taking the day off for my aunt's funeral. I shared the news of my father's decline and asked that they tell my boss that I had to find a nursing home for my father. I didn't know how long I would be off from work but my boss could call me if he had any questions.

My aunt's funeral service was held in the chapel of the retirement home and was well attended. My aunt and uncle belonged to a Bible church. Their minister conducted the service, assisted by the chaplain of the home and church members who had visited Aunt Ruth regularly. Each gave a eulogy or offered words of comfort to the family. The minister's wife sang Aunt Ruth's favorite songs—she had a beautiful voice.

I knew that I would miss my aunt, but I would miss the person she had been. That person had left us a few years before, and now her body was just catching up. I was glad that her suffering had ended.

After the service, we debated about going to the cemetery. We had an appointment at 1:00 to visit the next nursing home, but we still had time.

It was a very sunny day, but it took longer to get to the cemetery than we expected. Instead of taking the expressway, we wound our way slowly through the suburban streets. At the cemetery, the chapel wasn't heated. The sun didn't enter to warm the stone walls or floor, even the wooden benches held the cold and transferred it when a person sat down. Although a short service was held, I was glad when it was over. I wanted to be back out in the sunshine.

My uncle wanted us to join him for refreshments at the church. I expressed our regret and explained that we had a nursing home visit to make but we would be with him in spirit. He was hurt and replied, "A person needs more than spirit to live."

Terri and her husband decided to visit Pap at the hospital instead of attending the lunch. I knew my uncle would have many people from their church to comfort him, along with my father's brother and sisters. I didn't feel guilty skipping the luncheon and didn't want my children to feel guilty either.

After the funeral, we visited the second nursing home. I wanted to leave as soon as we walked through the door. It felt cold, the walls were sterile white. I decided, in order to be fair, we had to take the tour. We had to visit more than one place before making our decision. The receptionist gave us a folder to read while we waited. The folder was well put together—it described their services and answered important questions.

If this had been the first home I was visiting, I might have liked it. I got the feeling from our tour that they were concerned about their patients' welfare. The residents were all senior citizens and it looked and felt like a regular nursing home or hospital. The patients were sitting in wheel chairs watching the elevator; they were assigned to various floors according to their abilities and were transferred to another floor if their condition improved or regressed. I decided on the smaller home and Tom agreed.

I called the hospital, then the first nursing home to tell them our decision. It was too late to move Pap that day. I talked to the house doctor who told me Pap had seemed more depressed that morning. She said she had the feeling that he had been crying. I was worried about Terri's visit. I knew seeing Pap would be a shock for her, I hoped that her visit had gone well.

I needn't have worried. They must have started Pap back on Cognex that morning because Terri said that she stayed an hour and had a nice visit.

Here is Terri's story:

The Day at the Hospital

Pap's sister had passed away. We had spent the day at her funeral and the cemetery. When we were leaving the cemetery Pap's brother, Alvin, came up to me. I said goodbye and so did he. He also added that the next time he would see me would be at Pap's funeral.

Nice. Real nice.

My husband and I decided, after that was said, not to go to the lunch with everyone else but to go to lunch on our own and then go see Pap at the hospital.

He didn't look so good. He was skinny, bruised, and confused. But it was wonderful to see him. I don't think he knew who I was but he also didn't care. I could sit and talk to him all I wanted. Maybe he was lonely, or maybe he recognized me as someone he knew, but just didn't know who that was.

We sat and talked for a while, not about anything really, and I asked him if there was anything he needed. All he needed was a paper. I sent my husband to look for one. I stayed with Pap and combed his hair. He actually liked that. I didn't stay for long, it was kind of hard for me to see him that way.

11

Nursing Home

When I phoned the director of the nursing home on Wednesday to tell her that we had decided that her home was right for Pap, she requested certain documents in order to apply for public aid in Pap's behalf. She asked to see his Will, title to his car, deed to his house and cemetery plot, Social Security card, insurance policies, stock certificates, savings bonds, bank book, Social Security notice, and the monthly statement on his checking account for the past two years—proof of his assets and income.

I didn't go to work Thursday, instead I stayed home and searched for the papers the director had asked for. I didn't find all of them. Pap no longer owned a car or a house, he didn't have any stock certificates or savings bonds. I had saved most of his checking account statements and canceled checks. I couldn't find Pap's Social Security Card, life insurance policy, or the notice that he had just received from Social Security stating the amount of his monthly check. Several months before, we had found the deed for the cemetery. His Will was obsolete—it assigned my guardianship to a deceased uncle.

I found other things though. I knew the fire that killed my mother and brother was in January, but I didn't know the date. It upset my father too much to talk about it, so I didn't ask. I discovered that the fire was on January 19; the anniversary of my mother's death was the day before Pap fell. I found a letter that my father had written to his girlfriend. He talked about her fingers dancing before him, not wearing any rings when they had breakfast together. I found pieces of Snickers—in the chest by his bed, on top of his work table, downstairs in the three drawer chest in the little room. I decided that instead of driving myself crazy searching for the missing papers, I would wait a few days to see if they turned up.

Kathy phoned to tell me that Terri was hurt that I wasn't driving Pap to the nursing home. Terri thought I should pick Pap up from the hospital and take him to the nursing home, so he wouldn't feel abandoned. When I mentioned this to Tom, he called Terri to explain that I was meeting Pap at the nursing home. Then Terri became upset with me when I didn't know when Pap was leaving the hospital. I told her that I was going to wait for Pap to be settled at the nursing home and then I would visit him. I didn't know if she knew this, but I was having a hard time dealing with the situation.

What fun!

When I called the nursing home to inquire if Pap had arrived, I asked the person in charge what I should bring for Pap. He suggested I pack a suitcase as if Pap was going on a two-week vacation. We could also bring a television, radio, pictures, favorite objects—things that would make Pap feel more at home.

It hadn't occurred to me that I would need to take Pap's things to the nursing home. I started packing a suitcase. I found his robe and slippers; I packed a pair of pajama's that he had never worn. I put in more than a dozen handkerchiefs—so he wouldn't run out. I found a statue of the Blessed Virgin that Pap used as a night light. I took out the wires and packed the statue. I hunted for his harmonica. I found some photographs to take that I thought Pap might like. Packing gave me something to do. It kept my mind and hands busy.

The "WHAT IF'S" were raising their ugly heads to torture me. WHAT IF I hadn't taken Pap to see Dr. K.? WHAT IF his medicine hadn't been increased? WHAT IF they weren't able to see him at the Clinic on Friday? WHAT IF we visited him at the hospital? WHAT IF? WHAT IF?

I silenced them as best I could. I reminded myself that when you ask God for help, you don't give Him directions, you trust in Him. I reminded myself that I had been very close to looking for a nursing home for Pap. I reminded myself that I hadn't been happy when I couldn't devote time to playing with my grandchildren because Pap continually wanted my attention. I reminded myself that Pap was starting to cross the boundaries that I had set. I told myself in a very stern, loud voice that his moving to a nursing home was for the best. It was time. I didn't have to make the decision to put him in the home. Since the doctors and nurses told me I could no longer care for him, I didn't feel guilty. I told the "WHAT IF'S" to go away.

The day continued to slowly slip away. Pap wasn't moved to the nursing home until late in the afternoon. Since it was so late, Tom and I decided to have supper before going to see him. We wanted to give Pap time to get settled in.

We visited Pap around 6:00 that evening. We wanted to arrive before he was too tired. He had finished dinner and was laying in his bed and seemed to be content except he complained about the chest restraint that he was wearing. I sympathized with him but explained that it was for his safety. He was having a hard time talking to us. He had lost so much weight while in the hospital that his teeth didn't fit properly and kept slipping around in his mouth. We had trouble understanding him.

I put the statue of Our Lady and his harmonica on the bedside table where he could see them. I took out his robe and slippers before putting the suitcase containing his clothes in the closet. There wasn't enough shelf space for the framed photo's. We needed pictures that could be taped to the walls.

Pap didn't really know who we were. But when Tom told him that he was his son-in-law, a little later Pap called him by his name. We could tell that Pap was tired so we only stayed thirty minutes. He had had a long day and wanted and needed some sleep. We wished him a good night and said we would see him soon.

Before leaving, I stopped at the nurse's station and gave the nurse in charge the rest of Pap's medicine and explained his dosage. She said they had received Pap's prescription from the doctor at the hospital.

I told her that I had brought Pap's clothes but I didn't know where to put them, so I put the full suitcase in the closet. The nurse asked if Pap's name was on his clothes. When I replied that I hadn't thought of it, she said that she would unpack his suitcase and put his name on his clothes.

The nurse asked me to sign a paper agreeing to the chest restraint. It was a necessary precaution—Pap wouldn't be able to get out of bed unaided and hurt himself. They were going to get him up the next day.

Thursday night, Tom suggested I stay home from work on Friday. I was undecided until I had chills all night and once again the decision was made for me. I wanted to bring Pap's financial papers to the nursing home but I wasn't going to the home while I was sick. They would have to wait until I felt better.

Bill went to see Pap on Friday. Even though I had tried to forewarn him that the Pap we knew was gone, Bill wasn't prepared for the person that he visited. After the visit, he knew that Pap wouldn't be coming home to live again. If he improved, a short visit might be possible, but we would be able to take Pap's bed down from the attic. He wouldn't need it anymore.

I decided that I wouldn't visit Pap on weekends. I would leave those days for my children. During the week, they couldn't visit Pap until evening and then he was too tired to enjoy anyone's company.

Saturday, Terri and her husband took their children to visit Pap. Terri noticed a flyer on the bulletin board inviting the residents to join together each week to say the rosary and attend Mass. When Terri told the nurse that Pap was Catholic, the nurse said that she would see that Pap went to the rosary and the Mass. Here is Terri's story of the visit:

The Nursing Home

The nursing home was a nice place. Everyone was friendly. I visited Pap the first time to see where he was and how he was settling in. He was in a wheelchair because he could no longer walk. It's kind of strange to see someone who couldn't sit still for long stuck in a chair for who knows how long. But he was doing okay, even though he was sitting in the chair, he was walking it around himself, just moving his feet and going where he wanted to go.

We put some pictures up in his room. I noticed that Pap didn't have a handkerchief. He kept using his sleeve to wipe his eyes and nose. I gave him mine. After that, he wiped his eyes and put the handkerchief in his pocket. He did that a couple of times. The last time, after wiping his eyes, the zipper on his pants was open and he stuck the handkerchief in there. I told him that it didn't belong there. He should put it in his pocket. He answered, "I'd like to see someone take it."

Then we went for a tour with Pap leading the way in his wheelchair. I'm still not sure if he knew exactly who I was or if he was just being polite. We were in the hallway and there was a nice little nurse walking up the hall. Pap started to ask her a question and then started to mumble so she bent down and got real close to him to see what he said. He mumbled again. The nurse patted him on the shoulder, gave up on what he was saying and started to ask him questions instead. Who's this with you? How are you today? What cute great grandchildren you have. Well, anyway you get the idea. When she left, Pap just kind of smiled with a twinkle in his eye that he got the nurse to bend down over him. He enjoyed his view. He told me, "I wasn't saying anything." I thought he would be okay in his new home.

We went back to his room. He played his harmonica for us and then we decided to leave. He asked for some help to the hallway and from there he was on his way. Pushing himself back to the day room, he waved at everyone that he passed.

Sunday, we celebrated our grandson's first birthday. It was fun to put sorrow and pain aside for a little while, and just enjoy the day. Benjamin loves balloons and his parents gave him a big bunch of bright purple and yellow balloons filled with helium. He had so many in his hand that I thought he would fly away. We let most of the balloons rise to the ceiling and gave him one to play with at a time. Ben received many presents and ate a big piece of cake all by himself, but he enjoyed the balloons the best.

On Monday, I drove to the Center before going to work. I wanted to pick up Pap's clothes and sports bag. It was hard to make the drive without Pap. It was very sad to see everyone at the Center and know that I wouldn't see them everyday, anymore. I had always exchanged thoughts with many of the staff: weather and driving conditions with the bus drivers; diet, recipes, Pap,—life—with the staff. I would miss seeing them and talking with them, they had become friends.

The staff from the unit were already gathered in a circle for their morning meeting. They always got together before the buses arrived to plan the day, talk about their client's needs, or problems, and discuss better ways of interacting.

Everyone told me how sorry they were to hear of my father's decline, they already missed him. He was well liked.

I assured them that I felt that it was time for Pap to move on. We had all done the best we could for him. Because of their help and attention—the mental stimulation that they provided—he had lived with us longer. I believed that he was meant to be at the nursing home we chose and I was comfortable with the place. I mentioned that I didn't feel guilty about his going; now a staff member wouldn't have to tell us they were sorry, but Pap couldn't attend the Center anymore, he needed more care than they could provide, we had to investigate other options. The person who was in charge of making those hard phone calls thanked me for the thought.

As I left the Center with Pap's things in his bag, tears streamed down my face. They didn't stop until I parked the car in front of my office. I felt completely drained.

As usual, it was cold in the office, it always took longer on Monday to reach a comfortable temperature. I chatted with my fellow workers for awhile before I sat down at my desk and tried to catch up.

I decided that I would continue to leave work at the same time I left to pick Pap up. Instead of going to the Center, I would go to the nursing home to visit him. It would be late afternoon and he might still be alert.

Monday afternoon I went to see Pap by myself. I found him sitting in a wheelchair in the day room. He recognized me, not necessarily as his daughter, but as a friendly face that he knew. (Afternoons became my regular time to visit and I usually stayed a half hour.) It is hard to have a conversation with someone who has trouble thinking. Now it was even harder because I had trouble understanding what Pap said. I didn't know if it was because my cold affected my hearing, because the room was noisy, or because he was mumbling. He had lost weight, his teeth didn't fit; they kept slipping down and getting in the way of his speech. I gave Pap a piece of hard candy and tried to do most of the talking. I told him about Benjamin's birthday party and described how he had played with the balloons. I stayed until the noises in the hall indicated dinner would soon be served; it was my signal to leave.

Before I left the home, I looked for the director and gave her Pap's financial papers. I had his bank statements for most of the past two years and his saving book. I hadn't been able to find Pap's insurance policy but I had a receipt with his policy number. Nor had I been able to find out the value from the insurance company, but the director said that she would be able to get it. After she looked through the papers I brought, she said that she wouldn't need anything else. The rest of the papers were sufficient to prove his income and assets. She would be able to apply for public aid on his behalf.

The director explained that Pap had been assigned a doctor who was a member of his medical plan and Pap would receive monthly examinations. If I stopped at the nurses station, I could get the doctor's name, address, and phone number.

The director said she was notifying Social Security but it would take a few months before the check came directly to the home. Until that time, I should transfer the money after it was deposited in Pap's account. Thirty dollars from Pap's check would go into a savings account to pay for laundry, sundry items, and the barbershop. She asked if I wanted to do Pap's laundry myself or have the nursing home do it. I decided not to do Pap's laundry.

I stopped at the nurses' station and obtained the name and phone number of Pap's new doctor. While I was standing there, I saw our family doctor's name on the listing. I decided to talk to our doctor, to see if he would take care of my father. He wasn't a stranger, I knew him.

I felt better after dropping off the paperwork; it was one less thing that I needed to do. It was nice to come home from work...sit down...do nothing. I didn't have to worry about getting Pap's coffee, fixing something for him to eat right away, or wonder what he was doing.

Tuesday night, Tom went to see Pap. He said that he had a nice, short visit. Pap was tired so he didn't stay long.

I met my former co-workers for dinner. I told them about my father's hospitalization and his transfer to a nursing home, and about my aunt's death. As we were leaving the restaurant, an owl landed in the snow.

Since I had a writing class on Wednesday, Sue and her boyfriend visited Pap. It was a good visit but Pap was confused, he wasn't sure who they were and they had trouble understanding him. They arrived while he was eating and he wanted to share his supper with them. He was tired, so they cut their visit short.

Thursday afternoon, I visited Pap. I went to Pap's room but he wasn't there. I chatted with his roommate for a few minutes before searching for Pap. His roommate told me they had started the day by singing "Glory, Glory, Hallelujah."

I found Pap in the day room. He smiled when he saw me walking up to him. He looked better. He wasn't as thin and his funny mustache was gone. He wasn't wearing his teeth so I could understand some of the things he said and we had a nice visit. As I was leaving, I told the nurse that Pap looked better. She said that he was eating more. They had discovered that he was a slow eater so they were giving him more time to eat.

Arriving home, I found a message to call the social worker at the nursing home. When I reached her, I mentioned I had just returned from visiting my father. She told me they wanted to move Pap to a private room. Did I have any objections? I asked why, since he seemed to be doing so well. She replied that the original occupant of the room was being released from the hospital. The two men were used to each other, so they were going to move him back into his old room. They noticed that Pap kept unbuttoning his shirt so they were going to move him closer to the nurses' station so the nurses could keep an eye on him. I didn't know what to say. I told her to do what she thought was best but I emphasized that Pap was doing well with his roommate, adding that I wasn't sure that being in a room by himself would be good for him.

The social worker asked me to stop in her office the next time I visited Pap because she had some papers for me to sign. I told her about the papers I had just brought to the home but she said that her papers were different.

I went upstairs to our bedroom and got another surprise. One of our dogs had gone to the bathroom on my side of the bed—a big, brown, smelly pile rested there. Neither of our dogs had accidents in the house, let alone on our bed.

Pap always said good-bye to each of our dogs in the morning as we were leaving, told them to be good, and gave each one of them a scratch. Pap shared his food with them at night.

I concluded that our male dog was expressing his feelings. He woke me up at night when Pap was roaming. I took Pap away and I didn't bring him back. How do you explain to a dog that it isn't your fault?

I told my family about Pap's move to a private room and that I was concerned that he wouldn't have a roommate. I thought we should get him a television for company. I didn't know if we needed to buy a color set or if a black and white would do. The matter was settled when Bill offered to donate his old black and white television.

By Friday, Pap had already been moved to his new room, which was directly across from the nurses' station. When I arrived, he was alone in his room, sitting in his wheelchair and he wanted to go to bed. He wanted to take off his shoes and socks. I explained that it was almost time for dinner, he needed to stay in his chair. I told him to leave his shoes and socks on, his feet would get cold. Once again, I was trying to convince him to do things. I felt drained.

I checked to see if his pictures, statue, harmonica, and clothes had been moved. They forgot to take a few of his things, so I went back to his old room and retrieved them. The old roommate was already back in bed, he didn't appear to be well.

As I was leaving the home for the evening, I stopped to see the social worker, but she wasn't in her office.

Terri suggested that since Pap was in a nursing home, I could get to know him as a friend. I didn't have to be his caregiver anymore. It was a good idea but the visits were becoming more difficult. It was hard to find things to talk about, hard to hear, and hard to understand what he was saying. I kept a happy face in my pocket and put a smile on as I entered the nursing home.

Members of my family went to see Pap when they had time. It was hard emotionally to see his decline. The happenings of those visits were best forgotten. We wanted to remember the man Pap had been, not the ghost he had become. Terri expressed it best when she said: "I promised I'd go and see him again and I did. During the few visits I made I could see him slowly deteriorating."

Monday, when I visited Pap, I noticed that he was getting a cold. Visiting with him was even harder because his voice was softer, more muffled. His head hung down, his chin rested on his chest, as if it were too heavy to keep up. I only stayed a short time, then tracked down the social worker. I mentioned that Pap didn't seem to be doing as well as he had when he had a roommate. She agreed and said they would try to find a two-bed room.

She had papers for me to sign, authorizations for many things including emergency care. I signed a paper requesting that Pap not be resuscitated. I didn't want him placed on life support. When it was his time, let him go, with dignity.

I cried all the way home. Tough decisions. I had been thinking about visiting a funeral home to inquire about final arrangements but I kept putting it off.

On Tuesday, I had chills at work. I informed my boss that I didn't feel well and I was going home and if I didn't feel better on Wednesday, I was taking the rest of the week off. I wasn't going to come to work for one day. He wasn't happy with the news. (He still lowered the thermostat every evening to save money. I was the first one in the office on Friday and the office was always very cold.)

I reminded him that I would be the only one in the office the next week, everyone else would be out of town. I would be there to man the ship but I wanted to be feeling better.

I didn't go to work on Wednesday and spent the day in bed, which was unusual for me. I was glad that Pap wasn't home so that I could sleep the day away.

I was feeling better Thursday, but I stayed home from work anyway. I couldn't see any reason to go to work to freeze for a day.

During the afternoon I decided to visit Pap. Before going to the home, I stopped at the store to get a plant to brighten up Pap's room. I found a beautiful azalea plant. It was so full of blooms, it didn't look real.

Pap was in a wheelchair in his room. The nurse explained that he kept taking his shirt off. They were keeping him in his room to keep a better eye on him. I was glad we had brought a television to keep him company. I put the plant next to the television where Pap could see it. Once again our visit was short, I wasn't feeling well and neither was he.

Friday was a beautiful day. Bill went with me to visit Pap. He said Pap always seemed to do better when I was there. I didn't agree. I didn't think Pap was doing well.

Pap was very congested from his cold. I gave him a tissue, and told him to blow his nose. After we talked for a while, he seemed to be more alert. He kept singing, "You are so beautiful to me," over…and over. As we left, he said, "I love you. Take care of yourself."

Just a small glimmer of the man we knew, but only for an instant, and then he was gone.

I received a phone call from the nurse at the nursing home on Saturday. Pap had fallen out of his wheelchair even though he was restrained. He seemed to be unhurt but they called his doctor to examine him anyway. They put him in bed and they were ordering a Gerry chair. It was like a chaise lounge, he wouldn't be able to slide out of it.

On Saturday, Tom invited me to go to the camper. I wanted to go but decided to take care of my cold instead. So he went and I stayed home.

Sunday was very cold, the temperature was below zero. I attended Mass in the morning, stopped for coffee, and then proceeded to the nursing home to see Pap. I arrived as they were pushing the lunch carts down the hall.

As I walked through the vestibule doors, I could see directly into my father's room…Pap's legs lifted into the air. What in the world? Then I realized he was exercising while he lay in bed. As I watched from the doorway, he did a few knee bends before pedaling a bicycle in the air. Entering his room, I took the opportunity to tease, asked if he was getting in shape and advised him to watch out because all of the girls would soon be chasing him. We sang a couple of his favorite songs: "Be Not Afraid", and "Peace is Flowing Like a River." When his lunch arrived, I left.

Since I was already out, I decided to go shopping in an enclosed mall. It was Tom's birthday and I wanted to pick up something for him. It was nice to be able to take my time shopping, not to worry about going home. I didn't find what I was looking for, so I drove to another shopping center.

My first stop was a craft store. A little brown bear was sitting on a shelf and he called my name. He said that he wanted to keep my father company. I bought him to take with me the next time I visited Pap.

After I found Tom's present, I headed home. As I drove down one of the main streets toward our house, I thought I recognized the car ahead of me. It looked like Tom's car, but he was in the country, 100 miles from Chicago. When I got closer, I recognized Tom's license plate and realized that he had come home early. I was surprised—after all of our years of marriage, he still drew me like a magnet.

The office was very cold on Monday when I arrived at work. My fellow workers had forgotten to turn up the thermostat. When I sat down at my desk, I found a note from my boss, telling me about a mistake that I had made. The note reminded me to be more careful; my mistakes were undermining the credibility of the company. He was right, I had made a mistake. I realized I was making more mistakes lately. Then I found a note from our new office manager. She wanted me to write down the steps of some of my jobs for a procedure manual and provided the forms.

I called Tom. I told him about the notes and that I thought I should write a letter of resignation. Did he mind? "Go for it," he said. "I've wanted you to quit for a long time…you're not happy there…I'm glad that you are finally going to do it. We'll make it somehow."

I wrote a letter giving two weeks notice and put it on my boss's desk. He would get it Thursday when he returned to the office. I returned the nice, blank forms to our office manager with a note that we would do them together. She would get them when she returned to the office later in the week.

I packed my personal belongings to take home. I wasn't mad, but enough was enough. I realized how tired I was. I was tired of the job, tired of freezing, tired of being sick—just tired. Then I started to clear up the mess that was my desk.

When I left work on Monday afternoon, I drove to the nursing home. I gave Pap the little teddy bear and told him that the bear would keep him company when the rest of us weren't there.

Pap was reclining in the Gerry chair, which looked quite comfortable. We sang a couple of songs: "Peace is Flowing like a River", "I Ain't Got No Bananas". I didn't stay long. I wasn't feeling good and neither was he. I didn't want him to catch what I had. I tried to stay far enough away so I could keep my germs to myself. When I left, Pap told me, "I love you, take care of yourself."

On Tuesday, I felt so rotten I decided to go see our family doctor instead of visiting Pap. I was tired of the sore throat, the congestion. I was tired of being sick. The nurse said that the low side of my blood pressure was up eight points and asked if I was tired.

After his examination, my doctor said that there were so many viruses going around, he wasn't sure which one I had. He prescribed some medicine he thought would help.

While I was there, I told Dr. T. that Pap was at the small nursing home where he visited some of his patients. He was aware of Pap's mental dementia from all the times we had talked. I mentioned that Pap had fallen out of his wheelchair and now was in a Gerry chair. Then I asked if he would take Pap on as a patient. Dr. T. agreed but said I would need to inform the nursing home before he was able to see him.

I didn't go to the nursing home on Wednesday. I felt rotten. I went to work and then headed straight home to rest. I couldn't stop coughing and I made a hot toddy and went to bed.

Thursday wasn't much better but I went to work anyway. I wanted to be there when my boss found my letter. By midmorning, I knew he had found it, but he didn't say anything.

Before noon, I received a call from the nursing home. Pap wasn't doing very well. He wasn't swallowing his medicine, instead he was holding it in his cheeks like a chipmunk. His doctor's instructions were to keep him comfortable and they were putting him on oxygen. I told the nurse that the reason I hadn't been there was because of the congestion I had. I didn't want to share it with the residents of the home.

Tears spilled from my eyes. I knew Pap wouldn't be with us much longer. I called Tom and then called my children. I told all of them that Pap could recover, but I didn't think that he would. If they wanted to see him, they should do so soon. I wanted to see him, but I knew that with my cough it wouldn't be a good thing to do. I was with him in spirit. I asked My Friend to help Pap, not to let him suffer.

A fellow worker asked my boss if he found my letter of resignation. He said that he had but he wasn't going to talk to me because he could see that I was upset about Pap.

I still didn't feel well on Friday. I didn't want to go into a cold office but I didn't want the talk with my boss hanging over my head all weekend. We talked about many things during the day, but we didn't discuss that I was leaving. It was a normal day.

For this I went to work in a cold office—to spend a normal day? I was available, and if my boss didn't want to talk about my letter, that wasn't my fault.

I called the nursing home to see how Pap was doing. His doctor had been in to see him. He had ordered suction, to help him breathe better. They were trying to keep him comfortable.

Terri knew I wasn't feeling well. She called to tell me that she would visit Pap that evening. I told her what the nurse said, so she would be prepared.

Terri stopped by our house after she left the nursing home. She said Pap had slept most of the time she was there but she was glad she went.

I knew she was upset. I told her sleep was healing, it was good that he was sleeping. Here is what she told me:

My Last Visit

Pap wasn't doing well. He had been put on oxygen. I got a call from the family saying if I wanted to see him I'd better do it soon. I was already planning to go Sunday with the children but something about the call made me decide I should go now. I called a friend for a ride and went.

When we arrived, visiting hours were almost over but we went in anyway. Anytime was better than none. Pap was asleep and didn't look so good. I tried to wake him so he would know that I was there but he didn't want to wake up. I sat with him for a while just watching him.

Then I decided to sing to him, the songs we sang on our car ride quite a while ago: "Be Not Afraid", "Peace is Flowing Like a River", and "Amazing Grace." They were his favorites. Then I talked to him, telling him how stubborn he was being by not waking up. I even tried tickling his toes to wake him. Twice he woke up and looked into the distance with the most peaceful eyes. He tried to say something to me but it was just mumbles. At least in my mind he knew I was there and he was not alone. I decided I was going to say my goodbyes so that if something did happen I would have at least had a conclusion with him but I also told him I expected him to be feeling better when I returned with his great-grandchildren on Sunday.

I wrote him a little letter before I left so the nurses could read it to him when he woke up and I left with a heavy heart.

We drove a couple blocks away and pulled over. I knew it was the last time I was ever going to see him alive and I cried. I tried to tell myself that I would see him Sunday.

Saturday morning, I received a call from the nursing home. They were moving Pap again. I asked, "Why?" They replied that he was in a private room, and the money from Social Security didn't pay for a private room. I wanted to say: "But he is dying, leave him die in peace," but I didn't. I asked what the room number was. It was the original room that he was in when he first came to the home. Maybe they didn't want him to be alone when he died.

I still didn't feel well, I was taking medication, but it didn't seem to be helping. I didn't know if I was getting worse, but I knew I wasn't getting better. I debated about going to the home to visit Pap. If he was sleeping, he wouldn't know I was there. I didn't want to spread the germs of whatever I had in that environment. I was younger, possibly stronger, but whatever I had made me feel very old and very weak. The people at the home were already in a weakened state, I didn't want to share my germs. I asked myself the big question. Would I feel guilty if Pap died without my being there, if I didn't see him before he died? After much soul searching, I realized that I wouldn't.

I talked to the nurse many times that Saturday. Pap wasn't doing well. A nurse called around 9:00 P.M.—Pap was lethargic, he didn't cough when she used suction on him. I asked if he would know that I was there. She said no, he was too lethargic. I replied that if he didn't know that I was there, I wasn't going to come. I asked her to call the priest for Last Rites. She called back after 10:00. She had to call four parishes before she found a priest available, but he was on his way. I thanked her for going through the extra effort for us. Tom told Sue and Bill, then phoned Kathy and Terri. He said that if Pap passed away during the night, we wouldn't call them until the morning.

I went downstairs to the kitchen. Tears streaming down my face, I talked with my Friend. I knew that many people recovered when they received the Sacrament of the Sick, as Last Rites was now called. I asked myself, recover to what? To sit in a wheelchair, not to be able to walk, or think, or do things, or enjoy life. When Pap was living at home and going to the Center, he still enjoyed life. It was restricted, diminished, but he was able to visit with people, joke, enjoy eating, and get into trouble. I felt it would be much better for Pap if he left us for a better place. I said a chaplet for strength and for a gentle passing for Pap.

The nurse called at 12:50 on Sunday morning, Pap had passed away. Did we want to come? I told her that since we hadn't seen him while he was alive, I didn't feel that it was necessary to see him after he left.

I said a prayer of thanksgiving and tried to sleep.

12

Service

As I finished writing the last chapter, I thought, I can stop now. I was writing about Pap's life, our interaction with him, and now it had ended. But it hadn't ended and neither has my writing.

When I woke up early Sunday morning, I phoned the nursing home to find out what I needed to do. Tom wanted to call Kathy and Terri, but it was too early to wake them, so I suggested we wait until 9:00. After we called our children, I called Aunt Connie. First I asked her to notify the rest of the family, then I shared my idea. "If none of my children object, we are planning to have Pap cremated. I'm also thinking of having a closed casket or just a memorial table for the wake. Before I decide, I want to see what my kids think about it. If they agree, I'll proceed. But if anyone is uncomfortable with the idea, we will have an open casket at the wake."

"I don't want everyone standing there, looking at Pap, and telling us and each other how thin he was, how it doesn't look like him. I want him to be remembered as he was. I know that Aunt Edna and Uncle Alvin have a long way to travel. When you talk to them, please tell them what I'm planning, and that I will understand if they don't want to make the trip."

I knew that my father's death would be hard on the family. Less than a month had passed since Aunt Ruth's death and in four days, Pap would have been 85.

I phoned a funeral home in our neighborhood to inquire about arrangements. I had never planned a funeral so I asked many questions and inquired into the cost of various options. I wanted to discuss my

ideas with my family, get their opinion, and make an informed decision. I made an appointment with the funeral director for early afternoon and asked them to retrieve Pap's body from the nursing home.

A few months before, I had seen an ad in the newspaper stating that
since 1963 cremation has been an acceptable alternative to ground
burial for Catholics and the Catholic cemeteries could handle the
request. Both my husband and I had talked about cremation for ourselves, now I was considering it for Pap. I had been relieved to read that
it was approved by the Church.

When Tom and I discussed cremation, I explained that after my
death, I would no longer be in my body, it would be just an empty
box, the contents would be gone. I felt that if God, in His power,
could create my body at birth, He surely could do the same on Judge-
ment Day. He didn't need my old bones to remind Him who I was.

Since Pap had received the Sacrament of the Sick, I felt he was
blessed while he was still in his body. This thought made planning
much easier. I was glad I had delayed making arrangements for Pap's
wake and funeral.

My children gathered at our house, for comfort and to help. I told
them I was thinking of having Pap cremated and asked each one how
they felt. I asked if they objected to a closed casket or a memorial table.
It was a hard decision for them to make.

After thinking about it, Kathy, Bill and Sue told me to go ahead
with my plans. Terri admitted that she didn't like the idea of a closed
casket. If the casket was going to be closed, she felt more comfortable
with the cremation before the wake.

Bill offered to go to the nursing home. I turned down his offer,
explaining that I wanted to get a thank-you card and some candy for
the staff. I wanted to bring it myself, to personally thank them for
everything they did for Pap. Terri decided that she was going to the
nursing home, since I had enough to do. She would thank the staff on
behalf of the family. I reluctantly agreed—I didn't feel like arguing. I

wrote a letter to thank them for all of their help and care and asked Terri to pick up a box of candy.

It was a good thing that Terri went. The staff had packed Pap's suitcase. They had his stuff together, ready for us to pick up—but not all of it. Terri took it upon herself to check both rooms looking for Pap's harmonica. She went through the drawers until she found it. I wouldn't have had the energy.

When I spoke to the funeral director that morning, he had realized that I was leaning toward cremation before the wake, rather than after. He had explained that before cremation could take place, a law required that the body be identified by a relative. He arranged for a viewing of the body when we came for our appointment that afternoon.

I hadn't mentioned that we needed to identify the body to my family. With everything that was happening, I didn't think of it. Terri and her husband went to the funeral parlor with Tom and me. After we discussed some of the arrangements, we asked to see the chapel. We weren't prepared when we walked into the chapel and Pap was lying on a table. He looked very peaceful—he had a smile on his face.

We identified the body and I signed the papers authorizing the cremation. We chose the day and the time of the wake. Since we decided on cremation before the wake we weren't restricted to a certain timetable. But I still wanted to have the wake and funeral Mass within the normal time frame for the convenience of my family and out of town relatives.

Then we discussed the details. They had a long table that we could use to display our pictures. Two tall lamps would provide a soft light on either side. Tom saw a tall cross that he asked them to place behind the table.

We composed the notice for the newspapers, picked out the Memorial Card, decided on the flowers. We did the paperwork.

When we arrived home, I asked Sue if she would pick out pictures of Pap for the table and get the frames. (Photographs have always been important to Sue. She has many framed photos of family and friends in her room.)

We planned the rest of the table. Pap had written a poem titled "Peace," set it in type and printed it on card stock. I found a copy when I was looking through his papers. We decided to frame that too. I also wanted to use Pap's harmonica and the statue of the boy pulling the goat that Pap had received as a boy.

Terri offered to get the flowers and candles. Bill took charge of the refreshments for the wake: pop and cookies. I had a portable stereo system, we needed to pick out the music. Kathy was going to provide the glue to keep us together.

Monday, I continued to prepare for the memorial service. I called work to tell them of Pap's death. I called the rectory to schedule the Mass. Since the body wouldn't be present, the woman asked if I wanted a week day Mass said in Pap's name. I explained that I wanted to arrange for a funeral Mass, except it would be a memorial—we would have a picture instead of the casket. We picked a time for the service.

My father had bought grave sites when my mother and brother died. I knew he had three, but where were they? I had only visited the cemetery a few times when I was very young, my father didn't like to go there. I knew the cemetery was somewhere "out in the country."

I called information, and asked for the phone number of the cemetery. When I dialed the number, I talked to a person in the parish school office who gave me the phone number of the rectory. I remembered a regular cemetery, not one attached to a church. Was my memory wrong? Had the cemetery disappeared? The person who answered the phone at the rectory knew the place I was looking for. She explained that a couple of cemeteries had been combined for administration purposes and gave me the phone number. At the administration office, the person who answered the phone not only knew what I was talking about, she knew where the grave sites were and gave me directions. When I told her that I was having Pap cremated, she asked if I wanted him interred in the same grave as his wife and son—there was room. I liked that idea.

I asked if we could have the interment on Wednesday, since my family would be off from work for the Mass. The crematorium informed her that they wouldn't have his remains available on Wednesday. How was Thursday? Thursday was Pap's birthday, I thought it would be fitting.

Tom and I wanted to find a restaurant close to church for a luncheon after the services. I thought of a neighborhood restaurant where we went with Pap after Mass. I knew the food was good and the prices were reasonable. We stopped for breakfast and talked to the manager. Would they be able to accommodate 20 to 30 people on Wednesday at lunchtime? He told us they would push tables together, there would be enough room, and he would bring in an extra waitress. One less thing to worry about.

I called Aunt Connie to give her the rest of the details. She had finally reached Alvin in Wisconsin and he wouldn't be in for the wake or the Mass. If we had a viewing, he would attend, but for a memorial table he was going to pass. Aunt Edna, who lived near Joliet, said something similar. I was disappointed but I understood. I knew that they would be present in spirit, and their journeys would have been long. Our small gathering would be even smaller.

Bill and Sue spent Monday morning going through old pictures. Many pleasant memories surfaced as they picked out the ones for the table. We had many small pictures, but few large photos. Sue found a place that enlarged pictures in an hour. After she received the larger photos, she picked out frames to complement each one. When everything was assembled, we realized that a flat table would never do. Our collection of pictures told Pap's life story. A curly haired toddler in a dress peered at the camera from the safety of his mother's arms. A happy young man stood next to the new car he had won. A proud father sat with his wife and young children on a couch. Pap, a grandfather with a receding hairline, posed with his daughter at a wedding.

Pap, a great-grandfather but still a child at heart, stuck out his tongue at the camera as he sat with his sister, Connie. Two sisters and two brothers of the aging Witting clan mugged for the camera at Christmas.

Tom and I discussed the best way to display our collection of memorabilia. He assembled a set of steps from wood, providing three different levels. I found a white lace tablecloth that we used for family gatherings to cover the steps. We worked on the arrangement of the pieces, adding Pap's statue of Our Lady along with a small photo album holding all the good pictures that we didn't have enlarged.

Tuesday, I went for an early morning walk to visit Angel, our crossing guard. I told her of Pap's passing and gave her the times of the wake and Mass. I asked her to plan to come to breakfast with us after Mass. I also asked her to invite the people Pap knew from church. Angel called him Pap, a name she got from our family. No one really knew Pap's name, so the newspaper and the church announcement wouldn't mean anything.

When I returned home, Sue had left for school. Tom, Bill, and I went to the neighborhood pancake house for breakfast. While we waited for our order, we joked about many things. Tom remarked, "It'll be nice to find things where we put them. Pap won't be moving them on us anymore."

I warned Tom not to be so sure about that, gremlins were still roaming in our house. Then Bill added, "But the head gremlin is gone."

After breakfast, I dropped Tom and Bill off at our house before running some errands in preparation for the wake that evening. When I arrived home, Tom, Bill, and the dogs were all in the front room watching a movie. Tom was sitting in the swing chair, talking to Sue on our cordless phone. Since she wanted to talk to me, I took the phone and walked into the dining room so that I could hear what she was saying.

I heard a loud clunk; the noise came from the kitchen. ??? No one was in the kitchen. What fell?

I walked into the kitchen to investigate...my pancake turner was laying on the floor. It had fallen out of the deep, three-tier turntable where I kept my kitchen utensils. I stared at it in astonishment. How did it fall? I had to laugh. Was someone hungry?

Tuesday night, we gathered at the funeral home. We were worried that the table wouldn't be large enough to hold our collection. As we set up the stairs Tom made, we realized that the table was not only big enough for the photographs, the boy and the goat, the poem, the harmonica, Our Lady—memorabilia of Pap's life, we even had room for a basket of living plants sent by a friend. Terri placed votive candles in the nooks and crannies, their flames flirted with the photos and objects. The tall cross at the back was perfect, as were the flower arrangements on either side. The tall lamps provided the finishing touch.

After we finished, I took pictures of Pap's table. I wanted to send the photo along with the memorial card and a letter sharing my father's illness and death to those who weren't able to attend.

Our parish priest had never seen a memorial table. I explained our idea of wanting to remember the man and his accomplishments rather than the worn body. We talked about the pictures, the statue, and the poem. He remembered seeing my father at morning Mass.

The memorabilia brought many happy stories to mind for everyone. I was glad that we had decided on the table; it was much better than an open or closed coffin. It was warm, alive with memories. It was fitting.

Our gathering was not large. My cousins, with whom I had lost touch, saw the notice in the paper and attended. I was glad they came, our fathers had been very close. The absent relatives were missed. Co-workers stopped by; friends of our children dropped in.

A small group gathered Wednesday morning for Mass. I put the large picture of my young father with his wife and children on a table in front of the altar along with one of the flower arrangements. Then I received a very nice surprise. The Resurrection choir was going to sing for Mass. (I had never expected to have musical accompaniment, let alone a choir.) I asked the director if they would sing one of my father's favorites, "Peace is Flowing Like a River." Their voices added so much to the Mass. We wished there was time for more than four songs. They sang the one I requested plus "Amazing Grace", "On Eagles Wings" and one other. (I couldn't remember the last song, neither could my family. I ran into a choir member at the bank later in the week. I told her how glad I was to see her and asked if she remembered the name of the fourth song. She said, "Of course I do, it was 'How Great Thou Art.'")

The Mass was very hard for me. It was made harder by the photo that I had chosen. I hadn't been able to attend the funeral of my mother and brother. As I looked at the picture, I felt the Mass was for the three of them. Tears flowed.

Our priest's homily reflected on the faith of the older generation—they used their faith to nourish their bodies, to get strength for the troubles in their life, and to say thank you for the good times. The person lived on in the memories of those remaining, and in the teachings and values that the person had passed on. Their faith and values do not die away unless we let them.

I was glad that I was a Catholic and believed in life after death. I liked Father's eulogy and found comfort in the liturgy. Receiving Holy Communion had become more important to me as my father's memory diminished. Each Sunday I thanked God for the help I had received during the previous week and asked for His help to get through the next one. Now I thanked God for Pap's passing and the help He had given my family. I asked for His help in the days ahead.

After the service, I thanked both our priest and the choir. The Resurrection choir is comprised of senior citizens and some of the members recognized Pap from his picture. They remembered him from morning Mass but they hadn't known his name. (Later, when I told someone that I was surprised by the choirs' attendance, she was amazed that I was surprised. She explained that since Pap always attended Mass, the Lord took care of it. Why was I surprised?)

We gathered at the restaurant for lunch, enjoyed each other's company, and reminisced. Our grandson took the opportunity to win over more hearts.

After the luncheon, Tom and I took some of the flowers to the nursing home and the Center. I met the director of the home as we were entering. She thanked me for our letter and the candy. The letter was posted on the bulletin board so that all the shifts would see it. They were surprised that I had sent it since Pap wasn't there that long. I replied that the length of time wasn't important.

Then we proceeded to the Center. I felt going there would be rough for me but it was just the opposite. I gathered hugs like a bouquet of flowers. Tom was surprised that I knew so many people. I didn't understand his surprise. I went there daily. Why wouldn't I know the staff?

We had neglected to order thank-you cards when we ordered Pap's memorial cards. On the way home from the Center, I decided to use Pap's poem as the front of our thank-you card. My children and Aunt Connie had asked for a copy of the poem. I thought it would be fitting to share it with everyone. I took the poem to a local printer, explained what I wanted to do, and asked for his suggestions. He had a heavy card stock that would be perfect for the card. I asked him to insert the dates of Pap's life and death below his name on the card. He would also be able to print my letter and he had envelopes that were big enough to hold the complete package.

Pap was interred on his birthday. Our children gathered with us at the cemetery. It was no longer out in the country, now it was surrounded by a suburb. I had confided to the woman at the office that I didn't know the location of the grave, since my father hadn't bought a headstone. She arranged to have someone there to guide us.

I had a poem that I wanted to read at the grave side but I couldn't find it. I remembered some of the lines and said what I remembered, "Do not stand at my grave and weep. I am not here, I do not sleep. I am a thousand winds that blow. I am a diamond glint on snow, I am the gentle autumn rain. I am not here, I do not sleep."

Our plot was located in the old part of the cemetery. A grotto to Our Lady of Fatima was close by. Before leaving, I walked over to the grotto. If I lined myself up with Our Lady's statue, I looked out on my family's grave. It was comforting to know that their remains were symbolically in Her sight. It was fitting.

Before driving back into the city, we met for lunch at a country restaurant that had just opened. During the meal, we talked about the cemetery. Since our graves were in the older section, we weren't restricted to a headstone that was level with the ground. We made plans to get together to order a headstone for my parents and brother and we resolved to do it soon, not to put it off like my father did.

After we returned from the cemetery, I searched my wallet again, looking for the poem. It was there all the time, just overlooked:

Do not stand at my grave and weep.
  I am not there; I do not sleep.
  I am a thousand winds that blow.
  I am a diamond glint on snow.
  I am the sunlight on ripened grain.
  I am the gentle autumn rain.
When you wake in the morning hush:
  I am the swift uplifting rush
  of quiet birds in circling flight.
  I am the soft starlight at night.
Do not stand at my grave and weep.
  I am not there; I do not sleep.

–Anonymous

After I found the card, I sat down to write the letter to our family ⁿd friends. I didn't want to put it off. Many of our distant relatives not aware of the details of my father's illness, or his death. I ˙everyone who was with us in person as well as those who were with us in spirit. I briefly recapped the highlights of the past few years: cerebral arteriosclerosis resulting in a memory loss which was severe enough to require day care, the fall that led to the hospital stay, and finally, the nursing home. To lighten the news, I wrote "My father's death was one month after the anniversary of my mother's death. I feel that she was tired of his flirting with the ladies and called him home." I included a brief description of our memorial table and shared some memories of the service. "A funeral Mass was said where the Resurrection choir added beautifully to the service. They included, at my request, *Peace is Flowing Like A River.* This was the song my father was singing the last days of his life. We laid his earthly remains to rest with his wife and son on his birthday."

Our thank-you card, with my letter, memorial card, and the photo of the table was well received by those who were unable to attend as well as by those who were there.

When I asked Terri to make a note of some of the things that happened when Pap was in her care and when she visited Pap, she included her remembrance of the past few days.

Sunday

Sunday morning my husband came to wake me. I just looked at him and knew something wasn't quite right. I knew before he said it that my grandfather, my only grandparent, was dead. I looked at the clock and noticed that it was much later than I normally slept. My husband sat in silence. Finally he said that he thought I needed to sleep in because I was going to need the rest. My grandfather had died.

At first there were no tears. There were things to do, I had to go see my family. My friend was going to take the kids and me to see Pap but my husband said he would take me. It was just as well because I didn't really want to talk to anyone or be a mom for a little while. I had to sort out what was happening.

The day was really easy. Mom carried the biggest burden. Making arrangements and everything. Be the rock for everyone else to lean on. No one seemed to be needing it, except maybe Mom. So we were all strong for her. My husband and I went to the nursing home to collect Pap's things and then to the funeral parlor with my parents. It was strange to watch my Mom take care of business like a little soldier. Knowing that deep down the pain I was stifling had to be 20 times greater for her.

We all managed and my Mom did a wonderful job arranging for services and the beautiful memorial/wake.

Wakes, funerals and burials are all for the living not for the dead and my Mom at the grave side had a little something to read that said just that. "Cry not for me because I am not here." Pap is no longer here. The way his health was makes that easier to live with, if any loss can be easy. The fact that when you are born you start to die is never so real as when you see someone you love no longer taking the breaths of life. Life continues on day by day whether or not you live it to the fullest or idly watch it pass by. Pap tried to his last day to be as much a part of life no matter what. He took the good with the bad and struggled like the rest of us but at least now he no longer struggles.

Pap is not there, he does not sleep. He is alive in our memories. His spirit is still very busy—helping.

After I finished writing our story, I visited the Center. They have started a "We remember" book. A picture of my father is included in the book, as well as the dates of his stay and death. This note remembers the man:

> "William enjoyed socializing and was most often seen participating in a sing-a-long or dancing. He was always caring and helpful to other clients."

Before leaving, I stopped to visit the staff in the unit. A staff member told me that she had just written an article about my father as a person who made a difference in her life.

May our story make a difference in your life.

Epilogue

I n May of 1996 I attended the Ninth Annual Conference of the Rush Alzheimer's Disease Center, (part of the Rush Presbyterian St. Luke's Medical Center, a leader in the research and treatment of Alzheimer's disease). In just one year I noticed some positive changes. For example, when I attended my first conference, after my father's death in 1995, Cognex was not mentioned as a treatment for mental dementia. In 1996, the Alzheimer's Association had a flyer *Facts About Cognex And Alzheimer's Disease*. At the Tenth Annual Conference of the Rush Alzheimer's Disease Center new medications and vitamin therapy had already replaced Cognex as the treatment of choice. Medical technologies and research continue to develop new understanding of the disease—causes and treatment. The best way of treating the disease today will be replaced by the knowledge of the future.

Some things will not change—the love and care that is given to the affected person will remain a constant, as will the stress on caregivers that accumulates and doesn't easily dissolve. Every family will have to make their own decisions about what is right for them: independent living, assisted independent living, living with a family member; or living in a retirement community, specialized care facility, or nursing home. As the person's ability to make decisions declines, someone will have to step in and make those decisions. A *Durable Power Of Attorney For Health Care* is a document which delegates to a trusted family member or friend the power to become the agent for any health care decision that the individual is unable to make during periods of physical or mental incapacity. It has become the document of choice over a *Living Will* which is only activated when the person's condition is terminal. Forms are available from hospitals, doctors offices, libraries, and organizations. The *Durable Power Of Attorney For Health Care* can be filled out by the individual and witnessed, it does not need to be nota-rized. It should not be confused with a notarized Power Of Attorney, which is necessary for legal and financial issues.

Each person and family will need to make the decision that is right for them, what worked for us might not work for someone else. The length of the illness is a factor, it varies depending on the individ-ual—from only one or two years...to twenty years and counting. Many home services are now available—Meals on Wheels, CNAs (Certified Nursing Assistants), Professional Homemakers, and Hospice to name a few. These services will continue to evolve as the need changes. The National Association of Area Agencies On Aging located in Washington, D.C has an Elder Care Locator, phone 1-800-677-1116. They are aware of all the services that are currently available in an area and were a tremendous help to our family. The Alzheimer's Association is another important resource. They conduct educational meetings and run support groups. They now have a *Safe Return* pro-gram for missing persons that is nationwide and are always updating their book list and brochures to include the latest information on ways to provide the best care and the safest environment.

Rather than repeating information which is constantly being updated by these organizations, I would like to share some of the things that I learned that won't change:

- Love yourself and each other.

- Have patience with yourself and others.

- Rely on God, or a Higher Power, for strength to face the chal-lenges of the day.

- Take care of yourself—exercise, see people, don't cut yourself off.

- Remember that you are human, allow yourself to make mis-takes—then forgive yourself, admit that you made a mistake and go forward.

- Pretend you have mental dementia, forget the hurtful things that were said and done—the person affected with dementia has.

- Respect the dignity of the person, allow them to retain their feeling of self worth.

- Speak to the Individual's feelings—the question or complaint might not be the real problem. Feelings of loss or worry might be the real concern.

- Involve the individual in the decision making process or when possible give safe choices—create a feeling that he or she is making the decision.

- Help the person to remain active in body, mind and spirit. Visit friends, continue to go to church, don't withdraw from the world.

- Exercise their body and mind with simple tasks, adjusted to reflect their changing abilities.

- Alert the person to trips or doctor's visits so they feel they have some control, don't feel rushed, or left out. But adjust the time period to reflect their current ability and not create long periods of anxiety.

- Allow the person to be as self-sufficient as possible—for as long as possible.

- Remember—everyone needs to be needed.

- Remain flexible, remember what worked this time, might not work in an hour.

- Don't allow yourself to be backed into a corner, learn how to be a "politician," hedge your answers.

- Accept changes. Realize that your relationship will change: from spouse or son or daughter…to parent, lover, or friend. Try not to be hurt by the change.

- Have the courage to intervene and assume responsibility. Be alert to problems that might endanger the person or property and take appropriate actions.

- When necessary, acknowledge the person's frustration, assure them that it is not their fault that they don't remember.

- Don't try to do everything yourself, ask for and accept help from: family, friends, crossing guard, postman. This disease is not something to be ashamed of or to be hidden.

- Consider alternatives. Look at the problem from a different perspective. If the answer you receive doesn't make sense—ask a different question…to the doctor or to yourself.

- Create a peaceful home environment, free of fighting, enhanced by music and good companions.

- Talk in soft tones. Speak slowly, give simple directions.

- Slow down. Allow ample time to leave the house, get in the car.

- As the disease progresses—take a more active part in decision-making and health care issues. Go into the doctor's examining room with the patient if necessary.

- Become an advocate—It is okay to respectfully discuss issues that you don't agree on with a professional caregiver.

- Relieve yourself from the responsibility to keep the person grounded in the present—you can't do it. Give yourself the freedom to agree with the person, even when the time frame is wrong, as long as it is not hazardous to their health.

- Discuss the situation and disease with everyone, especially the young children. Let them know that it is not their fault that they are not recognized or are yelled at. Help them to understand that the person doesn't have control over his or her actions. It is the disease that causes the behavior.

- Young children have a marvelous ability to interact with a person afflicted with mental dementia. But supervision is needed.

- Don't burden yourself by making promises that changing circumstances won't allow you to keep.

- Set boundaries, but be willing to adjust them. Know your limitations. Accept that you can't do everything, you have not failed, the disease has progressed.

- As my father always said, "Have a good day, be good to yourself, take care of yourself."

About the Author

Diane McDonald is a wife, mother and grandmother. She is an active member of the National Writers Union, Society of Children's Book Writers and Illustrators, National Storytelling Network, Northshore Storytelling Guild and Northlands Storytelling Network. Life has given her many stories which she shares with the people she meets.

Do you know a child who would enjoy reading a story about a girl whose grandfather has Alzheimer's disease? In *Treasure Chest*, Mr. Button's, a magical bear, helps Jenny understand the disease that is causing her grandfather to forget. Mr. Buttons helps Jenny understand the changes that are taking place. He helps her understand that it is not her fault. The book has pages to color so a child can personalize the story.

Treasure Chest was written for children ages 4 to 7. As of this printing the book is not available in stores. More information can be received by contacting me at:

e-mail: Dianemc114@aol.com

web-site: Hometown.aol.com/Dianemc114

mail: Diane McDonald
              P.O. Box 622
              Sublette, IL 61367 .

0-595-22749-X